PRAISE FOR *FABULOSA!*

'A fascinating and complex story, beautifully told with clarity, passion, and humour.' – DAVID CRYSTAL

'Shot through with his nicely dry wit, this is a fascinating and important study.' – PATRICK GALE

'Glorious! This fascinating account of Polari, the Lost Language of Queens, is utterly absorbing. It's history at its best: alive, vivid, fluid, warm, human and humane, and it gets as close as any book I've read to penetrating the mystery-wrapped-in-an-enigma that is camp. Not just fabulous. Not just fabulosa. But completely *fan-tab-u-losa*!' – NEIL MCKENNA

'Vada this! By turns deeply edifying and hugely entertaining and unusual for succeeding at being both – a future classic!'
– DAMIAN BARR

'Brilliant, readable nonfiction is out there too . . . for those who want to be in the know, *Fabulosa! The Story of Polari, Britain's Secret Gay Language* by Paul Baker (Reaktion) is a compelling history of the linguistic lengths to which gay people had to go to hide in plain sight within an aggressively homophobic culture.'
– *OBSERVER*

'Baker's intriguing and often amusing book is the work of a writer interested in language who has been led by his subject to think about social oppression . . . [he] writes well about the milieux in which Polari flourished – the theatre and the merchant navy. He is especially acute on the political uses of vulgar innuendo . . . And Baker's interviews radiate warmth and good humour.'
– *SPECTATOR*

"It is as much for its vocabulary as for its sociological vagaries that we read Baker's always illuminating book"
– *TELEGRAPH*

'Baker intersperses his account with snippets of interviews with Polari speakers, whose first-hand recollections are invariably arresting and funny. He is partial to a spot of innuendo himself, and manages to slip one in every now and then . . . [T]here is some evidence that the language persisted into the 1980s and '90s in theatre circles, and it continues to enjoy a healthy afterlife as a cultural curio – of which this delightful book is just one manifestation.' – *FINANCIAL TIMES*

"Though a language smacking of Carry on films and saucy seaside postcards, it's the tragic torment and harassment that gave rise to Polari in the first place that must not be forgotten and that is why this book is important." – *DAILY MAIL*

'For anyone interested in finding out more about Polari—Britain's 'secret gay language', *Fabulosa!* Provides a thought-provoking look at how the language came about and fell in and out of favour with the gay community from the days when homosexuality was illegal. Academic Paul Baker details how Polari was based on a mixture of sources, including the common sailors' language of lingua franca and thieves' cant.' – *I* NEWSPAPER

"Book of the Month: A funny and joyous insight into the story of Polari.... This is an essential book for anyone who wants to Polari bona." – *ATTITUDE* MAGAZINE

CAMP!

PAUL BAKER

THE STORY OF THE ATTITUDE THAT CONQUERED THE WORLD

FOOTNOTE

First published in 2023 by
Footnote Press

www.footnotepress.com

Footnote Press Limited
4th Floor, Victoria House, Bloomsbury Square, London WC1B 4DA

Distributed by Bonnier Books UK, a division of Bonnier Books
Sveavägen 56, Stockholm, Sweden

First printing
1 3 5 7 9 10 8 6 4 2

A CIP catalogue record for this book is available from
the British Library and the Library of Congress

ISBN (hardback): 978-1-804-44032-2
ISBN (ebook): 978-1-804-44033-9

Book designed and typeset by VictoriaHeathSilk.com
Printed and bound in Great Britain
by Clays Ltd, Elcograf S.p.A.

FSC www.fsc.org MIX Paper from responsible sources FSC® C018072

I'd like to raise a glass of (hopefully non-burnt) champagne to my friends, especially the ones who've engaged me with endlessly entertaining conversations about old movie stars. Without you, Joan Collins would just be a noun, as opposed to an adjective or a verb.

Contents

List of Illustrations

p.99: 'Her hair's as fake as she is!' Neely O'Hara exposes Helen Lawson's secret in *Valley of the Dolls*. PictureLux / The Hollywood Archive / Alamy Stock Photo.

p.108: Is that my camera? Norma Desmond (Gloria Swanson) finally gets her close-up in *Sunset Boulevard*. Granger Historical Picture Archive / Alamy Stock Photo.

p.112: 'Butchya aah Blanche! Ya aah in that chair!' Joan Crawford and Bette Davis in *Whatever Happened to Baby Jane?* Warner Bros. Studios.

p.120: 'Tina! Bring me the axe!' Faye Dunaway as Joan Crawford in *Mommie Dearest*. Alamy Stock Photo.

p.123: Cooking up a storm: Fanny Cradock in trouser suit and headband. Mirrorpix / Getty Images.

p.130: Don't libel me, bitches! – Liberace camps in a cape. Photo by Alan Light, CC BY 2.0.

p.139: Killing it. Beryl Reid and Susannah York mucking around in Laurel and Hardy drag. Everett Collection Inc / Alamy Stock Photo.

p.148: These queens mean business. A crowd attempts to stop police arrests outside the Stonewall Inn. New York Daily News Archive / Getty Images.

p.157: Go ahead – put me in your electric chair. The cast of *Female Trouble*. Everett Collection Inc / Alamy Stock Photo.

p.175: 'Damn you, Alexis!' The camp of *Dynasty* summed up in a single image. AJ Pics / Alamy Stock Photo.

p.180: Screamer! Mark Patton in the shower in *A Nightmare on Elm Street II*. Maximum Film / Alamy Stock Photo.

CHAPTER 1

Hello, Pussycat

Picked last again. It's 1981 and every week I dread games class, which always starts with two of my Alpha-male classmates being assigned the roles of captains and picking teams. I cannot hide my embarrassment as the gym teacher, Mr Camp (in name only), gestures at me to join my unwelcoming team-mates. I am nine years old and, although I'm the star pupil in every other subject, when it comes to sports, I am bottom of the class. But at least I am not alone. I have a friend, Ian, who is also one of the boys picked last. As a result, we are usually on opposing teams and frequently get paired up on the Siberian reaches of the football pitch, where the ball rarely troubles us. But while I view being picked last as humiliating, and brood on the sidelines, Ian is more resilient – he simply does not care. Instead, he makes it his mission to cheer me up and, for the whole period, he cracks off-colour jokes about our classmates and their mothers, imitating them to make me laugh girlishly. At one point, someone accidentally kicks the ball into our vicinity and some of the more earnestly masculine boys in the class shout at us in disgust because we allow it to merrily sail past us and off the pitch. Ian shakes it off, like the irrelevancy that it is. He made those lessons more than bearable, fun even, and he was the first person who showed me the power of camp.

Since those days, camp has been a magic door to many of my most valued friendships. Whereas some men might bond over a discussion of their favourite football players and which ones perform the best kicks, or whatever it is they do, my common ground involves whether Bette Davis really did kick Joan Crawford on the set of *Whatever Happened to Baby Jane*? Football conversations, when I have overheard them, can be impassioned, but they are rarely funny. Camp is a form of humour, and for me it is the *best* form of humour. There's a reason why camp people are described as shrieking, screaming or hysterical with laughter – it's because their humour provokes such an extremely pleasurable reaction in a way that other forms cannot. I am always sorry for people who have no appreciation of camp – it feels as if they are missing out – and while I believe that some people are more inclined to find pleasure in camp than others, I also think that we all have the potential to enjoy it.

You don't need to be clad in a towel at the New York Continental Baths watching Bette Midler sing 'Chattanooga Choo Choo' to connect with camp. My father, a butch booming giant, has regularly demonstrated his ability to be camp and to appreciate it. When I was growing up, I sometimes felt that, in the son stakes, I was a bit of a damp squib. I didn't care about Dad's model railway or want to go fishing with him. Still, he never made me feel I'd let him down and it was apparent from an early age that I had a camp ally. On Christmas Eve 1980, the whole family sat down to watch the Disney film *Pollyanna*. It was a secular but morally inspiring tale of an eternally optimistic orphan who comes to a small town full of miseries and changes *everyone's* lives for the better. The scriptwriter, David Swift, admitted that, to off-set the saccharine nature of the film, he would also spend a few hours each day working on a horror play called *The Deadly*. We all watched *Pollyanna* with the kind of silent focus that my sister describes as 'under exam conditions'. At the film's end, Pollyanna falls from a window ledge, loses the use of her legs and becomes depressed. But then all the townspeople come to her house to tell her how much they love her and, as the orchestral soundtrack reaches its crescendo, Pollyanna is back to her annoyingly chirpy old self again. For one member of my family, it was all too much. My father ran to the bathroom, locked himself in and cried his eyes out, while we all cruelly laughed at him. My Christmas present that year was the knowledge that big tough men could be camp too. When I told my father that I was writing a book about camp, he began regularly phoning me with his favourite examples. Actually, I have been blessed with not one but two camp parents. While my father's sense of camp is more extroverted, usually requiring costume changes and an audience, my mother possesses a rich inner life of high drama that she occasionally allows me to glimpse. When, aged seventeen, I tried to prepare her for the fact that I was gay by telling her I had a secret, she (a little too quickly) asked me, 'Have you killed someone?' And on suffering a stroke and heart attack in 2021, she awoke in hospital a week later and was asked by a nurse, 'Do you know where you are?' 'Yes, I'm in prison,' she replied. When she had recovered, I asked her what crime she thought she had committed. She said, in all seriousness, 'I'd defied the system.' Really, with that pair, what choice did I have but to embrace camp? I think it would be lovely if you embraced it too, or at least recognised the camp in yourself. At the risk of sounding a little too earnest, I hope I can convey to you my love of camp and fascination with it, and that my enthusiasm will rub off on you a little so you might see the world as I see it or be inspired to seek out and try some of the camp confections that I'll be telling you about. And despite being seen as a frivolous or unimportant topic, several of the camp artistes, films and songs mentioned in this book have been selected for preservation by members of the US Library of Congress as being 'culturally, historically, or aesthetically significant'.

In the last hundred years or so, camp has become an increasingly important part of popular culture, particularly as the status of queer people has improved in many parts of the world. As Bruce LaBruce puts it, 'Camp is now for the masses. It's a sensibility that has been appropriated by the mainstream, fetishized, commoditized, turned into a commodity fetish, and exploited by a hypercapitalist system.'[1] In the space of a century, camp has gone from being a secret form of humour used by despised minority groups to part of the mainstream. This has not happened in a straightforward way, though. Camp has been continuously pushed and pulled, reacting to different social and political trends, encountering unexpected friends and enemies, regularly occupying the centre of controversy and never ceasing to surprise. And despite numerous proclamations that camp is over or even (gasp!) *dead*, today it is more powerful than ever. The story of camp's rise to dominance is one that is worth telling – it's played a key role in political protests and helped oppressed people get through some pretty dismal times. It's also fascinating to chart how camp went from being a minority sensibility to a thing so ubiquitous that current commentators, like Andrew Bolton, costume curator at the Metropolitan Museum of Art, have described it as 'everywhere'.[2]

BUT WHAT IS IT?

Camp can be seen as an attitude, sensibility or lens through which to view the world. It can also be a personality characteristic or mannerism, a type of humour, or an aesthetic, style or fashion. Or it could be a combination of some or all of these things. Because of this, it can be applied to a very wide range of phenomena – we can talk of a person as being camp or an aspect of a person, like their voice, hairstyle, dress or walk. We can also label any form of media or entertainment as camp: a song, film, joke, computer game or comic. Abstract phenomena can be camp – allowing us to speak of camp language, camp horror or camp silliness. Of course, there are certain words where if the descriptor *camp* is applied, the effect would be a case of pleonasm or redundancy. We don't need to be told that musical theatre, a beehive wig, kaftan, hostess trolley, poodle or pineapple-shaped cocktail shaker is camp. They just are. Additionally, certain words act as camp signals – if you call something *delicious*, *fabulous*, *outrageous*, *tedious*, *dreary*, *horrid*, *vile* or *vulgar* you're telling us more about your own camp proclivities than about the thing you're evaluating.

Because camp can be applied to such a wide range of contexts, it is difficult to fully define it. It is also tricky to find a single word that sums up its opposite meaning. Words like *macho*, *butch*, *natural*, *restrained*, *sincere*, *dull*, *ordinary* or *sensible* key into different aspects of what camp is *not* about, but none of them fully capture the whole picture. Sometimes, when gay men write personal adverts, they refer to themselves as *non-camp* – indicating that they can't come up with a good opposite word to camp so they have just lashed *non* to the start of it. With these kinds of adverts, *non-camp* has a specific meaning, often synonymous with straight-presenting masculinity. So that would imply that camp means gay-presenting femininity. However, as we will see, there are plenty of women who are camp, and more than a few straight men. Additionally, inanimate objects that have no gender or sexuality can also be seen as camp, so the personal advert use of *non-camp* only gets us so far.

Perhaps then, idiomatic uses can give us clues. *Camp as a row of tents* doesn't appear that helpful at first, although as we'll see later, the humorous meaning of camp can perhaps be traced to the literal camp spectaculars mounted by Louis XIV when he was conducting battle practice, so, etymologically, it is at least on-message. I like *camp it up* because it suggests that something is being raised to a higher plane of existence – and camp can provide a natural high, like sex, exercise or meditation. *Camp as Christmas* might set off a chain of thought regarding *why* that particular holiday season is camp. If we put the alliteration to one side as a red herring (after all, we don't have camp as Columbus Day or camp as Candlemas), we might want to ask why Halloween is not seen as the campest holiday. On the surface, a good case could be made for 31 October as the campest day of the year – the dressing up, the candy, the daft horror films like *Hocus Pocus* and the *Nightmare on Elm Street* series. However, this takes us to a key distinction: Halloween *knows* it is camp, and revels in it – and that makes it campy as opposed to camp. On the other hand, Christmas is unaware of its camp status. What can you say about a holiday where you drag a tree indoors, cover it in lights and hang ornaments on it? It's the sincerity of Christmas that makes it camp. But, at the same time, it's the most excessive holiday of them all. The one where the message about celebrating the birth of Jesus Christ through the tradition of giving gifts has become an unashamed orgy of capitalism and socially sanctioned gluttony. In 2012 I went to Radio City Music Hall's Christmas *Spectacular* (its official name) in New York. The Spectacular features the Rockettes, a troupe of talented women known for their synchronised high kicks, who, halfway through this book, are going to play an inspirational role in a riot that kicked the gay rights movement up a gear. The Rockettes perform a signature dance routine while dressed as toy soldiers and it is obviously, intentionally camp. But what I found most camp about the Spectacular was the shameless product placement throughout the show and the way that audience members were not disgusted by this but literally *applauded* the references to various well-known purchasable goods, affording them real affection. Halloween might be campy, but Christmas is camp.

Both camp and campy require some sort of recognition on behalf of an audience, although with camp the producer is not aware of the effect, while campy is on purpose. It could be argued that campy is a natural progression from camp. We see examples of unintentional camp around us, find them funny and then proceed to recreate the effect to amuse others, but because we are self-aware, it is campy. However, I think it is also possible for someone to be naturally camp without actually trying, as well as being aware of this – Larry Grayson, discussed later in the book, would be a good example of someone who blurs the distinction between camp and campy. Campy seems to be a particularly American concept, being much more frequently used in the US as opposed to the UK, so this suggests that the distinction is not universally understood. Another complicating factor is the extent to which camp and campy existed before these labels came into usage or before people were aware of the labels. Camp must have existed prior to it being labelled as such, otherwise nobody would have thought to give it a name.

It was certainly a word that, once upon a time, you wouldn't have dared to use in polite society. In 1909, a British author of detective novels called James Redding Ware produced a dictionary called *Passing English of the Victorian Era*. This dictionary was the first one to define camp as an adjective, giving the example: 'How very camp he is.' Ware also rather sniffily notes that the term is 'Used chiefly by persons of exceptional want of character'. By the 1920s, we begin to find examples of the word occurring in American contexts. An issue of the entertainment magazine *Variety* has a review of an act called 'Bits of Millinery' in 1920, where the reviewer writes: 'The man during the talk leans a little too much to "camping" for laughs. The day is past when that "nance" stuff will get anything for anybody and it doesn't belong.'[3] Despite the fact that camp has now become a verb, take note of the distancing quote marks, disapproving tone and the fact that people have been proclaiming that 'camp is over' since the Jazz Age. In 1923 we find camp occurring as a noun, to label someone. The American author and poet Robert McAlmon published a collection of short stories called *A Companion Volume*. In it, one of his characters says, 'You only wanted six absinthes one after another . . . You old camp.' We start to see examples coming into the British popular press in the next couple of decades – so in 1940 *The Illustrated Sporting and Dramatic News* has a round-up article that refers to the singing duo Marianne and Jane. One of their new songs is called 'They won't have Robert in the Guards', which is described as a 'very "camp" saga indeed'.[4] The use of quote marks around camp might indicate that the author does not expect every reader to be familiar with the term.

It isn't until the 1950s that an attempt to define camp appears in any sort of serious literary context, in a novel by Christopher Isherwood called *The World in the Evening* (1954). Like the inter-war architects of camp that we'll get to in Chapter 3, Isherwood came from a privileged background and went to Cambridge where he became friends with W H Auden, spending time with him on the hedonistic gay scene in Berlin, which functioned as a camp finishing school for fey British graduates in the 1920s and 1930s. The world's first gay village was in the Schöneberg district of Berlin, a popular haunt of the film star Marlene Dietrich and cabaret singer Claire Waldoff. Despite being illegal, homosexuality thrived in Berlin, and British queer people went there to experience a sense of freedom that was impossible back home. The party was to be cruelly cut short though – with the rise of fascism in the 1930s, Berlin's gay community would be brutally obliterated, and many of those involved would be murdered in prison camps. Isherwood enjoyed the party while it lasted, fleeing Germany in 1933 with a boyfriend who was later arrested by the Gestapo and sentenced to three and a half years' forced labour.

Isherwood's subsequent fiction made use of these experiences – his semi-autobiographical novel, *Goodbye to Berlin*, inspired the musical *Cabaret*, which made a star of camp icon Liza Minnelli. *The World in the Evening* also contains aspects of biography although it appears to be about a (somewhat shaky) heterosexual relationship. As the novel progresses, things get decidedly queer. It is the story of Stephen Monk, a handsome, rich young man who marries a much older English novelist. On holiday the couple befriend a German man who falls in love with Stephen. They have sex but Stephen doesn't return the man's intense feelings. Stephen also befriends a gay couple called Charles and Bob, and during a conversation with Charles, the topic of camp comes up, with Charles providing a distinction between High and Low camp (which could be seen as a precursor to camp and campy).

> You thought it meant a swishy little boy with peroxided hair, dressed in a picture hat and a feather boa, pretending to be Marlene Dietrich? Yes, in queer circles they call that camping . . . You can call [it] Low Camp . . . High Camp is the whole emotional basis for ballet, for example, and of course of baroque art . . . High Camp always has an underlying seriousness. You can't camp about something you don't take seriously. You're not making fun of it, you're making fun out of it. You're expressing what's basically serious to you in terms of fun and artifice and elegance. Baroque art is basically camp about religion. The ballet is camp about love.

This criterion of intentionality comes up repeatedly – the idea that camp can be something that is intended to be taken seriously but some people see it as funny, while other forms of camp are intended to be funny from the outset. Isherwood's treatise on camp only lasts for a few paragraphs and doesn't have much impact on the plot of *The World in the Evening*, although it helps to establish Charles as a kind of mentor figure to Stephen.

By the early 1960s, *campy* has become a distinct thing from *camp*. So, in 1962 we find *campy* being used in the play *Veronique*, written by the American author John O'Hara. A character called Townsend Ringwald tells another character, Earl, 'save your campy humour for some other time.' We also see *campy* occurring in other contexts in the 1960s – *TIME* magazine has an article about annual television screenings of *The Wizard of Oz*, where it refers to 'Bert Lahr's campy lion',[5] whereas, surprisingly, *Christian Science Monitor* refers to 'jaunty, low-pressure, sometimes campy displays of the most powerful nation' in an article about a simulated space ride at Expo 67.[6]

This growing acknowledgement of 'on purpose' camp in the 1960s helps to explain why it is in 1964 that we find our next camp milestone with Susan Sontag's ground-breaking essay 'Notes on "Camp"'.[7] Sontag was an American academic, intellectual and philosopher who became a freelance writer. With 'Notes on "Camp"', she hit on a killer idea – take something that is becoming increasingly mainstream but has received hardly any serious attention because up to now it was seen as culturally unimportant. The 1960s were a time when old certainties were being questioned – artists like Andy Warhol showed how concepts like art and taste were increasingly open to interpretation, and definitions of 'High' and 'Low', or serious and popular culture were starting to break down (Warhol would direct an underground movie called *Camp* in 1965). There were glittering seams of unmined material ripe for exploitation if you were willing to get your pickaxe out and dirty your knees. Sontag's little essay made her famous.

After an opening few paragraphs, the essay is divided into fifty-eight numbered sections. It is not clear that their ordering has been carefully considered, rather, they could be a series of thoughts that gripped Sontag and she simply jotted them down in that order. They are written as a series of certainties, some of which do not hold up to scrutiny. This somewhat flippant manner is perfectly in keeping with a camp style of writing. The essay attempts to define camp as well as provide examples, many of which have functioned as touchstones for the camp tour guides who followed her. A synopsis of Sontag's definition of camp would have it as a sensibility, a love of the unnatural, artifice and exaggeration, a mode of aestheticism, either unintentional, innocent and naïve (with a seriousness that fails), or wholly conscious, a spirit of extravagance, glorification of character, playful, often out of date, a comic vision of the world, generous and a kind of love for human nature. That's a lot to process, and Mark Booth in his 1983 book, *Camp*, starts off by being quite cross with Sontag's essay, complaining that her epigrams are too inscrutable, while some of her examples are questionable or simply inaccurate. But worst of all, he says, she has far too many definitions of camp, which results in her casting her net rather wide (Sontag's examples include the nineteenth-century poet Alfred Tennyson, the 1950s radio comedy *The Goon Show*, the Spanish surrealist artist Salvador Dalí, the President of France Charles de Gaulle and children's cartoons).

Booth decides to resolve the issue by distinguishing between people and objects that are properly camp of themselves and things that are not intrinsically camp but would appeal to camp people – he calls this latter group *camp fads and fancies* – it's what Sontag might refer to as *naïve camp* and Isherwood might call *High Camp*. This results in two lists. So 'proper' camp would involve people like Oscar Wilde, Bette Davis, Tallulah Bankhead and Dirk Bogarde, as well as *The Rocky Horror Show*, pop art and a solid gold safety pin, while the camp 'fads and fancies' list would include Mozart, King Kong, Jean Genet, Judy Garland, Shirley Bassey, Catholicism, feather boas and Joan Crawford.[8] I get the impression that he's trying to make the distinction between campy and camp, although I'm not sure I agree with some of his categorisations, and the trouble with these lists is that they don't allow for shades of grey (or pastel). Imagine inviting your friends round and asking them to put things into boxes as camp or not camp, or even as intentionally camp or not. Before long, everyone will be talking at once in raised voices, there will be frenzied gesticulating, and it is likely to end in people sulking or flouncing out (don't worry, something called postmodernism is going to parachute in dramatically in Chapter 7 and resolve this for us by allowing, encouraging even, everyone to have different yet valid interpretations of the same thing).

Booth then boils things down to a single definition: to be camp is to present oneself as being committed to the marginal with a commitment greater than the marginal merits. I can see where he is going with this, and he notes that the marginal is traditionally feminine, giving an example of a very committed Bette Davis impersonator. Yet how do we determine whether something marginal doesn't merit the commitment we are giving it, and how much commitment is too much? Where Sontag's definition has a shopping list of ingredients that result in something inedible, Booth's definition gives minimal nourishment – it doesn't name-check the humour or exaggeration that I would associate with camp.

The following year, Philip Core wrote *Camp, The Lie that Tells the Truth* – an adaption of a paradox from Jean Cocteau who was quoted in *Vanity Fair* in 1922 as saying, 'I am a lie that tells the truth.' Core takes an encyclopaedic approach to the topic, with examples of camp arranged in alphabetical order. He begins his book by defining camp as a list of twenty-five rules. These include 'Camp is a disguise that fails', 'Camp is a lifeboat for men at sea', 'Camp is first of all a second childhood', 'Camp is gender without genitals', 'Camp is an art without artists' and so on.[9] They all sound suitably witty and I can imagine that these statements could be programmed into a little doll of Oscar Wilde and, if you pressed a button on his back, he would say one of them at random, followed by a cackle. But they don't really get us anywhere near a workable definition. It isn't until the 1990s that we find an explosion of academic interest in camp, occurring as a sub-field of the newly minted Queer Studies. The essays that emerged during this period were very concerned with being taken seriously – and sometimes had difficulty in capturing camp's essence as a result. With camp becoming more ubiquitous and mainstream, moving far beyond its association with oppressed minority groups and tending to be of the 'knowing' variety, later writers on camp have taken a rather pessimistic perspective. Daniel Harris proclaimed the death of camp in 1996, whereas, in 2012, the Canadian film director Bruce LaBruce referred to camp as 'the white noise of the new millennium'.[10] Call me blasé, but I still think camp is alive and kick-kick-kicking. And I'm happy to share camp with anyone who wants to enjoy it. Everyone's got their own pain – camp won't necessarily take it away, but it'll make it easier to bear, and who can argue with that as a philosophy.

THE INGREDIENTS OF CAMP

The summaries above indicate that some attempts to define camp have been too narrow and limiting while others are gratuitously broad and lose coherence. Another set of writers have tried to boil camp down to a few essential ingredients. In 1972, Esther Newton defined camp as containing theatricality, humour and incongruity,[11] Jack Babuscio, in 1977, described four features basic to camp: irony, aestheticism, theatricality and humour,[12] whereas in 1995, David Halperin named the most important traits as being parody, exaggeration, amplification, theatricalisation and literalisation of normal codes of conduct.[13] Gary McMahon, in 2006, offers flippancy, excess and artifice.[14] These lists contain quite a bit of overlap, so I've tried to tease out the more distinctive traits. For me then, a definition of camp would include at least quite a lot of one and possibly all of the following qualities.

Too much. Camp is excess. It is off-the-scale. Imagine smiling on a scale of one through to ten. Now try smiling at level fifteen. There's camp for you. Susan Sontag says camp is a woman walking around in a dress made of three million feathers. The subtitle of this book describes camp as conquering the world – an obvious exaggeration shamelessly designed to grab your attention. In his dictionary, James Redding Ware defines camp as 'actions and gestures of an exaggerated emphasis'. Excess is attention-getting, and, as we'll see in the following chapter, such excess can involve showy displays of wealth. A hyper-masculine man – like body-building actor Arnold Schwarzenegger in his 1980s films, like *Predator*, *Terminator* and *Commando* – could be seen as camp because his gender presentation is too much. But bear in mind that excess can also mean too little of something. So, while we can think of most camp as being over-the-top, an excessive *under*-reaction can also be seen as camp. Having three names is camp (Sarah Jessica Parker, Jennifer Love Hewitt, Helena Bonham Carter) but so is having only one name (Cher, Madonna, Beyoncé). And, in

Chapter 3, we'll see how a camp trick of the British upper classes was to use ironic understatement.

Artificiality. The natural world is rarely camp, even unintentionally, although there are exceptions like peacocks and flamingos. Instead, camp is usually manufactured by human hand. It is demonstrated by a codpiece, lipstick or a wig, or the outlandish curves of Art Nouveau that attempt to appear like something you would accidentally find in nature. In the 1995 film *Showgirls*, an evenly spaced row of four neon lights at the side of a swimming pool are shaped like palm trees and usually evoke audience titters when Kyle MacLachlan's sleazy entertainment director switches them on. Theatricality is camp, both due to its artificiality and its exaggeration. We might be tempted to class drag as camp because it is artificial, but this is only partly correct – as RuPaul says, 'We're all born naked, the rest is drag.' So *all* clothes are artificial, not just drag. Drag queens and kings often play with the notion of excess but drag also fits into our next category.

Acting against type. Camp involves people behaving in ways that are not typically associated with their identity traits and are likely to draw amused attention: a chap with a high-pitched or overly inflected voice, or one who is overly emotional or dresses to turn heads; an old woman who flirts with much younger men; anyone who wears drag or fashions that are twenty years out of date. A way of interpreting 'against type' could be to use the term *queer*, which in 1990s academia referred to anything that is against what a particular society decides at any given point is 'normal'. Queer theorist Judith Butler views gender as a performance – one that we carry out by (usually unconsciously) copying the performances of others. We work out who we should be copying through internalising the messages we get from society about what's appropriate behaviour for us. So camp can be what happens when that performance is based on something other than what's meant to be normal for us. Either we copy the wrong target or we get the right target but our copying is so exaggerated that it draws too much attention to itself.

Silliness. While we'll see how camp has been used in political protest, its essential nature is flippancy or playfulness – camp is funny and thus entertaining – either intentionally or not. Although camp is associated more with adults than children, camp adults can sometimes come across as childish because they are non-serious or flighty. Sometimes they are beyond the norms of society, either because they are very rich or very poor, so they don't appear to abide by the rules. Characters like the omnipotent Q in Star Trek are camp, as is wealthy socialite Karen Walker in *Will & Grace*. And pretty much everyone who lives in the Capitol in *The Hunger Games* book series by Suzanne Collins is camp. They are bored and rich so their actions have few consequences. On the other hand, the homeless drag queens who kicked back against the police after the Stonewall Inn was raided were so far on the margins of society that they had little to gain from following the rules – so why not laugh at them. Camp can also be brought out through parody – making fun of those who follow the rules a little too closely or try to uphold them, like Joe Orton's insufferable Little Englander, Edna Welthorpe, described in Chapter 5.

WHAT'S IN THIS BOOK?

As this is the 'story' of camp, the chapters come in a loose chronological sequence, and in each one I have focused on the new ways that camp was developing at a certain point in time. Think of the developments as a series of layers, building on top of one another, with the older layers still showing through at later dates. Some of the older works on camp discussed in this chapter have taken a monocultural perspective, something that reflects the time in which they were written but fails to tell the full story. In the early 1970s, writers like Esther Newton and Dennis Altman viewed camp as the remit of gay men, giving it a role analogous to soul for Black people. Both camp and soul were seen as strategic but separate methods that the respective identities used for reclaiming pride. However, more recently, this perspective has been challenged, with historians pointing out how Black people were using camp in their own ways well before the start of the twentieth century. Part of the reason for writing this book is to take a more inclusive outlook, covering instances of camp that are non-white or non-western, as well as thinking about some of the wider issues that come up when we talk about camp in relation to culture, sexuality, gender and race.

I have tried to cover instances of camp that I've found most interesting – each chapter has at least one case, for example, where someone or something tries to be camp and it fails miserably. I've also focused on the contexts where there has been resistance to camp. These failures and backlashes can both reveal much about the limits of camp at different stages in time. The relationship between camp and oppression is a recurring theme – and, make no mistake, we'll be going to some rather dark places at various points in the story – slavery, prison, murder, war, pandemic – they're not subjects that spring to mind when we think of camp, but all the same, they're here. I don't want to argue that camp is always a benevolent force either. Like anything, in the wrong hands it can be used for nefarious purposes, and it can have unintended consequences.

It is not possible to cover *everything*. I could have written this book as a list of everything that has been seen as camp and perhaps devote a couple of sentences to each one, but it would still be incomplete. So, instead, I've tried to cover as much as possible in a way that allows for depth as well as breadth. I'm very sorry that I may have missed your favourite camp thing and I hope we can still be friends.

Susan Sontag gives the 'soundest starting point' for camp as the late seventeenth or early eighteenth century. This is when we have written evidence of the term camp to mean flamboyance, being used in French theatre. But what else would you expect from a country that has also created eclairs, sewing machines, Roulette, Rococo, cabaret, neon lighting, hot air balloons, bikinis, French hoods (think Anne Boleyn), pencil skirts, A-line dresses, champagne, margarine, and hairdryers, not to mention *bof* (the Gallic shrug) and *faire la bise* (air-kissing the cheeks). So, in Chapter 2 we're going to camp out at Versailles and meet its owner, the original King of Camp, Louis XIV. We then cross the Channel to eighteenth-century England, taking special note of Beau Brummell whose life was one long grooming routine, and then we'll look at a colourful selection of Victorian court transcripts, which provide a firm answer to the question, is it a good idea to use camp when you are had up in the dock? Our early origins chapter ends with a discussion of how camp was utilised in dance contests by Black slaves as a defiant parody of plantation owners in nineteenth-century America and how this led to the House of Swann – one of the first drag families.

In Chapter 3 we travel back to the UK and consider how, in the earlier decades of the twentieth century, camp became associated with British elites who were able to use their privileged social status to break taboos when writing about the antics of outrageous characters, which would have been otherwise unspeakable. The upper classes are frequently camp in themselves, so it is easy to paint them as frivolous figures of fun, as writers like Nancy Mitford and Evelyn Waugh did with alacrity. There is camp seeping out of the murder mystery novels and plays of Agatha Christie, the gay romantic fiction of Mary Renault and the comedic, aromantic characters in E F Benson's tales of village life. Additionally, we see how camp helped the British keep a stiff upper lip (albeit one that had just brushed against a cocktail glass) during the horrors of World War II. Our star character in this chapter is Noël Coward, who acted as a kind of one-man camp propaganda machine, presenting a beamingly nonchalant face to Mr Hitler. We'll also take a look at one of the first camp divas, the wonderful Josephine Baker, who had the sense to realise that if anyone was going to appreciate her brand of camp it would be the French.

Chapter 4 starts in Hollywood where we interrogate the ways that the star system used and abused its women for our amusement. We begin with the extraordinary story of Judy Garland, who provided more than a little inspiration for Jacqueline Susann's blockbuster *Valley of the Dolls*, an early case of camp that critics failed to appreciate. We then move to the genre of 'women's films' and ask, what happens when a starlet gets old? It was a question that several films of the 1950s and 1960s tried to answer, providing inspiration for countless drag queens along the way. A key entry is *Whatever Happened to Baby Jane?* whose twist ending is only slightly less remarkable than the off-screen rivalry between its two stars, Bette Davis and Joan Crawford. We also consider whatever happened to the divas who did it their way – Mae West, who had been camp longer than anyone else and was happy to age disgracefully, Fanny Cradock, a television chef who mistook bullying for camp, and Donna Summer, a disco diva who was seen as letting down her biggest fans when they needed her the most.

Camp has always had a strong association with gay men, and in Chapter 5 we look at the ways that mid-twentieth-century gay entertainers settled into comfortable pigeon-holes as mainstream camp figures of fun, hiding in plain sight so they could provide wholesome entertainment to all the family, even children. Not everyone approved of these comedy queens though, and, in the 1970s, there was a backlash against camp from within the gay community, replete with angry pickets outside theatres. In other quarters though, camp itself was weaponised as a way of playfully annoying the establishment by Joe Orton and Kenneth Halliwell, or, more tenaciously, as a means of fighting back against police oppression by queer patrons of the Stonewall Inn, like Sylvia Rivera and Marsha P Johnson. We consider how the gay filmmaker John Waters created camp films that were purposefully aimed at a queer audience, making stars of camp titans like Divine and

Edith Massey, and how his growing popularity signalled a shift in mainstream tastes.

Chapter 6 is our neon pink 1980s chapter – we'll begin by laying a wreath on the grave of disco, which had been cruelly slaughtered, on a sports pitch of all things, just a few months before the decade began. The '80s were characterised by the cold glare of neo-liberalism and a reassertion of material excess brought about by the new world order. We see how soap operas like *Dynasty* showed us how the rich and powerful did everything extra, although interestingly, the *least* camp characters in *Dynasty* were the gay ones. This was an era of renewed homophobia as politicians, religious leaders and newspaper editors reacted hysterically to the HIV/AIDS pandemic. The horror film A *Nightmare on Elm Street 2* is a strange example of the complicated relationship between camp and homosexuality in this decade, with its light-footed young hero suffering almost as much off-screen as on. Drag queen Lily Savage used camp to keep calm and carry on when she found herself in the middle of a police raid during one of her performances, whereas another British comedian, Julian Clary, engaged in a camp boundary-testing exercise during a televised awards programme, resulting in him becoming a tabloid target. This chapter also tells the story of the fabulous queens of the Harlem ball culture, Pepper LaBeija, Venus Xtravaganza and many others, who used *Dynasty* as inspiration. These queens invented a dance craze called vogueing, which would come to the attention of the pop star Madonna, resulting in a debate about the line between appreciation and appropriation.

In Chapter 7 we consider the trend for nostalgia in the backward-looking 1990s. In this period, with higher awareness of camp, it was becoming harder to find authentic present-day examples, so aficionados hopped onto the postmodern bandwagon to ransack the past, exclaiming with glee over the outré fashions of the 1960s and 1970s. Generation X rediscovered easy listening music while popular soaps like *Melrose Place* recycled old Bette

Davis films, sometimes line for line, to give audiences their camp fix. We should not assume that everyone was in on the joke though – the mainstream film *Showgirls* flopped spectacularly as audiences and critics simply couldn't or wouldn't celebrate it as unintended camp. This is also the decade where camp was deployed by queer activists like the Sisters of Perpetual Indulgence, who also took inspiration from the past, reworking the secret language Polari into their ceremonies. Such shenanigans were observed with interest by queer theorists who were inspired to adopt camp as a serious subject of academic interest – they penned mysterious tracts on the subject in their own secret language, which rendered camp practically indecipherable for a time.

Finally, Chapter 8 examines the first two decades of the twenty-first century. This is an era where anyone can become a camp superstar thanks to platforms like the internet and reality television. We see camp re-establish its link with fashion, most notably as the theme for the 2019 MET Gala, although the groundwork had been laid out in films like *The Devil Wears Prada* and the comedy soap opera *Ugly Betty*, an adaption of the telenovela format popular in Latin America. Camp is now mainstream, being the driving force of numerous television series created by Ryan Murphy and the long-running reality competition franchise *RuPaul's Drag Race*. Its ubiquity raises questions about its value though, and there are accusations that camp has been co-opted by darker forces in order to distract us from political and economic realities, or simply to get us to buy stuff. This is also a period of increased sensitivity around the ways that we treat minority groups, so camp is both expanded, to enable wider participation and acknowledge its diversity, and simultaneously problematised, with aspects of it seen as offensive. Our story is necessarily incomplete – camp isn't going anywhere, so we end with a look at the future, or rather a set of possible futures, all of which are, of course, likely to be very wrong.

One of my favourite camp movies is *Auntie Mame* (1958), a gloriously technicolour life-affirming comedy featuring Rosalind

Russell as Mame Dennis, an exuberant guide who takes her young nephew, Patrick, on a whirlwind tour of camp, vastly enriching his life in the process. 'Life is a banquet!' Mame is fond of saying. 'And most poor suckers are starving to death.' She's always been an inspiration and I hope you see touches of her here and there in the pages of this book.

So, put on your most colourful glad rags, zhoosh your riah, grab a cocktail and make yourself comfortable in a peacock chair. You may also want to have a macaron tower to hand – our first stop on our story of camp is France, *naturellement*, *chérie*.

"Paaaahtrick!" Rosalind Russell in tour guide mode in *Auntie Mame*.

CHAPTER 2

Your Actual French

If it has to start somewhere, let's plump for seventeenth-century France, with the mother of all house modernisations. This was not just any old house and it did not involve knocking out a wall to create a kitchen-diner. No, it was the conversion of Dad's old château into something much more fabulous – a remodelling job that would result in the most lavish, awe-inspiring, ridiculous palace that had ever been built.

France boasts a thousand years of kings called Louis, stretching from Louis I, who was called the Debonaire (814–840) to Louis-Philippe d'Orléans (1830–1848). But the most famous and longest-reigning (seventy-two years and 110 days) was Louis XIV, known as Louis *le Grand* (the Great). He was a late gift to his parents, who had been trying for a child for over two decades. There had been four older siblings, all stillborn, before Louis, and his mother, Anne of Austria, worshipped the ground he walked on, helping to develop his interest in the theatre and food – two elements that played no small role at the palace that Louis was to build. French politics was a tricky affair, but fortunately Anne was a good teacher. In 1643, when he was only four, Louis's father died, and Anne managed to snatch power for herself, annulling her husband's will and exiling his ministers. Louis was only able to take control of the government in 1661, after the death of Anne's chief minister, Cardinal Mazarin.

Lucky for him, Louis XIV turned out to be an incredibly successful ruler, not only establishing France as the centre of Europe but centralising power to the extent that he was known as *le Roi Soleil* (the Sun King), around which *everything* revolved. And this all happened at the Palace of Versailles, originally Louis XIII's hunting lodge, twelve miles west of Paris, converted to a relatively modest château in 1634. It was envy that inspired Louis XIV to upgrade Versailles to a full-scale palace during a visit to a spectacular château built by Nicolas Fouquet, his Superintendent of Finances.

The French style of décor epitomised by Versailles was an example of camp as excessive ornamentation. Surprisingly, the style – known as French Baroque – was relatively restrained compared to the theatrics of Rococo that were to follow. At least French Baroque was formal and favoured symmetry, but it can in no way be described as understated. Interior design featured a good deal of outsized furniture, gilding, marble, gold, bronze, mirrors and paintings, along with columns and niches that were covered with carved leaves, flowers, batons and crowns. Fussy geometric patterning was everywhere and, as time went on, designs started to incorporate seashell motifs, arabesques and Chinoiserie.

These bold choices were incorporated into the Palace of Versailles, making it the last word in show-off grandeur, with over 2,000 rooms, a private zoo and roman baths. The most dazzling part of the palace was the seventy-three-metre-long marble-clad Hall of Mirrors. In the seventeenth century, mirrors were a status symbol, mainly being manufactured in Venice, so Louis XIV imported a team of Venetians to make mirrors in France, just for him.[15] If you like mirrors, then this is the hall for you – there were seventeen arches, containing 357 mirrors, along with a vaulted ceiling fresco that took four years to paint. Louis XIV was not a modest man and the fresco depicted seventeen of his military victories over the Dutch with images of him posing alongside classical figures. The gardens of this ode to opulence amounted to 800 hectares, landscaped to death with elaborate fountains, grottos and a canal. The fountains cost a third of the total budget of the palace. As there was no water source nearby, artificial ponds had to be created, but, even so, there were water shortages. So, when Louis promenaded in the garden, his servants whistled to one another to signal that the fountains should be switched on as he approached, then turned them off when he went out of sight.[16] With 210,000 flowers and 200,000 trees it must have been hell in the spring if you suffered from hay fever.

Because it was such a grand project, there were bound to be a few oversights. The kitchens were placed so far away from Louis's dining room that his meals were often served cold (at least he could console himself that his cutlery came in a gold box), while all of those marble walls and pillars were a devil to heat, even with 1,200 fireplaces. As a result, winters weren't great fun and it was not unknown for your glass of wine to freeze over just as you were getting to the punchline of a banquet anecdote. Additionally, the lack of plumbing meant that toilets were in short supply. Some of the royals, like the outrageous Princesse d'Harcourt, would simply relieve themselves in the hallways, not even bothering to stop walking. While all the excess is camp enough, for me, it's those failures to pull it off that take Versailles to Boss Level.

By 1682 the palace had become Louis XIV's court and home of the government, with apartments built so that leading nobles could live there. Lavish entertainments were constantly put on – plays, pageants, parades, concerts, banquets, balls, hunts and a lot of gambling. If you wanted power, you had to court Louis and be prepared to spend your own money in doing so. As time went on there were exceedingly elaborate rituals to engage in, like whether you were chosen as one of the lucky 100 or so men who got to attend his grand getting-up ceremony, during which he got dressed and had soup for breakfast. Louis loved flattery – the more obvious the better – and he required his courtiers to be constantly in attendance. If someone was missing with no convincing excuse, he noticed, and would react with pettiness, effectively cancelling the miscreant.

There were a whole set of rules around doors. Many of the rooms in the palace boasted double doors, and there were ushers to open them. But only the King and his close relatives got to have *both* doors opened for them. Everyone else had to squiggle through one door. And you weren't allowed to knock on doors with your knuckles (how common!). Instead, you were required to grow one fingernail into a giant *claw* so you could scratch the door frame to announce your presence. Even sitting was co-opted into a hierarchy – Louis XIV, his queen and any visiting monarchs got to sit in armchairs. Princes and princesses were allowed chairs without arms. Poor duchesses had to make do with stools; Princesse d'Harcourt caused a minor scandal when she decided that *she* wanted to sit on a particular stool occupied by a duchess, and forcibly removed her.

Let's move on to clothes. I am reminded of the 2004 film *Mean Girls*, where a nasty all-girl high school clique invents arbitrary rules like, 'On Wednesdays, we wear pink.' The Fashion Club in the animated series *Daria* (1997 – 2002) also comes to mind – one girl had to have extensive plastic surgery before she was allowed to join. Fashion at Versailles was equally ridiculous and expensive, and there were many traps to fall into. For example, courtiers at Versailles had to wear high heels – men and women alike. But watch out if you decided to zhoosh up your look with red heels. That was Louis's favourite heel colour and you had to be of sufficient nobility to be allowed to wear it. Another aspect involved the court dress that women had to wear when they were presented to the King: whalebone corsets strangulated the waist, over which skirts with long trains were draped. They were so heavy that women had to practise moving about in them in advance. To make matters worse, women were required to do a lot of curtsying while in the presence of Louis, making such audiences the equivalent of a demanding session of squats at the gym. The scariest part occurred at the end, just when you thought it was over. It was a no-no to turn your back on the King, so you had to back out of the room, as gracefully as you could, all while trying not to get yourself tangled up in the flowing train of your dress. Wigs were also a must – Louis XIV put his on as soon as he woke up and never appeared without it, so, naturally, everyone had to have one: doctors, the clergy, magistrates, even some children.[17] These wigs were heavy and could bring on headaches and dizziness, not to mention skin irritations.

Another aspect of Louis XIV's vanity was his desire to be seen as a conquering hero. Under his rule, France was involved in several major wars: the War of Devolution, the Franco-Dutch War, the War of the League of Augsburg and the War of the Spanish Succession, as well as various minor ones. Versailles was full of images of Louis XIV as a conquering hero and he loved going out on manoeuvres. This was an event that required all the courtiers to pack up and accompany him as spectators. Life at an army camp wasn't hugely different from Versailles – there was still a lot of showing off in your finery. Is it a coincidence that the word camp is said to be derived from the French verb *se camper*, which is most likely derived from the noun *le camp*, referring to an army encampment? Mark Booth describes how, in the late seventeenth century, French camps were not small utilitarian things made of drab tarpaulin but rather more showy: 'billowy creations of shining fabrics – satins and silks studded with jewels, tapestries and gold banners.'[18]

However, there is another possible meaning of *se camper*, which is to do with standing firm, which is what army camps are supposed to do. Perhaps from this its meaning migrated a little, to refer to a defiant attitude, and then to mean a bold provocative position, which started to gain traction as a way of referring to exaggerated stage performances involving over-acting and upstaging other actors. Perhaps the origins of camp can be traced back to the theatre then, where actors perform on a stage and audiences gather in large auditoriums, having paid for an enjoyable evening of escapism. Stage acting involves having to exaggerate your performance so even those in the back row can appreciate it. Actors have to be slathered in stage makeup to enhance their features so they can be seen better. Without it, those bright lights will give them a most unattractive washed-out appearance. Unlike in boring old real life, where most people tend to just say things in monotone while standing or sitting in one position with their hands hanging meaninglessly at their sides, actors have to throw their whole bodies into it. It is a profession that not only rewards but *requires* exaggeration.

Court life at Versailles could be seen as a kind of endless immersive performance on a giant open stage where the boundaries between actors and audience were blurred, and, as part of the divertissements, Louis XIV put on innumerable plays, ballets and concerts. These performances were extravaganzas with outrageous costumes, fantastic special effects, live animals and elaborate stages that were set up both inside the palace and in the gardens. Louis himself was an accomplished dancer, having had two-hour daily lessons since the age of seven. When he was twelve, he performed in public for the first time in the *Ballet de Cassandre*, and everyone had to admit he was actually very good at it.[19] Then, aged fifteen, he appeared as Apollo (which helps to explain how he got the moniker Sun King), in *Ballet de la Nuit*. As its title implies, the ballet ran through the entire night, lasting approximately twelve hours, being a test of endurance for both the performers and the audience (God forbid that anyone nodded off). Louis's Apollo costume was an explosion of gold brocade, ostrich feathers and gems laid into silk. The headdress was designed so that Apollo's head appeared to be emitting rays of sunlight from it in all directions. The sun motif also appeared on his shoes, sleeves, shoulders, waist and knees. By all accounts, it was not a very restrained performance. He officially retired from dancing at the age of thirty-two, but continued to dance at balls at Versailles and was a steadfast patron of the arts.

One of Louis XIV's favourite theatricals was Jean-Baptiste Molière, a playwright, actor and poet; Louis took roles in some of his comedy-ballets. Mark Booth traces the first use of *se camper* to mean 'camping it up' from a line in one of Molière's plays, *Les Fourberies de Scapin* (Scapin the Schemer), first performed in 1671. The main character in this play is a valet, the deceitful and pompous Scapin, who manipulates the other characters and steals from his employers. In one scene, Scapin is helping another character called Octave get out of trouble with his father and coaches him on acting like a stage villain. He tells him: '*Enfonce ton bonnet en méchant garçon, campe-toi sur un pied, mets la main au côté, fais les yeux furibonds.*' This translates to: 'Wear your hat like a bad boy, camp about on one leg, put your hand on your hip and flash your eyes.' Booth also gives another theatrical example from French, almost 200 years later in a nineteenth-century novel called *Le Capitaine Fracasse* (1863) by Gautier. The novel is set in the seventeenth century and is concerned with a young baron who joins a troupe of actors who are heading to Paris. One of the comedians in the troupe is a man called Matamore who falls in love with a woman above his station called Isabelle (she certainly isn't interested in him). Gautier writes, '*Matamore se campait dans une pose extravagamment anguleuse dont sa maigreur excessive faisait encore ressortir le ridicule*,' or, 'Matamore camped in an extravagantly angular pose, which his excessive thinness made all the more ridiculous'.

Louis XIV died in 1715, and his great-grandson, Louis XV came to the throne in 1722, taking over Versailles. Where Louis XIV had been excessively proud, his successor was comparatively modest and shy, with his greatest vice being his mistresses (like the infamous Madame de Pompadour) who he often relied on for (rather wobbly) financial advice. Louis XV abandoned many of the ceremonies of the former king, and adopted the Rococo style, which was less about formal grandeur and more about conveying comfort and informality. If anything, Rococo was even more camp than Baroque, embracing frivolity, playfulness and elegance. Louis XV wasn't so interested in living out his life with a constant audience of courtiers, so he had his private rooms rearranged and new furniture commissioned – designed less to impress and more for comfort. Sofas, as opposed to chairs, came into fashion, because they allowed more people to sit down in the presence of the King.[20] Legs on furniture had to be curved though – Rococo had an eye for the theatrical and the unexpected with lots of curves, volutes (scroll-like ornamentations), flower patterns and asymmetry that was designed to inspire surprise and awe. While Louis XV's reign is seen as a high point for French culture and art, things were not handled so well in the spheres of the military, diplomacy and economics, and, after he died, his successor, Louis XVI, was to pay the price for the French monarchy's imperious style of government. In 1789, an angry mob of Parisians attacked Versailles, aiming to kill the royal family, particularly the Queen, Marie Antoinette – an extravagant Austrian who had one of the highest wigs in the land and was disliked by ordinary French people. Both Marie and Louis XVI were found guilty of high treason and beheaded by guillotine in 1793.

The French may have gotten rid of their aristocracy, but they wisely hung on to camp, with the style continuing to flourish in theatre and design in the nineteenth century. The artistic style Art Nouveau was characterised by the asymmetrical flowing shapes and curves found in nature, particularly flowers and plants. The whiplash line, which often resembles an S-curve, is one of my favourite aspects of Art Nouveau. It is naturally found in plants like the iris, orchid, thistle, holly and water lily, or in birds like the peacock or swan. The whiplash has many applications in camp art and architecture – depicting a swirl of cigar smoke, a woman's hairstyle, a sweeping staircase, the handles of a vase, a dragonfly pendant or a decorative comb. The nineteenth-century camp artist Aubrey Beardsley was master of the whiplash line, using it outrageously to shape the poses of the characters he drew.

Art Nouveau became the signature of the entrances for the Paris Metro, which began construction in 1898. Hector Guimard created amazing canopies using Art Nouveau curves for 141 of the subway entrances. The effect is to announce that you are not just going on any old train ride, you are embarking upon an enchanted adventure. The fanned glass used in some of the entrances reminds me of the delicately transparent wings of a dragonfly, while some entrances had curved lights that look like

Magic Journey – an Art Nouveau Metro sign in Paris.

ferns. Even the lettering style is delicious – it feels like each letter of the alphabet has been invited to attend a fancy costume ball and is trying to outdo all the other letters. The sweeping tail of the R, the snooty stance of the P and the unexpected direction of the last part of the N deserve special mention for the drama they convey. During the 1900 Paris Exposition, millions of visitors marvelled at a travel experience that was both technologically and artistically ahead of its time. I like to think that all stations in

Paris eventually lead to the Palace of Versailles – if not literally, then at least figuratively.

The styles of Versailles, Rococo and Art Nouveau have stretched, whiplash style, across the whole of the twentieth century. In 1935, an American filmmaker who specialised in animations made a trip to Paris with his family, stopping off at Versailles. His name was Walt Disney and he had gained an inkling of Francc's potential for artistic fabularity during a stint as an ambulance driver in Paris in 1918. During his family holiday, Disney took special note of architectural details that would find themselves transposed into films like *Snow White and the Seven Dwarfs* (1937), *Cinderella* (1950) and *Sleeping Beauty* (1959). Even much later, after Disney's death, films like *Beauty and the Beast* (1991) would draw on the style of Versailles in creating the Beast's castle and the characters who inhabited it – servants who had been magically transformed into objects – Lumière the candelabra, Cogsworth the mantel clock and Mrs Potts the teapot. Inanimate objects in Rococo and Art Nouveau were already modelled on living things so it makes perfect sense to use this style when animating objects that were once people.[21] Keith Harvey has noted that in typical English camp, people will sprinkle their speech with elements of French, a practice that has grown out of an appropriation of aristocratic gestures, signalling values of refinement.[22] This can be an intentionally camp strategy, with some speakers aware that their French is purely idiomatic and unlikely to convince – the joke is that you are parodying someone who thinks they are impressing others with their appearance of sophistication.

So if we have anyone to thank for camp, it is the French. In 2022, I went on my own family trip to Paris, dutifully doing my Auntie Mame act. At Versailles I got trapped in the Venus Salon by a coach-load of modern-day Marie Antoinettes, all with inflated lips and posteriors, bedecked in Versace zebra print, pouting for selfies among the gold and marble. One of my nephews was sufficiently impressed to announce that he had fallen in love with

Paris and intended to move there as soon as he could. 'That's nice,' I said. 'You'll have to learn French.' 'The French will have to learn *me!*' he replied – suggesting that the sensibility had already begun to work its magic on him.

MOLLIES, MACARONIS AND DANDIES

We must cross the Channel now, to consider how camp was expressed in eighteenth-century Britain, where it would be associated with several new classes of men, for very different reasons. Camp has long been linked to a gay sensibility, or gay mannerisms; although the word *gay*, when used to refer to same-sex attraction, is a relatively new label, only really taking hold in the twentieth century. Earlier words like *homosexual*, *invert* or *Uranian* attempted to capture the identity, and, while we should see them as related to *gay*, they are not synonymous – sexual categories emerge and change as societies develop, and taboos and ignorance can mean that various forms of sexual desire or behaviour do not get remarked upon. Despite this, by 1710 a new sexual category had emerged, one that could be considered as a forebear to *gay* – the Molly. Their home was London, which by the early 1700s had a population of around 630,000 and was one of the largest cities in the world. With numbers sufficiently large to establish a secret subculture, the Mollies, as they called themselves, met in a network of clubs, taverns, inns and coffee houses, which were referred to as Molly Houses. In 1709, Ned Ward published a book called *The Secret History of London Clubs*, writing in it that the Mollies 'rather fancy themselves women, imitated all the little vanities that custom has reconcil'd to the female sex, affecting to speak, walk, tattle, curtsy, cry, scold, and mimick all manner of effeminacy.'[23] The Mollies were early aficionados of camp, in other words. Some would dress in women's clothes, and there was a humorous use of slang with words relating to obtaining sexual partners (strolling and caterwauling), sex (riding a rump), a masculine lover (trade) and other Mollies (sisters or queens). A typical greeting from one Molly to another would be, 'Where have you been, you saucy queen?'[24] Mollies called each other by female names and used female pronouns on one another – practices that would continue as a form of camp among gay men into the present day. The Molly Houses often had a private room, sometimes referred to as 'the Chapel' where 'marryings' between men would occur, and there was occasionally a camp performance where a Molly dressed as a woman would pretend to be in labour and give birth to a wooden baby, which would then be christened.

With homosexuality being illegal, the Molly Houses were relatively safe spaces for men to meet one another, have a camp laugh with their friends and possibly a bit of intimate contact. Many of them were located around Covent Garden, Moorfields, Lincoln's Inn and the Royal Exchange. However, by the 1720s, Britain was knee-deep in one of its recurrent censorious moral periods and a number of 'Societies for the Reformation of Manners' had cropped up around the country. The Mollies became targets, and between 1726 and 1727 there were sixteen raids on Molly Houses, the most famous of which was the raid on a private residence that doubled as a coffee house in Field Lane near Holborn, run by a woman called Margaret 'Mother' Clap. The raid took place one night in February 1726. Forty men were arrested, of which three (Gabriel Lawrence, William Griffin and Thomas Wright) were hanged at the infamous Tyburn gallows, close to the current location of Marble Arch. The *Caledonian Mercury* reported that Margaret Clap was put in the pillory 'for keeping a disorderly House for the Entertainmene [*sic*] of Sodomites'. A century later, in 1825, the *Morning Chronicle* claimed that 'many persons in England in former times have been convicted of these revolting offences on false evidence', accusing members of the Reformation of Manners societies of lying. Despite these raids, which continued well into the twentieth century, it is unlikely that the Molly Houses ceased to operate. In 1810, the *London Star* reported that 100 policemen raided a Molly House called the White Swan in Vere Street, Clare Market. It was claimed that the White Swan had its own Minister, John Church, who performed 'mock' marriage ceremonies for male customers. Two men who had visited the White Swan (sixteen-year-old Thomas White and forty-two-year-old John Newbolt Hepburn), were hanged. Several of those arrested were put in the pillory, including James Amos (also known as Sally Fox), who showed the remarkable insouciance that is characteristic when camp comes under fire – he laughed back at the watching crowd. The pilloried men were pelted with mud, potatoes, turnips, offal, dung and dead cats, and such was the feeling in the crowd that as they were returned back to the prison a mass of furious people surged forwards and attacked them. The harsh public reaction to Amos suggests an indignation regarding camp and what it represented – the wilful refusal to buy in to society's sexual and gender norms or even to express shame when caught out.

But in eighteenth-century Britain, camp was not only a sensibility of men who had sex with men – plenty of men who wouldn't have been seen dead in a Molly House also came to epitomise camp, although the reasons for that lie squarely with Europe. There is nothing like travel to make you realise how typical of your nationality you are, and how your nationality measures up to others. When I visit America, I am usually struck by how socially awkward and self-deprecatory I appear. I can get away with it in the UK, but stick me in a room full of Americans and my self-confidence is drained away in seconds. On trips to Italy, I rail at how glum and stodgy British food is by comparison, and in France I always notice how very plain and unstylish my clothes and hair appear. I suspect that the wealthy young men of eighteenth-century England experienced similar feelings of exposure and inadequacy when they embarked on their Grand Tours of Europe. Such trips usually occurred around the age of twenty-one – a most *impressionable* age – being popular from about 1660 to 1840, and seen as an educational rite of passage. A typical itinerary would take in the cosmopolitan cities of France and Italy, studying masterpieces of painting, sculpture and architecture, along with key archaeological sites around Naples. The more adventurous might go on to Sicily, Malta or Greece. Then, during the return trip, Austria and Germany would be taken in, finishing in Holland. Of course, due to inter-railing passes and cheap accommodation, the whole journey can now be done on a budget during summer break, without the need of an army of servants; the Grand Tour is still a recommended way of getting to know Europe while your body is young enough to withstand the pressures of travel and attractive enough to make other people want to talk to you.

During these tours, young men were bedazzled with new ideas and concepts. In Italy they developed a taste for macaroni, a tubular-shaped pasta that was barely known back in Blighty, and so, when they returned, bedecked in rather more daring European styles, they were disparagingly referred to as *macaronis*. This is a key moment in our story of camp – it is one of those early instances when unintentional camp is called out. French and Italian fashions might have been excessively flamboyant but, as this was the norm, nobody in mainland Europe thought to comment. Yet dour Brits, seeing their own young men mincing round in striped stockings, short coats, tight breeches, huge powdered wigs, tiny hats and fancy canes, found it all too hilarious. In 1764, Horace Walpole referred to upper-class social club Almack's as 'the Macaroni Club, which is composed of all the travelled young men who wear long curls and spying-glasses.'[25]

Macaroni was definitely an insult – the lexicographer Samuel Johnson, who was distinctly unfashionable, found himself accused of being a macaroni during a trip to Scotland in 1773, when he had trouble riding his horse. His companion, James Boswell, made fun of him: 'You are a delicate Londoner; you are a maccaroni; you can't ride.'[26] Macaronis were seen as feminine, with Mary Darly, a professional cartoonist of the 1770s, providing so many caricatures of them that her shop became known as 'the Macaroni Print Shop'. The lyrics of the song 'Yankee Doodle Dandy' were written in 1755 by a British army surgeon, Richard Shuckburgh, and the British troops initially sang it to make fun of fashion-obsessed American soldiers. The first verse of the song went: 'Yankee Doodle went to town, a-riding on a pony, stuck a feather in his cap, and called it macaroni.' The song was eventually adopted by Americans, during the War of Independence, who added new verses that mocked British troops, and by 1781 it had become a song of national pride for Americans.

The term *macaroni* gradually went out of fashion, being initially synonymous with, then supplanted by, *dandy* from around the 1790s. Dandy became popular during the Napoleonic wars, describing a man who was well groomed and well dressed, but not perhaps as outrageously dressed as a macaroni. The archetypal dandy was George Bryan Brummell, known as Beau. Brummell was an interesting character, not coming from an aristocratic background (his father had achieved wealth by becoming Private Secretary to Lord North, who served as Prime Minister from 1770 to 1782). The Brummell family were middle-class and had ambitions – young Beau was educated at Eton College and went on to Oxford University, leaving aged sixteen and joining the army as an officer of the lowest rank. Beau was not academically outstanding or particularly suited to military life, but he had oodles of charisma and a quick wit, which made him incredibly popular – had he been alive today it's likely that he would have had a lucrative career as a social media influencer. It was in the army where Brummell caught the attention of the Prince of Wales (later King George IV). The prince was an extravagant and somewhat unrefined man, whose interests were eating, hard drinking, horse-riding and women. He also had rather camp tastes and in 1787 he commissioned Henry Holland to turn an old farmhouse in the seaside town of Brighton into what became known as the Royal Pavilion. With its domes and minarets, the building resembles an Indian palace and its lavish décor earns my award for the Campest Building in the Campest City in the UK.

As a child, Prince George's father had only allowed him to eat the crusts of fruit pies, to keep his weight down – this was not a habit that continued into adult life, and the prince's favourite breakfast consisted of two pigeons, three beefsteaks, three quarters of a bottle of wine, a glass of dry champagne, two glasses of port and a glass of brandy. Not having the most becoming figure (his waist when girdled was fifty-five inches), he was fascinated with trim, handsome, sparkling Brummell, and the two quickly became best buddies. Having secured royal patronage, Brummell immediately resigned from the army, establishing himself in London as the fashion leader he was meant to be.

It was there that he established a 'look' that would be widely copied – dark coat, full-length trousers, linen shirt and a cravat. Compared to the macaronis it was understated, but, stylish and distinctly masculine, it continues to influence male tailoring today. Colours were muted – white, buff and blue-black. Breeches were made of tight-fitting marble-coloured wool that revealed the shape of your legs and made men look like Greek statues (if they had the physique to pull it off). Brummell didn't even wear a wig – a scarcity of flour in 1795, combined with a hair-powder tax (yes, really), had resulted in men eschewing their wigs in protest, and so Brummell instead epitomised the new sartorial style for men – your own hair, brushed forwards and zhooshed up to give it volume, in a 'Brutus' cut. He had a very rigorous grooming routine, always being clean-shaven, and he would examine his face in a dentist's magnifying mirror, removing stray hairs with tweezers. A lot of attention was given to cleaning his teeth, along with daily bathing. Ironically, his manly appearance was only achieved by a level of primping that is usually seen as excessively feminine. These grooming sessions had a sense of camp theatricality about them – they were conducted with an audience, often Prince George himself. Brummell was usually fully or partially naked and, while there was no suggestion of anything overtly sexual, the homoeroticism level was set to maximum.

Brummell's claims about his grooming regime became increasingly outrageous – it took him five hours to get ready to go out; he recommended that boots should be polished with champagne; he told a widow that it would cost £800 to keep her son fashionably dressed (at the time the average annual wage was around £52). It was these kinds of silly pronouncements, just as much as the fastidious grooming routines, that have resulted in Brummell being labelled as camp by twentieth-century commentators like Susan Sontag. When dining, a female companion noticed that he passed on the greens and she inquired if he ever ate vegetables. 'Yes, madam, I once ate a pea,' was his response. He even claimed to have ended a potential engagement to be married because the woman in question liked cabbage.

But the qualities that made Brummell camp would eventually bring about his downfall. His love of excess, the endless shopping sprees, the attempts to live the high life, the gambling – even with an inheritance equivalent to £2.5 million,[27] this lifestyle could not be sustained forever. Worst of all, Prince George gradually got tired of Brummell. In 1813, during a masquerade ball, of all things, that Brummell hosted with his cronies Lord Alvanley, Henry Mildmay and Henry Pierrepont, the prince 'cut' Brummell, staring at his face but only acknowledging Alvanley and Pierrepont. In the UK, this was, still is, and always will be, the gravest and most hideous of all insults, signifying a relationship that has irrevocably broken down. Brummell had no choice but to respond with a camp put-down, 'Alvanley, who's your fat friend?' The bold remark was widely repeated but the person who mattered most wasn't laughing. Social death was the result. By 1816, Brummell's over-spending had caught up with him and having lost the patronage of the prince, he fled to France to escape prison. Lord Alvanley eventually managed to get him a job as consul to Caen, but

Brummell spent the later years of his life penniless and, by all accounts, increasingly slovenly in his dress. *Quel dommage!*

THE VICTORIAN QUEENS

While Jean-Baptiste Molière's use of *se camper* in 1671 indicated that awareness of camp had been around in France for a couple of centuries, it appears to have taken some time for the term to make its way across the Channel. The dandies affected a languid wit while their fashion and grooming choices were excessive, but they are unlikely to have been called camp. The Mollies, with their cross-dressing performances and delight in wordplay were purposefully camp, despite not appearing to have a word to label what they were, and it isn't until we reach the nineteenth century that we start to see cases of intentional camp in England that had acquired the vocabulary for self-recognition.

Bruce LaBruce views camp as having become a secret language in Victorian England, particularly among men who sought sex with other men. He refers to camp as 'almost kabbalistic references and practices developed in order to operate safely apart and without fear of detection from a conservative and conventional world that could be aggressively hostile.'[28] I suspect that there was a bit more than this going on – camp wasn't just a code, like semaphore, that you could sit down with a pen and paper and learn, it was a sensibility and a form of behaviour that characterised the central identity of some gay men. It was a form of expression that perhaps best represented their authentic selves – this being despite our common understandings of camp being linked to artificiality.

Being largely a word associated with an underground and illegal subculture that did not write about itself extensively, during a period where recording technology did not exist, it is difficult to find on-record references to camp during the Victorian era. What we do have tends to come from court cases, which at least give illuminating insights despite the serious contexts in which they occurred. For example, on 28 April 1870, Frederick Park and Ernest Boulton (known to their friends as Fanny and Stella) – two cross-dressing actors who were probably also sex workers – occupied a box at the Strand Theatre, accompanied by two male friends. Some time ago their behaviour had attracted the attention of the police and, unknown to them, they had been under surveillance for over a year. This was the night that the police decided to make a move and they were arrested as soon as they left the theatre. The next morning, still in drag from the night before, Park and Boulton were charged with buggery, conspiring others to commit buggery, and to scandalously outrage public decency and corrupt public morals by disguising themselves as women. At Bow Magistrates Court, various letters they had written were read out. One was a letter by Park to Lord Arthur Clinton, who, up until a couple of years previously, had been a Liberal MP. Park wrote: 'I cannot echo your wish that I should live to be a hundred, though I should like to live to a green old age. Green did I say? Oh, ciel! The amount of paint that will be required to hide that very unbecoming tint! My "campish" undertakings are not at present meeting with the success they deserve.'[29]

Park's use of *campish* is notable for his use of quote marks round it – indicating he is aware of its colloquial status. It is not just the word campish that is of interest in the letter though, it's the style and subject matter – Park's flight of fancy in imagining how much paint would be needed to cover up his skin if it turned green, a colour described as 'very unbecoming', his dramatic French exclamation '*oh, ciel*' (oh, heavens). One hundred and fifty years later, this is recognisably camp discourse.

On 17 June 1870, Lord Clinton received his subpoena to testify in Boulton and Park's trial for sodomy. He apparently died the following day, officially of scarlet fever, although it is possible that he committed suicide or even faked his death and moved abroad to avoid scandal. There was no such escape for Boulton and Park, whose trial took place the following year in May. The pair had a very good defence, who argued that they were merely feckless and immature, while many of the witness statements went in their favour too. As a result, the jury returned verdicts of not guilty, enabling Boulton to snatch all the attention by fainting dramatically – although I suspect he would have fainted no matter what the outcome had been.

Another example comes a few years later in 1884, during what was known as the Dublin Scandals, which involved a campaign by Irish Nationalist William O'Brien against Dublin Castle, the seat of the English government in Ireland. O'Brien made accusations against several notable men, accusing them of engaging in indecent acts, including sodomy. A sex worker called Malcolm Johnston was one of the witnesses for the prosecution, and during the trial he gave evidence against the accused men, describing how he had arranged a 'drag ball' at his father's home in the wealthy area of Ballsbridge, and how the men had female nicknames for each other. Johnston himself was named Lady Constance Clyde or, more affectionally, Conny, another man was referred to as the Marchioness of Dame Street and a third was Ma Fowler. Johnston read a letter he had sent to one of the accused, James Pillar, who he referred to as his 'Pa' (perhaps a precursor to what today we'd call a *daddy*). Johnston described how he had been bribing police with sex. 'My dear, "Pa", I have been in the hands of the police (don't be frightened) or rather the other way, the police have been in my hands so many times lately that my lilly [*sic*] white hands have been trembling, and I am utterly fucked out. Such camp.' The word camp was clearly unfamiliar to most of those present because Johnston was required to explain that it meant amusement: 'It might mean proper amusement or it might mean improper amusement'.[30] Pillar initially pleaded not guilty, but then admitted to the charges, being sentenced to twenty years' imprisonment. He was discharged in 1894 on the grounds of ill health after serving half his sentence, dying six months later.

During other trials we are given full instruction in the meaning of camp without anyone having to say the word. Take, for example, the rather sorry case of Oscar Wilde, a nineteenth-century fount of camp epigrams: 'I am not young enough to know everything'; 'To love oneself is the beginning of a lifelong romance'; 'Everything in moderation, including moderation'. In the 1890s, Wilde was one of the most famous people in the world, with plays like *Lady Windermere's Fan*, *A Woman of No Importance* and *The Importance of Being Earnest*, and fiction like *The Happy Prince* and *The Picture of Dorian Gray* propelling him to stardom. Wilde's writings often focus on aestheticism, decadence and wit, with characters oozing quotable flippancy from every pore. Take Lord Darlington from *Lady Windermere's Fan*: 'Life is far too important a thing ever to talk seriously about'; 'It is absurd to divide people into good and bad. People are either charming or tedious'; 'I can resist everything except temptation'. Wilde's play *Salome* was illustrated in 1893 by the artist Aubrey Beardsley, who depicted the characters as heavily stylised, eroticised and flouting sexual and gender norms of the time, indeed, of *any* time. In these pictures everyone is dressed extravagantly, with complicated headpieces, over-the-top hairstyles, abundant jewellery and flowing gowns that don't exactly cover their bodies. Characters are depicted with satisfied, knowing looks on their faces. Brigid Brophy wrote of Beardsley's pictures of women, 'Are they female fops, these personages of Beardsley's: female dandies: female effeminates, even? Or are they male hoydens, male tomboys, boy butches?'[31] Combined with Wilde's plays, Beardsley's drawings depicted a most un-Victorian sensibility, one that was dangerously, alluringly camp, attracting as many critics as adherents.

It is perhaps unsurprising then, that Wilde became caught up in two of the most famous trials of all time, which, Chris Freeman has argued, illustrates the limits of camp, at least in terms of its ability to win the favour of juries in 1890s Britain.[32] And it was all over a pretty young man, how commonplace! Wilde had become infatuated with Lord Alfred Douglas (Bosie to his friends) and the two had conducted a somewhat public affair, with Bosie introducing Wilde to a series of male sex workers, which Wilde later described as 'like feasting with panthers'.[33] Bosie's father, unfortunately, was the Marquess of Queensberry, a butch brute of a man whose biggest passion was boxing (he helped found the Amateur Athletic Club and gave his name to the rules used for conducting boxing matches). When he found out about Wilde's relationship with his son, he was disgusted, demanding that Bosie stop seeing Wilde, on the threat of disinheritance. Bosie was dismissive, telegramming his father the message: 'What a funny little man you are.' Queensberry was furious and escalated the situation, showing up at Wilde's home in Chelsea with a prize-fighting boxer in tow, presumably for back-up. There

'The very essence of romance is uncertainty.'
Oscar Wilde and Lord Alfred (Bosie) Douglas 1894.

was an angry exchange and Wilde sent Queensberry packing, telling him, 'I do not know what the Queensberry rules are, but the Oscar Wilde rule is to shoot on sight.'

On 14 February 1895, Queensberry decided to disrupt the opening night of Wilde's play *The Importance of Being Earnest* at the St James's Theatre, but Wilde got wind of the plan and ensured that the theatre was surrounded by police. Queensberry hung around for about three hours but was unable to gain entrance, so he eventually left, muttering darkly to himself. Four days later, he called at Wilde's club, the Albemarle Club, leaving a card that read: 'For Oscar Wilde posing Somdomite [*sic*].' In hindsight, Wilde ought to have taken the advice of his friends, like George Bernard Shaw and Frank Harris, and gone travelling abroad for a year or so, but he reasoned that Queensberry wasn't going to drop the matter, so he decided to slug it out in court, suing the Marquess for libel. If Wilde was good at anything, he could put on a show – he would be his own star witness, the judge and jury would be bowled over by his brilliant performance and he would be vindicated amid applause and bouquets of roses thrown from the galleries.

But it didn't turn out like that exactly. Queensberry had employed a tenacious solicitor, Edward Carson, who knew Wilde of old and didn't think much of him.[34] At the Old Bailey, Carson cross-examined Wilde for two and a half days. It began with questions about Wilde's literary works, with Carson aiming to show how Wilde's writing was immoral or touched on homosexual themes. During this part of the trial, the exchanges were of the cut and thrust kind that showed Wilde at his wittiest. When Carson suggested that *The Portrait of Dorian Gray* was a 'perverted novel', Wilde replied insultingly, 'That could only be to brutes and illiterates. The views of Philistines on art are incalculably stupid.' Wilde was on reasonably safe ground here, but this wasn't the main show – Carson was toying with him, holding the real evidence back for later.

He had done his homework, and the second part of the cross-examination involved working through a list of young men whom Wilde had known, producing gifts that Wilde had given them, which garnered astonished reactions from jury members. He eventually got to a young man called Charles Parker. Wilde managed to get in a few zingers – when asked about Parker's age, he professed not to know: 'Really, I do not keep a *census*.' Carson then asked Wilde about whether he had hosted Parker for tea and Wilde gave one of his typically flippant responses:

> I delight in the society of people much younger than myself. I like those who may be called idle and careless. I recognize no social distinctions at all of any kind, and to me youth – the mere fact of youth – is so wonderful that I would sooner talk to a young man half an hour than even be, well, cross-examined in court.

Although this produced laughter from the gallery, the judge and the jury remained stony-faced. A few minutes later, Carson asked Wilde about a sixteen-year-old called Walter Grainger: 'Did you ever kiss him?' Wilde responded as if he was a character in one of his silly plays: 'Oh no, never in my life. He was a peculiarly plain boy. I pitied him for it.' As camp lines go, it was a good one. If this *had* been one of Wilde's plays, it would have been the point of triumph. But this was real life and Carson pursued the point, asking again and again why Wilde had brought up the young man's ugliness. As a result, Wilde became increasingly flustered, to the point where his speech became inarticulate – the worst thing that can happen when camp is your defence. Carson kept at him, like a yapping dog: 'Why? Why? Why did you add that?' Finally, Wilde's camp carapace cracked, and what he said next was depressingly sincere: 'You sting me and insult me and try to unnerve me; and at times one says things flippantly when one ought to speak more seriously. I admit it.'

It was going to get worse. In Carson's opening speech in defence of Queensberry he tantalisingly claimed that he would produce several young men who would testify to their sexual association with Wilde. He may as well have pulled out a smoking gun. That evening Wilde's lawyer persuaded him to drop the case. The Marquess was not magnanimous in victory – he sued Wilde for expenses incurred on lawyers and private detectives, effectively bankrupting him. And that was just the start. Queensberry sent his package of evidence to Scotland Yard, which resulted in Wilde being tried for gross indecency on 26 April 1895. Now the promised parade of young men appeared, most of them expressing shame for their actions. Four days later, Wilde took the stand. He had lost his confident pose and quietly denied the allegations of indecent behaviour. The jury returned the verdict of guilty on all counts (excepting those relating to one man called Edward Shelley). Some in the courtroom cheered while others shouted, 'Shame!' It was a crushing humiliation and the end of his life as he had known it.

Wilde served two years in prison, spending a couple of months in the prison infirmary after collapsing from illness and hunger, rupturing his right ear drum. When he was transferred to Reading Gaol from Newgate Prison, a crowd on the railway platform jeered and spat on him. On his release, he left the UK for France, never to return. He died three years later, on 30 November 1900, of meningitis, aged forty-six, having become increasingly infirm and impoverished. One of his last jokes was about the state of his hotel room: 'My wallpaper and I are fighting a duel to the death. One of us has got to go.' At least that remark trumps some of the disgrace and indignity that he had endured. Wilde might have been publicly shamed and incarcerated, but that show of camp at the end indicates that his spirit was unbroken. I hope that he had the foresight to realise that the world would change, and when his story came to be told, he would be the hero. It is his words and his works that we remember. A fitting epitaph would be one of his most quoted and campest sayings: 'There is only one thing in the world worse than being talked about, and that is not being talked about.'

YOU IS NO GENTLEMAN

While camp was becoming explicitly associated with the emerging identity of 'the homosexual' in the mid-to-late nineteenth and early twentieth centuries, in America, elements of camp were being incorporated by Black people, in a stylized form of entertainment that parodied the formal gait of slaveholders. In 1860, four million Black Americans (around thirteen per cent of the US population) were slaves, almost all of them in the South, many being made to work on cotton and sugar plantations or as servants. With pressure to restrict and ultimately abolish slavery from Northern states, led by President Abraham Lincoln, eleven Southern states seceded from the United States, with Jefferson Davis elected president of the new Confederate States of America. A bloody Civil War took place between 1861 to 1865, resulting in 670,000 deaths, many as a result of diseases like dysentery and typhoid. After the Confederate States were defeated, they were re-admitted back into the United States. On 8 April 1864, the Thirteenth Amendment to the US Constitution, abolishing slavery, was passed by the Senate, and ratified on 6 December 1865, although Lincoln didn't live to see this – he was assassinated on 15 April 1865 by an actor called John Wilkes Booth. And, of course, segregation laws and prejudice would continue to make life much more difficult for Black people in the US long after slavery was outlawed.

Both before and after this point, dance contests were held at social events around plantations, with the prize for the winner often being a cake. These contests were called 'prize walks' and dances were referred to as 'walk-arounds', 'chalkline-walks' and 'cakewalks'. Interviews with former slaves carried out in the

1930s gave first-hand accounts of the contests. Louise Jones from Virginia described how slaves would set the floor in turns and do the cakewalk most of the night, while Estella Jones from Georgia described how the women wore long ruffled hoop dresses while the men were dressed in high hats, split-tail coats and carried walking sticks.[35]

The contestants would exaggerate the dance styles associated with minuets and waltzes.[36] As Hafizah Geter describes:

> Black dancers puffed out their chests, held their heads comically erect on their spines. They marched in exaggerated high-knee steps while draping themselves in an air of propriety that reached toward hysterics – all of it mocking their white captors. Cakewalking required an attitude of exuberant pride.[37]

It is unlikely that the slave-owners realised that they were being mocked, most likely they thought the dances were straightforward attempts to emulate them. And so, the term cakewalk acquired a new meaning, to refer to something that was effortless or easy. It's where the idiom 'it's a piece of cake' comes from. A cakewalk might have *looked* easy to do, but even this was misunderstood – learning the steps and holding the body in the rigid positions was incredibly demanding physically.

The dance style became very popular – in 1876, it was exhibited at the Philadelphia Centennial, and, in 1908, at the International Conference of Dancing Masters in Berlin, it was selected as the dance of America. White people decided to have a go, appropriating the cakewalk, not realising that it was meant to mock them. They danced the cakewalk in minstrel shows, sometimes wearing black makeup. Even Judy Garland, who plays a key role later in our story, got in on the act, performing a cakewalk in 1944 with Margaret O'Brien in the musical *Meet Me in St Louis*. Wearing straw boaters and holding canes, the pair sing a song about 'a Zulu from

Vogue, nineteenth-century style.
Dancers performing the cakewalk in New York.

Mataboolooo' who falls in love with a 'maid of royal blood though dusky shade'. Towards the end of the performance, they engage in an exaggerated stepping dance, holding their hats aloft in one hand. In 1963, Amiri Baraka, writing as LeRoi Jones, said of the cakewalks, 'I find the idea of white minstrels in blackface satirizing a dance satirizing themselves a remarkable kind of irony – which, I suppose, is the whole point of minstrel shows.'[38]

Cakewalks were a form of camp subversion, but some of the dancers took the camp aspect to a new level. Enter William Dorsey Swann, born in Maryland in 1860. His entire family were enslaved to a plantation owner called Ann Murray. After the end of the Civil War his parents bought a farm and William took a job as a hotel waiter. In the 1880s and 1890s he organised balls in Washington DC for other men who had been enslaved. It was not easy to find out about these events – you might receive a whispered invitation about them at your local YMCA if you knew the right people. The balls were held in private homes and the men performed their cakewalks wearing dresses of satin and silk. William called himself the Queen of Drag and he and his friends were collectively known as 'the House of Swann', a naming that signified a chosen family. This was the start of a tradition that, as we will see later, has continued among drag queens to the present day.

On 12 April 1888, William held a very special ball for his thirtieth birthday, which took place in a house in L Street, a few minutes' walk from the White House.[39] He wore a 'gorgeous dress of cream-coloured satin'.[40] However, as the night got under way, the party was rudely gate-crashed by the police. To avoid arrest, members of the House of Swann put up a fight and during the melee William's dress was torn to shreds. He disgustedly told the police lieutenant in charge, 'You is no gentleman!' Twelve other men were arrested at the ball although around seventeen managed to escape. The raid caused quite a stir, with hundreds of people turning up at the police station where the men were being held, wanting to get a look at them in their finery.

This wasn't the first time that one of Williams' drag balls had been raided. A similar one had taken place on 14 January 1887, with six Black men in low-neck and short-sleeve silk dresses brought up in court the following day. There were reports of arrests made of drag queens en route to the balls, with descriptions of their bewitching fascinators and cashmere dresses.[41] Prurient descriptions of the raids on the balls in newspapers like the *Washington Post*, the *Washington Critic* and the *National Republican* whipped up a sense of scandal, trying to shame those involved by publishing the names of the men who had been arrested. As a result, William became a local notoriety, making it much more difficult for him to organise balls, although the news reports also helped to publicise their existence for those who wanted to attend. William was undeterred and continued to host balls in the following years. In 1896, he was sentenced to prison for ten months on the false charge of keeping a 'disorderly house' (a euphemism for a brothel), which the *Evening*

Star referred to as a 'Hell of iniquity'. The judge in the case told him that he wished he could have imposed a ten-year sentence. Then he said:

> I would like to send you where you would never again see a man's face . . . and would then like to rid the city of all other disreputable persons of the same kind. Thieving and petty assaults amount to nothing as compared with the conduct of these people.

William asked for a pardon from the sitting president, Grover Cleveland, putting in a petition that had thirty other signatures. His request was denied, with the Attorney, A A Birney, writing:

> This petition is wholly without merit. While the charge of keeping a disorderly house does not on its face differ from other cases in which milder sentences have been imposed, the prisoner was in fact convicted of the most horrible and disgusting offences known to the law; an offence so disgusting that it is unnamed. This is not the first time that the prisoner has been convicted of this crime, and his evil example in the community must have been most corrupting.[42]

William served out his sentence and eventually retired from hosting balls at the end of the nineteenth century. He is the first recorded American to pursue legal and political action for the right of LGBTQ+ people to gather and his story forms the first part of a thread of Black American camp, which we will trace throughout this book.

There is little more horrific than slavery. As Hafizah Geter writes, 'Camp is a negotiation of horror, grief, and the absurd – it requires allowing yourself the space to look at what else gazing into that abyss calls up in you.'[43] Cakewalks are an example of how camp was used as a form of defiance by the dispossessed, a way of signalling, 'You will *never* break me.' In Susan Sontag's famous 'Notes on "Camp"' essay, her second note is that 'the Camp sensibility is disengaged, depoliticized – or at least apolitical'.[44] Perhaps she had never heard of cakewalks.

Even this early in our story, it is easy to see how problematic it is to present a simple definition of camp. It is in the mannered ostentation of privileged Versailles, the defiant parodying of the cakewalk dancers, Beau Brummell's wit and elegance, Oscar Wilde's flippancy, and the dirty jokes of Victorian sex workers. Perhaps we need to get a bit more focused. The next chapter introduces a different set of people – who have proved to be rather influential on my own development, the Bright Young Things and their associates.

CHAPTER 3

Cocktails and Laughter

Aged thirteen, during the Easter Holidays in 1986, I am taken by my parents on a family outing to nearby Durham, north-east England's quaintest city. Durham has a fairy-tale feel to it and I always feel out-of-place among the book shops and twee cafés, not to mention its university, cathedral and castle. It is the latter that my parents opt to visit today, paying for a tour. The university tends to attract students from well-to-do families 'down south', while the bright local kids often end up at nearby Newcastle Polytechnic. Our guide round the castle is one of these misplaced southern students, a somewhat otherworldly young man sporting maroon trousers and a strangulated upper-class accent that none of us have heard before. He pronounces *house* to rhyme with *mice*, while *castle* is a single syllable with all of its vowels amputated. His social class is so alien and he is so fragrantly well-mannered that he comes across as effortlessly camp.

I am not intellectual enough to enjoy an interminable (actually sixty-minute) history lesson so halfway through I start to act up. My mocking is not openly disruptive but instead I try to make my family members laugh by stealthily conveying opinions with my own camp facial expressions. My little sister is the first to succumb and she has to cram her hands into her mouth and hide behind my father. My parents wisely try to avoid my gaze but I manage to get them too, and they both erupt with laughter at an impromptu moment, causing the other members of our tour group to issue glares in our direction. The poor guide is none the wiser, hopefully, or just too well brought up to remonstrate at my bad behaviour.

Afterwards, we stop off at the cosy stationery chain W H Smith and I squander all my pocket money on a calligraphy set, then spend the rest of the holiday trying to get the nib pen to make pretty letters with swooping whiplash lines. Despite my inverted class snobbery towards the student, I am secretly envious of him and my sudden interest in calligraphy is a misguided attempt at being posh. I shouldn't have felt too guilty about making fun of him though. A few years later, at university, my own accent and middle-brow interests would frequently be the subject of slightly sneering interest. 'Where are you from? Wales? No? Holland then?' Even now I am regularly informed that I have 'funny vowels', and I have to stop myself from snapping, 'Well, at least I don't pronounce funny as fanny, like you do!'

This chapter is about how camp became synonymous with the British upper class (and to a lesser extent upper-middles), from some point around the 1920s until after World War II. This was a relatively small, insular world, difficult to break into, with various unwritten codes of behaviour to keep people out, even those who thought they could buy their way in. Boys went to a boarding school like Eton or Rugby, then on to Oxford or Cambridge at a time when university participation was extremely limited. In 1930, only 9,129 people were awarded a Bachelor's degree in the UK[45] (the equivalent figure in 2021 was 359,115[46]). By the time they had left university young men were pretty much assured a fast-track to the top of any field of endeavour that they chose. Girls received a patchier education, sometimes being taught at home by governesses, although they might be sent abroad, often to one of the 'finishing schools' near Lake Geneva in Switzerland where they could be taught social graces and etiquette. When they were of marriageable age they would be presented at the Court of St James's as debutantes, a practice that wasn't abolished until 1958. This was followed by a season of afternoon tea parties, evening balls and polo matches so they could be introduced to eligible men – it was simply not *done* to marry outside your class. Although they had various estates or country piles dotted around the UK, many of them also had large homes in London and they moved in tight social circles. For those of a literary bent, their wealth and connections provided them with a platform to get their voices heard. And so, it was their stories that tended to be told – and, of course, they wrote about what they knew. So British literature of the 1920s to the 1940s is dominated by the 'uppers' – helped by the fact that everybody else wanted to read about the lives of the wealthy and powerful. And, because these writers were from the upper classes, they were more at liberty to break taboos.

Being upper class is one of the easiest routes to camp – the extravagance, the snobbishness, the boredom, the showing off, the excesses in taste, the assumption of privilege, the detachment from everyday problems. As one of our camp writers in this chapter, Nancy Mitford, casually observed of ordinary folk, 'People in towns are always preoccupied. "Have I missed the bus? Have I forgotten the potatoes? Can I get across the road?"' If you are upper class the answers to these questions are, respectively, 'I own the bus, I own the potatoes, and I own the road.'

KEEP CAMP AND CARRY ON

During this period, a camp sensibility suffused the cultural output of a small group of creatively minded people from reasonably privileged backgrounds. The exception, of course, is Noël Coward, who had a relatively modest start in life but was able to parody the role of an upper-class dandy in a way that was so perfect that nobody had any choice but to accept it. Coward's grandfather on his mother's side had been a captain in the Royal Navy, although his father was a somewhat lacklustre piano salesman and the family were not well off. As a boy, Coward had a flair for performing and an ear for sparkling dialogue, and these skills helped him gain access to High Society. By his mid-twenties, four of his plays were running simultaneously in the West End – *The Vortex*, *Fallen Angels*, *Hay Fever* and *On with the Dance* – and he was earning today's equivalent of £3 million a year. His plays had rather risqué themes for the times – *The Vortex* was about an ageing socialite who had affairs with young men, while her son was addicted to cocaine and also possibly gay. These were the kinds of people whom Coward was intimate with, although, like many 'bachelors' of the time, he refused to openly acknowledge his sexuality, commenting, 'There are still a few ladies in Worthing who don't know' in the 1960s.[47]

Many of Coward's characters were breezy stereotypes of upper-class society, which only someone who had been an outsider could concoct, and Coward himself assumed the persona of an effete wit, posing for photos in silk dressing gowns with either a cigarette holder or a cocktail glass. 'Why do I drink champagne for breakfast? Doesn't everyone?' is a typical Coward quote, demonstrating his signature combination of extravagance and flippancy. Coward was a talented songwriter, composing witty observational songs with titles like 'Mrs Worthington' and 'Poor Little Rich Girl'. In the latter song, Coward refers to cocktails and laughter, asking what comes after and declares that the titular character is weaving love into a *mad jazz pattern*. Did I mention he was on £3 million a year?

It is impossible to talk about this period without acknowledging the devastating impact of World War II. With reference to camp, we could be on very shaky ground here. Genocide and nightly bombings of cities are not topics we would immediately associate with camp, although sometimes, when our prospects are at their darkest, and our enemies appear at their most powerful, a camp sensibility can signal a show of strength. Coward threw himself into the war effort, running the British propaganda office in Paris and working for the secret service. One of his satirical songs, 'Don't Let's Be Beastly to the Germans' was composed in 1943. With typical flippancy, Coward tells his audience that because the war is pretty much won, we should turn the other cheek to the Germans and bring out their latent sense of fun. After all, it was those 'nasty Nazis' who got them to fight. Winston Churchill loved it, but the camp sentiment did not go down well with the general listening public who complained in droves. As a result, the BBC banned the song from being played on the radio.[48]

The Nazis certainly intended to be beastly to Coward. Assuming their success, they had a 'kill list' of Allied celebrities, which included Virginia Woolf, H G Wells, Paul Robeson and Noël Coward. When this fact was revealed later, Coward made light of it, noting a telegram he'd received from a fellow member of the list, Rebecca West: 'My dear – the people we should have been seen dead with.'

If 'Don't Let's Be Beastly to the Germans' didn't hit the mark, Coward had more success with the naval war film that he wrote and co-directed with David Lean. Polymath as he was, he also composed the music and had a starring role in it. *In Which We Serve* (1942) is a patriotic film about a British destroyer which is capsized by German bombers during the invasion of Crete. Coward played the ship's debonair Captain – an *interesting* casting choice. If you can buy that he is married to Celia Johnson and has managed to produce two children with her, then you should have no trouble accepting him as inspiring the respect of 244 burly sailors. When he makes a rousing speech to them in his clipped morning-room voice, they all stare at him in stunned silence. My favourite part of the film is when Coward and his men are evacuating troops from Dunkirk, and he gives the evacuees his favourite drink to warm them up. 'It's damn good,' says one of the officers. 'Just ordinary Bovril rather heavily laced with sherry,' Coward explains. Bovril is a beef-flavoured warm drink – exactly the sort of thing to fortify you during a wartime evacuation. But it is the 'rather heavily laced with sherry' part that summarises Coward perfectly and subverts this rousing war film into something more deliciously whimsical.

Coward's screen-wife, Celia Johnson, appeared in several of his other films, including the classic *Brief Encounter* (also directed by David Lean), which was ranked as the second-best film of all time by the British Film Institute. It was also the name of a gay bar in St Martins Lane, London, which was popular with office workers looking for a pick-up on the way home – earning it the nickname, Briefcase Encounter. But I digress. *Brief Encounter* is the somewhat melodramatic story of two people, Laura and Alec, who fall in love at a train station. However, any chance they have of a lasting relationship is doomed because they are married to other people, and Sergei Rachmaninoff's work was looted to provide a sentimental, over-the-top soundtrack. The film features several camp supporting characters, like Laura's gossipy friend, Dolly Messister, and the supercilious owner of the train station café, Myrtle Bagot, who gets some of the best lines: 'Now look at my Banburys all over the floor!', 'You saucy upstart!' and 'I don't know to what you're referring'. Actor and drama coach Steve Nallon stresses to his students that they should never be camp or knowing, nor try to be funny when they perform Coward's lines 'because it is the knowingness of camp that is the real enemy of Coward's style'.[49]

Celia Johnson always manages to show great restraint in her *Brief Encounter* monologues and voice-overs, her cut-glass accent almost masking her passion. Here's my favourite Celia monologue – and if anything sums up the dramatic stoicism of the British, then this is it:

> This can't last. This misery can't last. I must remember that and try to control myself. Nothing lasts really. Neither happiness nor despair. Not even life lasts very long. There'll come a time in the future when I shan't mind about this anymore, when I can look back and say quite peacefully and cheerfully how silly I was. No, no, I don't want that

time to come ever. I want to remember every minute, always, always to the end of my days.

Brief Encounter is also a perfect showcase for one of Coward's great camp techniques – over-use of degree adverbs, a grammatical class of words that ooze camp. And what a lot of work they are put to. Degree adverbs are words that describe the degree to which a verb or an adjective applies, often ending in *-ly* – *frightfully*, *terribly*, *awfully*, *dreadfully* etc., all of which act as boosters, helping to emphasise a statement, and, for repressed British people, they are an indication of flirtation. Uses in *Brief Encounter* include: 'You look terribly peaky'; 'I'm perfectly all right now'; 'How awfully nice you are'; 'I enjoyed the afternoon enormously'. However, another set – compromisers, like *rather* and *quite* are used as a form of understatement; a British way of not making a fuss. 'I tried not to show it but I was quite hysterical,' admits Laura at one point. However, to make things complicated, boosters and compromisers are frequently used ironically, meaning the opposite of what they're intended, so whenever you hear a Brit using a degree adverb, you can be sure you're in for trouble. Degree adverbs were more common back in Coward's day. For every three of them that you'd encounter in 1931, you'd only come across two of them in 2021.[50] Americans, on the other hand, were never that big on them in the first place – and I suspect that they will continue their decline, becoming a kind of camp echo of a more restrained age.

A more straightforwardly camp venture was Coward's *Blithe Spirit* (1945), another David Lean collaboration, which first enthralled me during a weekday television matinee when I was home from school with the flu. Unlike his other works, *Blithe Spirit* deals with the supernatural, being the story of Charles Condomine and his second wife, Ruth, who hold a séance that goes dramatically awry – his first wife, Elvira, is summoned back to Earth, though only Charles can see her. Elvira is played by Kay Hammond, covered in green makeup with a languid, adenoidal self-assurance. 'Well, I really think you might be a little more pleased to see me, after all, you conjured me up,' she tells Charles. Upper-class people are camp enough but imagine how even more bored and entitled they'd be if they were ghosts – there is no attempt to hide that this is anything but all-out comedy. Elvira turns out to be spectacularly catty, making poor Ruth's life a misery. Added to this magic potion is the superb character actress Margaret Rutherford, who plays a dotty medium called Madame Arcati, gurning and mugging her way through each scene. *Blithe Spirit* is perhaps the most accessible of Coward's works, and the ending has one of his trademark stings in it – the message being that a normal heterosexual marriage is a fate worse than death.

In the 1950s and '60s, Coward starred in a diverse range of films, playing a weirdo neighbour in the deliciously titled *Bunny Lake is Missing* (1965), an incarcerated crime boss in cult hit *The Italian Job* (1969) and Bill Ridgeway (also known as the Witch of Capri) in the rather less acclaimed *Boom!* (1968), which John Waters has described as 'Beyond bad. It's the other side of camp. It's beautiful, atrocious, and it's perfect . . . I never tire of it'.[51] *Boom!* is an adaption of a Tennessee Williams play with Elizabeth Taylor as Flora, a wealthy, terminally ill woman living on an island, who is visited by a man nick-named 'the Angel of Death', played by her then-husband, Richard Burton. Coward makes a bizarre entrance in a full dinner suit, being carried on the shoulders of a servant, calling 'Sissy!' to Flora. His line, 'My heart pumps blood that isn't my own blood but is the blood of anonymous blood donors' suggests he is somewhat vampiric, although in fact he tries (unsuccessfully) to divert the other characters from their tragic conclusion. Hidden inside the brittle, sparkling carapace, Mr Coward had a heart.

Like Oscar Wilde before him, Noël Coward had an enormous cultural influence over British society – bringing an upper-class camp sensibility into the homes of ordinary people for decades, despite neglecting to define the genre with a label. But, unlike Wilde, he was never disgraced. Coward's trick was to spot the camp

Is that what you're going to wear? Noël Coward and Elizabeth Taylor in *Boom!*

in British society and then to reflect it back upon itself – it was a case of ready or not, here I come, and audiences loved it. He was one of the first people who mainstreamed camp – I love thinking of how Home Counties wives dragged their stuffy old husbands to see his whimsical plays or how he introduced patriotic war-film fans to the idea of Bovril rather heavily laced with sherry (which actually isn't that bad a drink).

KEEPING UP WITH THE MITFORDS

Of course, all cocktails are essentially camp – even the ones that try to be butch like the Rusty Nail (Drambuie and Scotch Whisky). What can be said about a type of drink that has a tiny umbrella hanging off it? There have been claims that the umbrella provides shade to stop the ice melting or the alcohol evaporating, but this seems doubtful.[52] No, it is purely decorative – goodness knows what future alien civilisations will think we used them for. Cocktails were the epitome of classy camp in the 1930s, although they have a rather more dubious currency in modern times – when something called a Porn Star Martini appeared on supermarket shelves in 2018, I couldn't work out if I was more distressed by its name, the fact it was in a can, or that you could buy one from Marks & Spencer. It felt a bit like catching your grandmother in the bath.

At least Evelyn Waugh knew how to use them for character development. In *Brideshead Revisited* (1945), Waugh represented Oxford University (which he had attended from 1922 to 1924) as an elite hotbed of frivolity. His novel concerns the relationship of protagonist Charles Ryder with the members of the wealthy Flyte family who live in a mansion called Brideshead Castle. Charles meets Sebastian Flyte at university and becomes part of his flighty set of friends, which includes haughty homosexual Anthony Blanche. To Charles's inexperienced eyes, Anthony is described as 'ageless as a lizard, as foreign as a Martian'. Early in the book, Anthony takes a shine to Charles and asks him to dinner. He orders *four* Brandy Alexander cocktails[53] (there's a message of intent that's easy to decipher), and then gamely drinks them all himself when Charles chastely declines his two. 'Isn't this a delicious concoction? You don't like it? Then I will drink it for you. One, two, three, four, down the red lane they go. *How* the students stare!' Later, Anthony takes Charles to a 'pansy bar' called the Blue Grotto Club, which has gold and silver fish on the walls, and the pair have to fend off a youth who wants to know if Charles will dance the rumba with him. Anthony says, 'No, Tom, he would not, and I'm not going to give you a drink, not yet, anyway . . . That's a very impudent boy, a regular little gold-digger, my dear.'

Where Anthony's camp is knowing and jaded, Sebastian is childishly camp – he is unable to cope with adult life and carries around a large teddy bear called Aloysius. Early in the novel, Charles is at the barber's and Sebastian flounces in with the bear, wanting to buy a hairbrush – not to brush the bear's fur but to threaten him with a spanking when he is sulky. Yes, reader, these are our future leaders. It is a case of, aren't they outrageous, but what do you expect from the uppers? *Brideshead Revisited* was televised in the 1980s and several friends from working-class backgrounds told me they were put off applying to Oxford due to Sebastian and his sulky bear.

Three's a crowd. Anthony Andrews, Jeremy Irons and Aloysius in the 1981 television adaption of *Brideshead Revisited*.

The relationship between Charles and Sebastian is ambiguous – it is unlikely that Waugh's book would have received as much critical acclaim or even found a publisher if he had openly depicted them as lovers, but if that's what you want from the book, then there are hints – Charles writes that Sebastian is 'magically beautiful' and that when he met him he was 'in search of love'. This is followed by a metaphorical account of how he found a low door in the wall which opened onto an enchanted garden – was there ever a more fragrant account of gay sex? I don't think, though, that Waugh intended to write a gay love story – unlike some of the more shamelessly frivolous novels discussed later on in this chapter, *Brideshead Revisited* is viewed as a serious piece of literary fiction, dealing with themes of friendship, class, religion, innocence, suffering and rebellion. The camp feels almost like a trail of breadcrumbs, to lure you towards the heavier stuff, and while some of the languid narration could be interpreted as unintentional camp, the book is still widely admired as a classic. Indeed, Eileen Battersby, reviewing a film version of *Brideshead Revisited* in 2009, does not disguise her disappointment at the fact that the director camped up the relationship between Sebastian and Charles, allowing their scenes to collapse into camp melodrama.[54]

Waugh's friend and fellow author Nancy Mitford was appreciative of *Brideshead Revisited*. 'I am literally dazzled with admiration,' she characteristically wrote to him. Her only teeny criticism was actually a fairly major one – that the main character wasn't very glamorous and a tiny bit dim (he's a bit of a Mary Sue in today's fanfic parlance). She also couldn't work out why three of the other characters in the book would be in love with someone so dim. She does have a point – I think that Sebastian would have tired of Charles rather quickly in real life. Nancy may not be given credit for producing great literary works herself, but she was a more earnest devotee of camp, and her cataloguing of upper-class eccentricity showed that fact was often stranger than fiction.

Nancy was the eldest of seven children (all but one whom were girls), and the campest of the Mitfords, despite stiff competition. She once wrote: 'Life is sometimes sad and often dull, but there are currants in the cake, and here is one of them.'[55] She could have easily been referring to herself. The Mitfords were an upper-class family, and the children had a somewhat unconventional home life, with their father refusing to send them to school and hunting them on a horse, with hounds, for fun. Between the wars, the sisters were 'bright young things' and their exploits regularly got them into the papers. This was a period of volatile political movements and some of the sisters took it far too seriously, zinging off in all directions away from one another and causing no end of grief for their parents. Beautiful Diana married the British leader of the Fascist movement, Oswald Mosley, strong-minded Jessica became a Communist, and great galumphing Unity, who had been conceived in the town of Swastika, Ontario, in Canada, joined the Nazi party. She fell in love with Adolf Hitler and ran off to Munich in 1934 to become his stalker. He actually became quite fond of her and she joined his inner circle, appearing with him on the balcony in Vienna when he announced the Anschluss (Germany's annexation of Austria) in 1938. But when Britain declared war on Germany on 3 September 1939 Unity was heartbroken – she had believed her destiny was literally to create unity between Britain and Germany. With that dream shattered, she went to the English Garden in Munich, took out a pearl-handled pistol that had been a gift from her beloved Führer, put the gun to her head and shot herself. The bullet didn't kill her, and she was an invalid for the rest of her life, dying a decade later. Nancy, on the other hand, was unimpressed by the big political movements of the era, being more interested in people and the humour that could be found in everyday life. In 1935, she based the character of Eugenia Malmains on Unity, in one of her early novels, *Wigs on the Green*, making a joke of her sister's political fervour.

Nancy was a terrible tease, informing three of her sisters, Unity, Deborah and Jessica that their names respectively contained the words 'nit', 'bore' and 'sick'. During a general strike in the UK in 1926, Nancy and another sister, Pamela, ran a café, supplying tea to the emergency services. Poor put-upon Pam did most of the work, while Nancy would drift in late and exclaim that she didn't know how to make sandwiches. One morning, she turned up disguised as a tramp, leered at terrified Pam, then grabbed her, saying, 'Can I have a kiss!' According to one account, Pam ran away, fell and broke her ankle. I'm sure Nancy's shrieks of laughter could have been heard from the next street.[56]

But that was nothing compared to Nancy's relationship with Diana – Mrs Fascist, who had Hitler as a guest of honour at her wedding. Such devoted sisters, never were they. In June 1940, Nancy was required to attend the Home Office to give information about Diana. Obediently, she trotted along and informed Gladwyn Jebb, working for the Under-Secretary of State, that 'I regard her as an extremely dangerous person.' Diana was subsequently arrested and imprisoned without trial in Holloway prison for more than three years. Nancy never confessed to her role in her sister's imprisonment, but at least she wrote her jolly letters to keep her spirits up.

Nancy was a bit kinder to Jessica, who had run off to the south of France in 1936 with Winston Churchill's nephew Esmond Romilly, so they could be Communists and fight in the Spanish Civil War. Nancy and her handsome husband, Peter Rodd (she called him Prod), were despatched to get Jessica to see sense, coming down the gangplank in full glamour mode amid 'a barrage of popping bulbs' from the press photographers. Nancy's attempts to bring Jessica back are steeped in camp sensibility – 'You are a naughty little thing, worrying us all' and 'Nanny keeps saying you didn't have any suitable clothes to fight in.' The rescue mission failed. No wonder that Nancy's father, Lord Redesdale, remarked that each of his children was sillier than the last.

They say, 'write about what you know' and these politically enthusiastic sisters were great material for Nancy to exploit in her most well-known novel, *The Pursuit of Love*, which came out just after Waugh's *Brideshead Revisited*. *His* book had been taken seriously as a proper literary work, riffing on the dying aristocracy and Catholicism, whereas at first brush Nancy's looks as substantial as

Each one sillier than the last:
Jessica, Nancy, Diana, Unity and Pam Mitford in 1935.

cappuccino froth, although a closer look uncovers a much darker undercurrent – it is sometimes referred to as an anti-love story. Waugh was something of a literary mentor to Nancy and she sent him early drafts of her book. He was encouraging, but also rather harsh in his evaluation, advising, 'There is a work of art there, lurking in a hole, occasionally visible by the top of its whiskers.' He advised her to rewrite various themes and passages, much of which she sensibly ignored.

The Pursuit of Love made Nancy rich and famous. It tells the story of the highly emotional Linda Radlett, who leaves her boring husband for an idealistic Communist and, after that doesn't work out either, she is rescued by a foxy French Duke. Linda is the sort of girl who lives for drama. As a little girl she cries at the drop of a hat, something which her elder sister, Louisa, exploits by intoning a poem about a little houseless match that is guaranteed to induce tears. *The Pursuit of Love* features a parade of upper-class camp characters. Linda's father is one of those impoverished eccentric

Lords who is in a permanent rage, cracking a stock whip under the bedroom windows of governesses he doesn't like, referring to people as sewers and hunting his children like foxes (just like Nancy's own father), for fun. When he dislikes someone, which is often, he writes their name down on a piece of paper and puts it in a knife drawer, believing that this would make them die within the year. Most of the characters have the amused sangfroid of the excessively privileged. Take Linda's neighbour Lord Merlin, who has two black whippets bedecked in diamond necklaces. Merlin also has pigeons dyed in different colours for his annual party (they are dried out in the linen cupboard). 'What about their poor eyes?' asks Louisa. 'Oh, they soon learn to shut them,' she is told.

Linda's best friend and the book's narrator, Fanny, is by far the most sensible person in *The Pursuit of Love*, although her mostly absent mother is something of a notoriety, having run away with so many men that she is known as the Bolter. When the Bolter turns up at the end of the book, with a much younger Spaniard called Juan in tow, calling everyone in sight 'darling' (pronounced *dulling*), Fanny studies her with much curiosity, deciding that although she is silliness personified, there is something engaging about her frankness, high spirits and endless good nature. The Bolter is also a decade or so out of her time. Although it is 1939, the Bolter sincerely uses the slang of the late 1920s, her hair is a canary-coloured shingle (it's actually a wig) and she wears trousers as if she's flouting conventions, though Fanny (rather uncharacteristically cattily) notes that by this point 'every suburban shopgirl was doing the same'. Fanny comments how Linda's French Duke was the great love of her life. '"Oh, dulling," said my mother sadly. "One always thinks that. Every, every time."' It is the last line of the book, a curious mixture of blasé throwaway and hard-bitten wisdom, which sums up Mitford's oeuvre perfectly.

The sequel, *Love in a Cold Climate*, published in 1949, went even further, in terms of camp at least, while the plot pushed against the boundaries of what post-war British society was willing to accept, even despite the ministrations of Noël Coward. Mitford introduces us to Cedric Hampton, a screaming upper-class queen who is described as:

> . . . a glitter of blue and gold . . . a human dragonfly . . . a tall thin young man, supple as a girl, dressed in rather a bright blue suit; his hair was the gold of a brass bed-knob and his insect appearance came from the fact that the upper part of his face was concealed by blue goggles set in gold rims quite an inch thick.

Cedric has come to England from Nova Scotia to meet his wealthy ageing relatives, Lord and Lady Montdore, and soon has them wrapped round his little finger, insincerely declaring them both the two most beautiful people he has ever seen. Not everyone is impressed with him – Linda's father, on coming upon Cedric at a train station, spots that the seams of his coat are piped in a contrasting shade. It is too much – 'He fell upon Cedric and began to shake him like a rat.' Unusual for the time, Mitford doesn't even bother to code Cedric's homosexuality, instead she has jealous neighbours explicitly refer to him as an 'awful effeminate pansy'. But what is most surprising is the book's unconventional happy ending, with Cedric settled in a ménage à trois. 'Here we all are, my darling, having our lovely cake and eating it too.'

Nancy showed remarkable sangfroid herself during World War II. She refused to leave London, enduring the nightly bombardments of the city, and volunteered as a fire-watcher. After putting out an incendiary she was asked to give a lecture on the topic. However, her upper-class accent proved too much for the audience and she was asked to stop, being told, 'Well, you see it's your voice. It irritates people so much, they said they'd like to put *you* on the fire.'[57] She also took in Jewish evacuees from the East End, airily calling them 'my sweet refugees'. The experience resulted in some unexpected challenges, which Nancy met in her usual flippant way, as this excerpt from one of her letters to a friend indicates: 'Oh dear a little creature here aged 16 is in the family way . . . shall I be obliged to wield a knitting needle & go down to fame as Mrs Rodd the abortionist? (I might join Diana which would be rather nice).' Her attitude to the war was somewhat fatalistic – she swanned about London as normal, refusing to use air raid shelters.

Years later, on a radio chat show she joked about the air raids, telling an anecdote about her maid Gladys, who loved them.

> We used to sit in the kitchen listening to the news with the air raids going on. Then there were about two years in the war when there weren't any air raids. And then there was a small air raid. And there was the siren and almost immediately afterwards there was a bomb, rather near and everything was shaking about, and I was sitting up in bed rather sort of wondering. And Gladys put her head round the door and said, 'Isn't it a *treat* to hear them again!'

In 1942, Nancy worked in Heywood Hill bookshop in Mayfair, which quickly became a haven for her witty, gossipy friends like Evelyn Waugh, Cecil Beaton, James Lees-Milne, and Osbert and Sacheverell Sitwell. Nancy sent parcels of books to Diana (still in prison) and wrote to her that 'The shop is really very gay now, full of people all day'. The shrieks of laughter didn't always go down well with regular customers though, with one woman telling her, 'A little less *darling* and a little more attention please' while Nancy was engaged in a particularly engrossing phone call.

After the war, Nancy moved to Paris, having exactly the right temperament to appreciate French camp in all its outrageous glamour. She conducted a long-term love affair with Gaston Palewski – a French colonel (sadly, she was way more into it than him) – dressed in Christian Dior and wrote biographies of Voltaire, King Louis XIV and Madame de Pompadour. The critic Raymond Mortimer said that the latter book read 'as if an enchantingly clever woman was pouring out the story to me on the telephone'. I hope Nancy took that as a compliment, even if it wasn't exactly meant that way. Although she was sometimes seen as a literary lightweight, her biographer, Laura Thompson, rightly notes that it takes a lot more effort to make a souffle than a bread pudding. Being such a connoisseur of camp, it is no surprise that Nancy became so obsessed with Versailles that she ended up relocating there in 1967 – not to the palace itself, obviously, but to a house in the town, 4 rue d'Artois, where she worked on a biography of Frederick the Great.

Despite her privileged upbringing and literary success, Nancy's life had its fair share of sadness. She lost a baby and was told she could never have another one. As usual, she put a brave face on it, 'I love children, especially when they cry, for then someone takes them away' but it's doubtful that she ever got over it. She never got to live happily ever after, even with Gaston, and her brother, Tom, whom she idolised, was killed at the end of the war in Burma. She died of Hodgkin's lymphoma, in 1973, after several years of agony, writing to James Lees-Milne: 'It's very curious, dying, and would have many a drôle amusing & charming side were it not for the pain.' Nancy embraced camp in the most wholesome and healthy way possible, using it to keep herself and everyone around her cheerful, even during some of Britain's darkest years. As she writes of one of her characters in *The Pursuit of Love*: when she died 'a great light went out, a great deal of joy that could never be replaced'. Of all the beautiful, fascinating, maddening Mitford sisters, Nancy is the one who best epitomises the joy of camp.

MISS MILLINER MICHAEL-ANGELO

Nancy's Cedric was a stereotypical camp queen, a glittering forerunner to the gay men who will be discussed in Chapter 5. However, there are times in our story when camp will be self-consciously disassociated with homosexuality – particularly in the 1980s and 1990s. Throughout the twentieth century romantic heroes would rarely be camp, even if they were gay. When Mary Renault wrote her gay love-triangle World War II masterpiece, *The Charioteer*, in 1953, none of the three main characters have a camp sensibility. One, Andrew, is so naïve and sheltered that he doesn't even know he is gay. Another, Ralph, is a He-Man who everyone fights over – it could be argued that Ralph's gruff masculinity makes him unintentionally camp, but he certainly doesn't engage in any dishing. The third, Laurie, is a dreamy everyman (another Mary Sue) who is only allotted one or two uncharacteristic moments of acid humour while under duress. Laurie and Ralph are marked as upper class, having both attended the same boarding school where Ralph was expelled under a cloud of sexual intrigue. In keeping with the fact that homosexuality was illegal and not an appropriate topic of polite conversation, the more explicitly gay parts of the book are written in the heavily coded language of euphemism and implicature. The first time I read it, I didn't even *realise* that two of the men had sex because it was written in such a delicately veiled way.

The masculine characters at least did get to sleep together, even if you need to read between the lines to realise it. The camp ones don't; although at least their camp is laid out on display for us all to enjoy. There are a host of minor characters who circle vulture-like, sporting silly nicknames like Bunny, Binky, Bim and Toto. Renault contrasts butch Ralph's spartan room – shabbiness and simplicity and smelling like school – with queenly Bunny's interior-designed quarters, which have glossy magazines strewn about, low furniture (looks good but is rarely physically comfortable) and a cocktail cabinet. When Ralph turns off Bunny's radio without asking, Bunny exclaims, 'Oh *you*,' coquettishly. The set piece of the novel involves a birthday party for gay servicemen which gradually escalates its drunken drama quotient, resulting in the host's boyfriend trying to kill himself in the bathtub. At the party, Laurie is surprised to be reacquainted with Ralph, and the other party-goers jealously observe the obvious chemistry between them. One of Ralph's cast-offs, flight-lieutenant Bim, tries to sabotage the relationship before it is rekindled. Bim is described as small and handsome, with a tough steely kind of grace and a high girlish voice, feverish and taut behind the glitter. He gives a synopsis of Homer's *Odyssey*, which ends with, 'And all this while the poor queen has been knitting and knitting away *madly* in the bedroom, dropping stitches left and right, with suitors camping and screaming all over the house.' Sheltered Laurie is appalled at all of this effeminate homosexuality and Ralph, who has been residing on the periphery of this world, makes it clear that he's just been slumming it, hoping that someone better will come along.

Renault was an accomplished writer and had worked as a nurse, treating evacuees after the Battle of Dunkirk. She was also gay and her descriptions of camp gay men, although less complex than her 'masc' gay characters, ring true, even if they are undeveloped. But while *The Charioteer* is a sensitive portrayal of gay life in World War II, we are not expected to identify with or even like the camp characters, and one of them turns out to be quite the villain, providing a major complicating plot twist. In romance novels, camp men were not given Main Character Energy, the implication being that camp is funny but not sexy. At best, the camp man gets to be a hilarious member of the supporting cast, albeit the one who does receive those few additional decibels of applause at the finale.

However, outside the constraints of romance novels, camp can take centre stage. E F Benson's *Mapp and Lucia* books are unusual because *everyone* is camp. Set in the fussy fictional village of Tilling (modelled on Rye, East Sussex), the two main characters are a pair of battling middle-aged women who are hilarious from a distance – you wouldn't want either of them in your life. There's Emmeline Lucas known as (Queen) Lucia – an inexhaustible force of nature who pretends to speak Italian and makes her dinner guests sit through her plodding renditions of the 'Moonlight Sonata' when they'd just prefer another hand of Bridge. Lucia bullies her neighbours into submission with her bell-like laugh and perfect manners, eventually becoming Mayor of Tilling (one book ends with her trying on lots of hats to determine which one would be the most Mayoral). Her angry, jealous rival, Miss Mapp, constantly tries to expose Lucia's fake self-presentation, sometimes managing to pull it off but usually being thwarted. The pair manage to be outrageously malicious to one another, all the while appearing to be polite. And don't be fooled – this isn't the mock rivalry of two good friends like Auntie Mame and Vera Charles – Mapp and Lucia actually do hate one another. Forced to sit through a long evening of Lucia playing recitals, Mapp says, 'Lovely, wasn't it, the other night? And so many movements of Mozart. I began to think he must have discovered the secret of perpetual motion, and that we should be stuck there till Doomsday.' Lucia tends to mask her dislike of Mapp with pity, 'Poor Elizabeth! . . . My heart aches for her, for I am sure all that carping bitterness makes her wretched.'

Lucia's Best Friend Forever, Georgie, is a simpering man who wears a wig, dyes his beard, does embroidery and fusses over his decorative knick-knacks, which he calls *bibelots*. He and Lucia are perfect for each other – the fag and his hag, and they eventually marry, although it is made clear that there will be separate bedrooms. Benson never hints that either of them have any interest in sex, whatsoever. Another character, (Quaint) Irene Coles, inspired by the writer Marguerite Radclyffe Hall, is a striking example of lesbian camp, with her pipe smoking, men's clothes, perfunctory manner and bold art creations. Irene has a somewhat ironic crush on Lucia and hates Mapp, poking fun at her by drawing her as Venus rising from the sea. Other notables include Susan Wyse (MBE[58]) who wears massive fur coats, has a chauffeured limo to take her a few metres down the street and believes that her dead budgie is trying to contact her from the grave; retired army bore Major Benji, who loves hard liquor and golf; Diva Plaistow, a shameless gossip who is Mapp's 'Beta'. The usual greeting in Tilling is 'Any news?' and everyone's favourite word is 'No!' – which is usually uttered upon receipt of a particularly juicy bit of scandal.

Benson's characters are all comfortably off, nobody does a jot of work, even housework (they all have servants), they are all irritated by one another but their world is so cosily fascinating that nobody would ever want to leave. In one of the early books, Lucia decides to make a name for herself in London. She is hideously out of her depth and has to increase her efforts to maximum power, but is only successful because her smart new London friends find her social climbing to be hilarious and they form a secret society of 'Luciaphiles' to exchange the latest gossip about her. Although Benson pokes fun at his characters with their small outlooks and petty squabbles, there are brief moments when they break out of two dimensions. When Mapp and Lucia are feared dead during a flood, Irene reacts with real emotion, bursting into tears, while Georgie's loyalty to Lucia is admirable and their relationship is genuinely charming. These are gay novels without any sex or romance, and while Georgie's sexuality is sometimes the subject of innuendo (Major Benji calls him 'Miss Milliner Michael-Angelo'), the books were written at a time when homosexuality was not talked about publicly. In a foreword to the 1971 edition of *Queen Lucia*, Nancy Mitford commented on the asexual world that Benson had created:

> No writer nowadays could allow Georgie to do his embroidery and dye his hair and wear his little cape and sit for hours chatting with Lucia or playing celestial Mozartino, without hinting at Boys in the background. Quaint Irene, in her fisherman's jersey and knickerbockers, would certainly share her house with another lesbian and this word would be used.

But this just would not have been done in 1920. Instead, camp was the way that gay characters were made visible for those in the know and palatable for those who weren't. As we'll see later in the book, it is a limiting characterisation and one that eventually resulted in a backlash, but it was at least a foot in the door, a representation that, if not well-rounded, was a start.

THE QUEEN OF PARIS

While Waugh wrote of the Bright Young Things in his novel *Vile Bodies*, and the Mitford sisters personified them, in actual fact, the Brightest Young Thing was neither British nor upper class. She was born in a slum region of St Louis in 1906, and, while she did not boast any form of noble heritage, she earned the title of Queen, showing how values in the early twentieth century were starting to change – celebrity and fame were the qualities of a new social class, one that would soon overshadow the inherited titles. Readers, meet the fabulous Josephine Baker, *the* symbol of the Jazz Age and the Roaring Twenties.

There had always been something special about her, and, as a young girl, Josephine danced on street corners for money, eventually finding work with a performance group called the Jones Family Band. Aged fifteen, she left her second husband, William Howard Baker, when her vaudeville troop was scheduled to play in the Plantation Club in New York City. It was there that she secured a role in the Broadway revue *Shuffle Along*. Baker had immense stage presence and in her performances she combined sexuality and humour in a uniquely camp way that made it impossible to take your eyes off her. She learned the trick of appearing to be the 'pony' in the chorus line – the one who gets the dance wrong and makes everyone laugh, only to then perform it flawlessly. It established her as the most memorable part of the routine, and in 1925 she sailed to Paris to star in *La Revue Nègre* – an all-Black musical comedy, which later transferred to the Théâtre des Champs-Elysées. It was a turning point in her life. And so it is back to France that we must go.

Baker found that French attitudes towards Black people were complex. On the one hand there was no segregation – she could mix with who she wanted, get served in any shop, and dine where she wanted to – this gave her considerable freedom compared to back home. She was also much in demand, as part of a French fascination with and love of Black culture. However, this love was sometimes manifested in appropriation by white French artists, and French understandings of Black people were frequently marked by reductive stereotyping, even when trying to celebrate them. One reviewer, Pierre de Régnier, described Josephine's body as writhing like a snake or a dipping saxophone – 'she grimaces, crosses her eyes, wiggles disjointedly, does a split and finally crawls off the stage stiff-legged, her rump higher than her head like a young giraffe.' While this was supposed to be a positive review, the comparisons to animals showed how Baker was often casually dehumanised. Other reviewers referred to her performances as savage, exotic and primitive.

If there is one performance that sums up Baker's exuberance it is a dance scene set in a theatre in the film *Princess Tam Tam* (1935). Carried away by the music and egged on by a friend, Baker pulls off her shoes and throws them away (one lands in an ice bucket, the other on some poor man's head). She then descends a giant staircase, ridding herself of her wrap-round dress, and literally jumps down several feet onto the stage. She dances like *everyone* is watching. The sheer pleasure on her face is breathtaking.

Baker's costumes were heavy on rhinestones, feathers and eye-catching headpieces – Naveen Kumar describes her as having a drag aesthetic before such a thing existed.[59] Baker was also represented as a sexual object – she often performed or posed semi-nude or scantily clad, but there is a sense *she* is in control; you don't expect someone who's doing a sexy dance to suddenly cross their eyes and make a funny face. There's the impression that she's making fun of any members of the audience who are getting a bit too excited, and Baker used camp humour to reclaim and control her image.

She resisted people's attempts to categorise her again and again – whatever they said she was, she did the opposite. Call her a savage, she would act like the most refined lady in Paris society; if men wooed her with chocolates and flowers, she'd put on a man's suit; if she was referred to as a 'black Venus', she'd don a blonde wig. But if people thought she was too refined, she'd sashay down the Champs-Élysées with a pet leopard.[60]

One of her most famous costumes was a skirt made of a circle of rubber bananas, which she first wore in 1926. The skirt brings to mind racist stereotypes of the exotic Black person, as well as being suggestive of a circle of phalluses. Alicja Sowinska writes that it acted as a device that reflected and played on racial and sexual norms and also problematised the ways that Black women were looked at and eroticised.[61] The skirt also drew attention to her backside, something that Baker viewed with a certain amount of pride, saying, 'The rear end exists. I see no reason to be ashamed of it. It's true there are rear ends so stupid, so pretentious, so insignificant that they're good only for sitting on.'[62]

Despite the problematic ways that French people reacted to Josephine, she loved her adopted country. When Germany invaded France in 1939, she joined Charles de Gaulle's Free French movement, stating, 'France made me what I am. I will be grateful forever. The people of Paris have given me everything . . . I am ready, captain, to give them my life. You can use me as you wish.' At her home in the South of France she stored weapons, housed members of the resistance and arranged visas for them. She was also able to make use of her special status as an entertainer to move from one country to another. She attended events at embassies, charming ministers to get information from them, which she then passed on – writing down messages about airfields, harbours and German troop concentrations on her sheet music, using invisible ink.[63] The idea of this talented, beautiful, hilarious performer as a World War II spy on top of everything else can't really be beaten in the camp stakes, and it's why I chose Miss Baker as the cover girl of this book.

After the war, Baker returned frequently to the US, campaigning against racial discrimination, challenging segregation laws and marching for civil rights – both the CIA and the FBI kept files on her. She adopted twelve children from different parts of the world, living with them all at a château in the South of France. Baker's friend and biographer Jean-Claude Baker noted how, later on, her performances became even more camp, saying in an interview that:

> Onstage she looked like . . . a badly made-up drag queen – glitter over her makeup, too much mascara, extravagant gowns that exaggerated the feminine, extravagant gestures. Nobody else performing in Europe during the 1930s moved like she did. Later, here in the U.S., it would be called 'vogueing'.

And by the late 1960s, Jean-Claude estimated that gay people made up eighty per cent of her faithful audience.[64] Gay fans rarely desert their divas – and as we'll see in the final chapter, some of the campest ones are prepared to really put themselves on the line for them. What was that about camp being superficial?

DELICIOUS DEATH

It could be argued that the best-selling author of all time (putting aside the Bible and Shakespeare) should receive a Gold Award for Services to Camp. Between 1920 and 1973 Agatha Christie wrote sixty-six detective novels, more than twenty plays, and fourteen short story collections. They nearly all involved murder mysteries that were usually ridiculously difficult to solve. Christie's world was populated by quaint English villages, forgetful vicars, gossipy old ladies, manor houses full of envious, bitter relatives and glamorous hotels in exotic locations. The camp comic Alan Carr has spoken about how, during his childhood, his mother once asked him, 'Why aren't you like other boys?' so he just said, 'I am like other boys' and continued reading his Agatha Christie.[65] He would attend football matches at Northampton when his local team were playing at home, but would always take along one of Agatha's books in his bag. I can understand the attraction. I purchased my first Agatha (*The ABC Murders*) aged eleven and for the next two years I would trek to my local town centre every Saturday afternoon to buy a new one. Christmas and Easter holidays were always a source of delight when the TV listings magazines arrived and I would scour them, committing to memory the dates of any Agatha Christie films. By the time that my poor sister had learnt her ABCs, I persuaded her to read *Death on the Nile*, one of Christie's most complicated stories. She bridled, 'There's too many people in it!' and I made her create a list of all the characters so she wouldn't get them mixed up.

Christie's two most famous detectives were camp in different ways. Hercule Poirot was a vain little man with an egg-shaped head, brilliantined hair and an ostentatious waxed moustache. His mannerisms were based on those of Belgian refugees that Christie had observed during World War I. Although the term was never used in any of the books, I think a good case could be made for Poirot being an example of asexual camp. The same label might be applied to Jane Marple, an elderly spinster and inhabitant of another one of those twee fictional English villages, St Mary Mead. Characters frequently refer to her as an 'old pussy' and she appears deceptively sweet and unassuming. However, Miss Marple has a nose for murder and decades of village life have given her an exhaustive knowledge of the dark side of human psychology. She is always able to draw parallels between the present case and something that happened decades ago to a neighbour or one of her maids. There have been numerous old lady detectives but Miss Marple was the first and best. Camp connoisseurs may wish to sample Margaret Rutherford's 1960s interpretation in four films, all of which revel in their rinky-dink theme tune and are heavily played for humour, relying on Rutherford's disarming manner of bulging her eyes and shaking her head from side to side while blowing through her mouth. However, for those looking for a more authentic Miss Marple, the BBC series starring Joan Hickson, which aired between 1984 and 1992 is spot on, with this Miss Marple being both frightfully proper and vague. My favourite Miss Marple novel is *A Murder Is Announced* (1950). It has a typically preposterous set-up. In the village of Chipping Cleghorn a note appears in the local newspaper: 'A murder is announced and will take place on Friday, 29 October, at Little Paddocks, at 6:30pm. Friends accept this, the only intimation.' Half the village turn up at the appointed hour, thinking that there will be fun and games. But then the lights go out, a shot is fired and someone is actually killed. This is a murder mystery where the clues involve a shepherdess lampshade, a string of pearls and which word is pronounced in italics in the phrase 'She wasn't there'. The novel is also full of camp stereotypes, among which is Mitzi the cook, a forthright and emotional refugee from Eastern Europe who all the other characters belittle and accuse of lying. Mitzi makes a birthday cake which is referred to as Delicious Death, and to add insult to injury one of the characters actually dies shortly after eating it.

Violence is not camp and murder certainly should not be camp. But Christie pulls off the trick of backgrounding the murder to the point where it becomes incidental. Murders usually occur 'off-screen' and nobody bothers to linger over the grisly forensic detail of examining corpses. Quite often, the people who are murdered are heavily characterised with various moral failings, so it's implied that nobody is going to miss them anyway really (sometimes a second person is murdered because they are blackmailing the killer, so that's no big deal either). Instead, the focus is around the interplay between detective and suspects within the comfortable closed-off board-game world that Christie creates. There is also the pleasure in solving a puzzle, meaning that the books are as emotionally upsetting as a crossword. And, in several novels, when the murderer is unmasked, they obligingly commit suicide, so everything gets wrapped up jolly neatly, thank goodness!

For many people, Christie's most well-known stories are those set in glitzy holiday locations, which were ideal vehicles for big-budget films: *Death on the Nile*, *Murder on the Orient Express*, *Evil Under the Sun*, *And Then There Were None*. The 1978 film *Death on the Nile* features a trio of camp actresses: Bette Davis, Angela Lansbury and Maggie Smith. We will hear more of Bette's wisdom in the following chapter but for now we will have to be content with her staccato delivery of the line: 'This place is *beginning* to resemble a *mortuary*.' In 1982, Maggie Smith teamed up with another British camp icon Diana Rigg, for *Evil Under the Sun*, which is full of bitchy rivalry between the two. All the women in the film look as if they've made their outfits out of discarded wrappers from a chocolate box. They showcase a dazzling range of ridiculous turbans and outsize sun-hats, and Rigg is exceptionally catty to her teenage step-daughter, Linda, telling her, 'Do stop standing there like a cough-drop' and 'Scram, Cinderella!' When Linda runs away, Rigg laughs, 'She runs like a dromedary with dropsy.' The men are mostly stuffed-dinner-jackets, although Roddy McDowall plays a flamboyant biographer in sailor drag, while strapping Nicholas Clay spends much of the film crammed into a tiny pair of black bathing trunks. The proceedings are saturated in camp and feel like a pilot episode of *RuPaul's Drag Race* where the format hasn't been worked out properly. To top it all, the murder hinges on whether someone will be wearing a bathing hat or not at a particular point in time.

Christie's play *The Mousetrap* is the longest running in the world, being performed continuously from 1952 to 2020, at which point COVID necessitated a fourteen-month break. It is classic Christie fare – a country house, cut off from the world during a snowstorm, a disparate group of posh characters, a murder at the end of the first act, a clever twist, and everyone has a good laugh at the end. Written as a radio play in 1947, Christie encoded culpability into everyone's DNA, playing on the prejudices of post-war audiences of the time. Mr Paravicini is Italian (a foreigner!) and wears makeup! Miss Casewell, who has quite a bit in common with E F Benson's Quaint Irene, is described in the script as having 'a deep manly voice', has the audacity to live *abroad* despite being English, might have socialist tendencies and is caught writing a letter to a friend which begins, 'My Dearest Jess'. One of the owners of the Manor, Mollie, describes her as 'rather peculiar', while her husband, Giles, says, 'Terrible female, if she *is* a female.'

But this is nothing compared to the play's Most Valuable Player, Christopher Wren, who, in the script, is described as 'a rather wild-looking neurotic young man' with long, untidy hair, an artistic tie and a 'confiding, almost childish manner'. From the moment he arrives at Monkswell Manor, he is on fire – fluttering around the stage, exclaiming over everything and critiquing the furniture, asking if the owners have any wax flowers or birds of paradise, then saying, 'What a pity,' when they reply in the negative. This is clever characterisation – Christie isn't telling us that Christopher Wren genuinely likes wax flowers but that he'd experience a sneering, camp frisson if any were present. I wonder how 1950s audience members who owned wax flowers would have perceived the remark, whether they would feel embarrassed or outraged at the dig at their taste, or whether the insult would have flown straight over their heads. When a handsome young policeman arrives to warn the occupants that the house might be targeted by a killer, Christopher Wren goes weak-kneed, describing him as 'terribly hearty'. Mollie takes an instant shine to Wren, but he is disliked by Giles and one of the other guests, Mrs Boyle. However, his detractors do not refer to him as camp or homosexual. Instead, he is called 'extraordinary', 'peculiar', 'odd' and even 'unbalanced mentally'. Another character, Major Metcalf, says, 'Think he's escaped from a mental asylum.' It's a telling indictment of the time that common-or-garden camp behaviour gets interpreted as *insanity* and even as a possible defining characteristic of a murderer. Of course, Christie knew what she was doing – there were plenty of clues regarding the sexuality of Christopher and Miss Casewell, and she makes some of her other characters either bigoted or ignorant, reflecting the views of some audience members, but not all. In 1955, a reviewer in *The Times* described Christopher Wren as 'a garrulous young weakling', which appears like an almost purposefully blinkered portrait of him.[66]

By the end of the 1950s, upper-class voices were increasingly competing for attention with a range of others and their influence on popular culture had lessened, although the camp sensibility remained. Because writers like Coward, Waugh, Mitford and Christie held such powerful cultural sway, they adorned camp with respectability, contributing towards its gradual mainstreaming by showing audiences that it was funny and entertaining, if you could just get into the right mindset. Laura Thompson suggests that Nancy Mitford easily found a publisher for her novels because they liked the idea of 'this pretty, well-connected girl who wrote in the style du jour'.[67] To a large extent, her class opened doors during this deferential period of British history. Camp also enabled a somewhat unexpected take on the British 'stiff upper lip', helping people get through World War II with affected insouciance. I think the British, with their quiet dislike of earnestness and their talent for ironic understatement, were well primed to take the droller and less excitable aspects of camp to their hearts, even if many of them didn't exactly recognise what it *was*.

For the next chapter we travel across the Atlantic to America, to consider a period in the middle of the twentieth century where a completely different set of people are going to become the pure embodiment of camp for a time – female entertainers.

CHAPTER 4

Dolly, Diva, Sister, Hag

My early years were influenced by two elderly sisters who kept me fascinated and amused, their rivalry sometimes reminding me of Bette Davis and Joan Crawford. Nanna (Betty) Cochrane was born in 1912 and her sister Ethel (my great-aunt), arrived a year later. Betty was the dogsbody eldest child while Ethel was the upwardly mobile favourite who delighted older family members by tap dancing on the dining-room table, and years later married Hughie, a dashing World War II RAF pilot. Ethel liked to drink an aspirational alcoholic drink called Pimm's and she insisted on soup, a main and dessert at every meal (as a result, Hughie got quite big and had to go on a diet). She was so much like the overbearing roles played by comedy actress Patricia Routledge that one family member was unable to watch anything with her in it because it triggered them.

I always liked to visit Betty and Ethel and marvelled at how different their homes were, compared to my parents' modern 1970s council house. Betty's bungalow was a homage to kitsch with a gigantic arrangement of wax flowers on display in the living room and a crocheted doll toilet-roll holder in the bathroom. Ethel's home was more well appointed and I was fascinated by the fact that she had a box of matches that had different coloured heads –

she always let me play with them. At the end of the 1980s, Ethel sold her house and moved into a bungalow in the same street as her sister. Betty was ambivalent about the move; she had always harboured a slight jealousy towards bossy 'Jane Anne Fiddlesticks' as she called her. Now the two sisters were living practically on top of each other, and, worst of all, Ethel had secured a south-facing home. Betty's was west-facing. 'Mine is a tomb!' she kept saying mournfully. 'A tomb!'

Ethel brought Perry, her latest black poodle, with her. I think this was the fifth one. There had been the original pair, Mimsy and Trudy, who had died eventually, being replaced by two more (also called Mimsy and Trudy). After they had died, Perry appeared. 'I take Perry to get groomed by two *men*,' Ethel informed me when I was seventeen, apropos of nothing. It was her way of telling me she knew that I was gay and she didn't mind because she was a woman of the world. I have a lot of time for that generation, or maybe I just like old ladies. My mother felt sorry for Perry because Ethel insisted that the two *men* always give him a lion cut, which looked absolutely ridiculous. She wouldn't entertain suggestions of a lamb cut, which is only slightly less ridiculous. For extra pocket money I collected the sisters' pensions on Thursdays and did their grocery shopping, and I'm afraid that for a whole year I used them as a refuge when I played truant from sports class, telling these Geordie Golden Girls that the school was 'on strike again' so I could watch old movies with them and listen to their gossip when they had visitors.

While all of Ethel's poodles were neurotic, Perry was the worst of the lot. He lived his days in a state of constant hysteria, jumping up at Ethel's legs and going berserk whenever she had visitors. He suffered from separation anxiety and so Ethel took him everywhere. For her annual optician's appointment, she would get my father to drive twenty-four miles to Gateshead so that she could make a day of it and go to a restaurant. My father, never one to turn down free food, was happy to oblige. For the optician's visit, Perry had to be left at home and he was not happy. Somehow, he found himself in the kitchen, where he started trying to jump up onto the work units. Perhaps he thought he could get to a window or perhaps he had a more sinister intention. Somehow, he must have bumped up against one of the dials on the ancient electric oven, turning on one of the heating rings. Ethel used to keep a wooden chopping board on top of the oven when it wasn't in use. Gradually, the heat from the ring set it alight and within minutes there was a full-on house fire.

Fortunately, a neighbour sounded the alert, so when my father returned with Ethel in his car, they were horrified to see black smoke pouring out of the kitchen, and a crowd of pensioners agog at a burly fireman attempting mouth to mouth resuscitation on an unconscious black poodle disguised as a lion, lying on its back in the garden. You'll be glad to hear that Perry made a full recovery, outliving Ethel. Sadly, nobody in the family was able to take him on after she died, but I'm almost sure we found him a good home.

Like me with Betty and Ethel, in the middle decades of the twentieth century, gay men channelled camp through a select set of fabulous women, a sparkling collection of jewels, each one with a unique cut and colour. These women were not often conventionally beautiful, but they commanded attention wherever they went and their lives both on- and off-screen were a whirlwind of drama! As this chapter shows, the symbiotic relationship between these men and their beloved divas was sometimes complicated, and while the love was not sexual it was passionate.

Gay men were involved in every aspect of theatre and film but with homosexuality illegal and attendant social attitudes disapproving, it would have been unthinkable to give them major roles. They didn't expect to see themselves on celluloid or centre-stage, so women like Grace Kelly, Bette Davis, Tallulah Bankhead and a host of others became their stand-ins, appearing as female drag queens and role models. Daniel Harris has written of how, as a schoolboy in blue-collar North Carolina, 'a land of lazy southern drawls', he developed a British accent. It was an unconscious imitation of the above-mentioned women, who spoke in the 'gracious accents of an Anglophile argot concocted by the elocutionists at the major studios'.[68] With its elegantly elongated As and clipped Ts, the mid-Atlantic accent is a key component of mid-twentieth-century camp, placing the Hollywood stars in a distinct, glamorous class. Imitating this accent was a form of worship that didn't involve wanting to be female but instead to inhabit a sophisticated urban world, to mark oneself as a castaway from a better, more elegant place. Harris casts the films of these divas as a poor man's aestheticism, being much more accessible than the aristocratic ideals cultivated by the invulnerable *dandy* figure discussed in Chapter 2.

It was the camp in these women that attracted gay men to them – their excess, their theatricality and their combination of feminine and masculine traits. And it was also their suffering. Because, as we will see, being a star ain't easy, especially if you are a woman. These women faced enormous pressure to look and act a certain way – and, as they got older, it only got harder. Come take a Streetcar Named Desire with me, we're heading for a tour of the Valley of the Dolls – and the first stop is the marvellous Land of Oz.

A HANDFUL OF DOLLS

In 1990, aged eighteen, I found myself in a gay Bed and Breakfast in the seaside resort of Blackpool. The owner of the hotel was a gregarious matronly figure called Colin who made a fuss over everyone. At the end of breakfast, he produced an enormous photo album which contained pictures of him performing in drag. 'I take it we're all friends of Dorothy here,' he said, winking conspiratorially. It was my first experience of gay slang and I had no idea what he meant. The only thing I could think of was that perhaps he was speaking of Dorothy from the sitcom *The Golden Girls*. Dorothy, played by Bea Arthur, was the most sarcastic, compassionate and sensible of the quartet of fifty-plus ladies in my favourite sitcom. However, Colin wasn't speaking of this Dorothy but of one who had come before her, the greatest Dorothy of all time. Dorothy from *The Wizard of Oz*.

The Wizard of Oz regularly appeared on British TV schedules around Christmas or Easter and, along with (the almost as camp) *Carry On Screaming*, was one of the first films that had kept my attention all the way through. *The Wizard of Oz* is ostensibly a children's musical film, based on the book of the same name, about a girl from Kansas whose home gets whisked off in a tornado to a magical world.

For many gay men, *The Wizard of Oz* is more than just a children's film though. It is a coming-out parable. How many young gay men have dreamt of escaping their suffocating small-town environment to a more colourful, glamorous world, populated with flamboyant characters? Of course, Oz has its own dangers (there's an evil witch who controls an army of flying monkeys), but still, it's a much more exciting place than back home. Despite this, the film's message is that 'there's no place like home', and the film uses a clever casting trick of having the same actors play characters in both Kansas and in Oz – indicating that no matter how far you travel and how fabulous the costumes get, people are essentially the same deep down.

The Wizard of Oz is chock-full of camp, particularly in its look. In the film, Kansas is shown in sepia-toned black and white. But when Dorothy arrives in Oz (via tornado) the film switches to full three-strip Technicolor. The backdrop of the Emerald City is particularly stylised – depicting a futuristic-looking city made of sparkling tube-like towers. And what can you say about a film where the plot is premised on someone's desire to own a pair of shoes? An early sequence involving Dorothy meeting some of the inhabitants of Oz (the Munchkins), who sing 'Follow the yellow brick road', is a camptastic spectacular, ending dramatically when the Wicked Witch of the West, played by character actress Margaret Hamilton in green makeup, appears in a puff of brown smoke. The Munchkins immediately fall to the ground and I remember being absolutely terrified because I thought she had killed them all. Voicing threats like, 'I'll get you, my pretty, and your little dog too!' and 'I'll use you as a beehive!' she *is* pretty scary – a warning to gay men of what they might encounter once they escape their small towns, and also, perhaps, what they might one day *become*. One

My pretty! Margaret Hamilton terrorises Judy Garland as the Witch in *The Wizard of Oz*.

of her parting shots to Dorothy: 'As for you, my fine lady, I can't attend to you here and now as I'd like, but just try to stay out of my way. Just *try!*' is worth memorising, you never know when you'll need it. However, the witch's campest moment is her final speech after Dorothy throws a bucket of water over her: 'I'm melting! Oh, what a world, what a world! Who would have thought a good little girl like you could destroy my beautiful wickedness.' If one witch isn't enough for you, there's also Glinda, the Good Witch, who wears what looks like a wedding dress designed by a three-year-old who's had too much candy. Her key accessory is a cane with a star on it (OK, a magic wand). Despite being the nice one, she gets in a few shady lines too, such as when she warns the wicked witch: 'Rubbish! You have no power here! Now begone, before someone drops a house on *you!*'

Then there is Dorothy, played by seventeen-year-old Judy Garland, who was reportedly made to bind her breasts for the role. Garland was exceptionally talented, showcasing a magnetising mixture of vulnerability and gumption in films like *Meet Me in St Louis* (1944), *Easter Parade* (1948) and *A Star is Born* (1954). But the studio system was not kind to Judy – film executives criticised her looks and forced her to diet. To cope with the demanding pace and long days of filming, she was given amphetamines to keep her awake, then barbiturates so she could sleep, then more amphetamines the next day. No wonder that she was plagued with self-doubt, with a need for love that could never be satiated. No wonder that she became addicted to pills and alcohol and would die at the age of forty-seven, just a few months after her fifth marriage, as a result of an 'incautious self over-dosage' with Seconal capsules. No wonder that gay men took Judy to their hearts. Richard Dyer has referred to Judy's early performances as being camp due to their failed seriousness, while her later performances were 'wonderfully over-the-top'.[69]

In *The Wizard of Oz*, Judy's energy, innocence and goodness shine through, and, knowing her life story, listening to her sing the wistful ballad 'Somewhere Over the Rainbow' is likely to induce tears unless you have the coldest of hearts. Steven Frank wrote that the song was 'the sound of the closet . . . it spoke to gay men's consciousness that the image they presented in their own public lives was often at odds with a truer sense of self'.[70] Subsequently, the rainbow flag, that camp symbol of LGBTQ+ pride (it has far too many colours to be usefully applied in any sort of tasteful decorating scheme), has been said to be connected to the song. *The Advocate* magazine called Judy 'the Elvis of homosexuals'.[71] Towards the end of her life, when she performed in New York at the Palace Theatre in 1967, *TIME* magazine noted how 'the boys in tight trousers' would 'roll their eyes, tear at their hair and practically levitate from their seats'.[72] William Goldman viewed Judy as a kind of emblem for the suffering that gay men faced in the 1960s:

> Homosexuals tend to identify with suffering. They are a persecuted group and they understand suffering. And so does Garland. She's been through the fire and lived – all the drinking and divorcing, all the pills and all the men, all the poundage come and gone – brothers and sisters, *she knows.*[73]

At the Stonewall Inn, a gay bar that witnessed a defining moment of political camp, patrons often signed in as Judy Garland,[74] and it has even been suggested that Garland's death, in June 1969, was the catalyst that sparked this community to rise up against police persecution, a part of our story that is covered in more detail in the following chapter. One of the protesters, Sylvia Rivera, remembers how she had been saddened and amazed by the numbers of people who attended Garland's funeral; she hadn't felt like going out on the night of the funeral, but had changed her mind and gone to the Stonewall Inn.[75] She also recalled that there were several patrons at the bar who had been to the funeral and that there was a feeling in the air that something would happen that night: 'I guess Judy's death just really helped us hit the fan.'[76] It is a compelling story, although some have argued that it has been overstated and that the young, homeless and trans people at the Stonewall Inn had bigger problems (namely systematic homophobia) than Judy's death to face.[77]

In 1966, Jacqueline Susann worked Garland's life into an epic roman à clef of soap opera proportions, spanning two turbulent decades of the lives of three young women in the entertainment industry – nice Anne Welles, beautiful Jennifer North and talented Neely O'Hara. All three women end up being ruined by amphetamines and barbiturates, or 'dolls' as they are referred to. The book's title, *Valley of the Dolls*, ambiguously refers to both the drugs and the women themselves – they are the playthings of studio executives and managers who care little for their well-being. As well as the three 'dolls', there is a fourth woman, ruthless Broadway star Helen Lawson, and her jealousy of the younger characters drives the plot development at the start of the book. Amid the tragedy, exploitation and poor decision-making, there is camp aplenty – it's packed full of overdoses, comebacks and drunken cat-fights. The crowning glory is the chapter where Neely pulls off Helen Lawson's wig and flushes it down the toilet. The book was savaged by critics but queened it at the top spot on the

'Her hair's as fake as she is!'
Neely O'Hara exposes Helen Lawson's secret in *Valley of the Dolls*.

New York Times Best Seller List for twenty-eight weeks. By the time of Susann's untimely death in 1974, it was the best-selling novel in publishing history. It is also the campest novel in publishing history. It gets *everything* right.

With those kinds of sales, there was clamour for a film version and, on 2 March 1967, Susann appeared at a press conference with Judy Garland, announcing that Judy had signed to play Helen Lawson. Judy said, 'Let's face it: the role calls for an old pro over forty. That's for me. It's for sure I am no longer Dorothy in *The Wizard of Oz* . . .' She had wardrobe tests and pre-recorded Lawson's song, a gutsy show-stopper titled 'I'll Plant My Own Tree'. But Judy hated the song and wanted changes to the script. During initial filming, she wouldn't come out of her dressing room, and on 27 April it was announced that she had 'resigned for personal reasons'. It was a case of life impersonating art impersonating life. Susan Hayward replaced Judy, making a serviceable Helen Lawson. I love the scene where she 'reads' the riot act to Neely O'Hara: 'Look! They drummed you right of Hollywood. So you come *crawling* back to Broadway. Well Broadway doesn't go for *booze* and *dope*!' It would have been interesting to see what Judy would have done with the role, although I suspect she might have struggled to appear as hard-nosed as was required. She at least made off with the Travilla-designed sequin-encrusted pant-suit that Lawson's character was to wear, putting it to good use in her performances at London's Talk of the Town cabaret club.

Critics hated the book version, but their response to the film was even more brutal. The *New York Times* had a good old gloat: 'Bad as Jacqueline Susann's *Valley of the Dolls* is as a book, the movie Mark Robson has made from it is that bad or worse. It's an unbelievably hackneyed and mawkish mish-mash of backstage plots and "Peyton Place"[78] adumbrations . . .'[79] Roger Ebert prissily described the scene where Jennifer (played by Sharon Tate), does bust exercises as 'the most offensive and appalling vulgarity ever thrown up by civilization'.[80] At its premiere, Lee Grant, who had a role in the film, said, 'I almost fell out of my seat . . . I just kept laughing and laughing. It was what it was.'[81]

I first became aware of the film after reading about it in book called *The Fifty Worst Films of All Time*, which made me desperate to see it immediately. Anne, Neely and co. might have been addicted to dolls, but take pity on the poor fan who was addicted to *Valley of the Dolls*. It took years but I finally located a copy on VHS in a movie store – the late, lamented, Kim's Videos in St Mark's Place during a holiday to New York. However, due to the fact that America uses a different encoding format to the UK, I had to then arrange to have the film run through a machine that 'translates' it so that it could be played on British VCRs. This process resulted in a rather grainy version which added green and yellow wavy lines all over the screen. Of course, my imagined version of the film was never going to be as good (or bad) as the reality, and I found it an oddly stilted affair rather than the over-the-top screaming camp-fest that I had been expecting. With that said, Patty Duke gives good Neely O'Hara, sarcastically shouting, 'Sparkle, Neely, sparkle!' Her final scene, where she screams a roll-call of the cast, while rolling around in the gutter, is worth the wait. The film gained a cult following as well as an association with tragedy, not only through Susann's death but also because of the senseless murder of Sharon Tate and her unborn baby by members of Charles Manson's 'Family' in 1969. As a result, for me, watching the film is an unsettling experience, drawing out conflicting emotions. So, be warned – those surface pleasures can lead to us wanting to find out everything we can about our camp objects. But that can change the way that we engage with them forever.

NOBODY LOVES A FAIRY WHEN SHE'S FORTY

Judy is your starter for ten – the gateway doll there to get you hooked on the hard stuff. And, for that, we need to turn to a somewhat patronisingly titled genre called Women's Films ('Men's Films' are not referred to as such because they are the default, unmarked case). Women's Films had been around since the start of film-making but their heyday lasted from the 1930s to the 1960s. They tended to be low-budget affairs, shot in studio and featuring plots about love, family, motherhood, relationships, careers and emotions. The female protagonists were not traditional heroines but they had large personalities and demanded attention and respect in a man's world, just like the actresses who played them – a list that included Marlene Dietrich, Mae West, Tallulah Bankhead, Katharine Hepburn, Vivien Leigh, Ingrid Bergman, Jane Wyman, Susan Hayward, Jennifer Jones, Merle Oberon, Bette Davis, Joan Crawford and Barbara Stanwyck. Their male co-stars were often lesser-known actors who would not crowd out the female star. So, when Bette Davis appeared in *Another Man's Poison* (1951), she was cast alongside *two* B-listers: her real-life husband, Gary Merrill, a solid but unglamourous actor whom she had fallen in love with on the set of their previous film, and Anthony Steel, a young hunk with a rather stilted delivery who had earned the nickname 'the wooden dish'.

There was a lot of what my husband calls 'face acting' in these films, with the actresses making good dramatic use of their eyes and mouths in close-up to convey over-the-top emotions, particularly fear and rage. They would also do it when they had no lines, mugging away in the background to upstage others. Each actress had a distinct and often easy-to-parody style, making them a cut-out-and-collect template for aspiring drag queens. Joan had her severe eyebrows and shoulder pads; Bette had enormous glaring eyes and an odd delivery style, which involved pausing at unexpected points. Vivien had a direct and sultry way of looking at her leading man, combined with a whiny little-girl voice that concealed dangerous strength. Katharine had razor-like facial features and sounded like she was talking through her teeth; Marlene strutted around in men's suits and spoke in a Germanic purr; Mae glided majestically like an ocean liner and punctuated her lines with little orgasmic noises. There was an intangible quality to some of these actresses, a steeliness or grit that might be mistaken for manliness. These women sometimes earned reputations for being difficult, which meant that they knew how things should be done better than anyone else. They had no time to waste while other people figured it out. This made them divas – when men do this it's called leadership.

One of the basic tenets of camp is transgression, existing outside what counts as normal, breaking the unspoken norms that govern how different types of people are supposed to behave, sound or appear. In 1972, the English painter and Booker Prize winner John Berger wrote an essay on art criticism called *Ways of Seeing*, based on a television series of the same name. Perhaps the most famous part of the essay was Berger's highly perceptive view of gender roles:

> Men act and women appear. Men look at women. Women watch themselves being looked at. This determines not only most relations between men and women but also the relation of women to themselves. The surveyor of woman in herself is male: the surveyed female. Thus she turns herself into an object – and most particularly an object of vision: a sight.[82]

In mainstream society, at least, women's bodies were the default object of desire, pornography was not made for women, and, if they did find men's bodies attractive, they weren't expected to go on about it. So, because the women in these films didn't always act like women were supposed to – they acknowledged their desires for men – they could be read as camp, and from today's perspective many of them are. But, as often as not, at the time they were taken seriously, with the women critically acclaimed as actresses who commanded armies of fans.

Women's Films verged on being feminist because they placed strong women in central roles, even if the plots were often driven by their love of men. They broke Berger's rule – these were women who might have been looked at, but they also did their fair share of looking back. Take Tallulah Bankhead, whose most famous role was journalist Constance Porter in Alfred Hitchcock's perfect 'bottle' film *Lifeboat* (1944). Everything takes place on that one boat, after the cast's ship is sunk by a German U-boat, which is then itself destroyed. It is an ensemble piece rather than a true Women's Film – although Constance embodies many of the aspects of the strong female protagonist, with her husky smoker's voice, habit of calling everyone 'darling' and complicated asymmetrical hairstyle. She is *alive*, bringing colour to the black-and-white tones of the film. With her mezzo-basso voice (the result of childhood bronchitis apparently) and mid-Atlantic drawl, she might come across as a terrific snob, but it emerges that she has worked her way up from the gutter, climbing a staircase built of men along the way. Constance falls into conflict with handsome engine-room crewman John Kovac, who wants a German survivor of the U-boat thrown overboard. However, she can't help but notice Kovac's rather manly chest, asking, 'What are those letters on your diaphragm?' then expressing disapproval that he is covered in tattoos of the initials of former girlfriends. But, when it looks like the lifeboat is going to go down during a storm, Connie reasons why the hell not and embraces him. The next morning, she writes her own initials in lipstick on his chest. Over the course of the film, she embarks on a character-transforming journey as she is gradually stripped of all of the accoutrements of success and sophistication – her camera, her typewriter, her mink coat and her Cartier diamond bracelet. Yet, in the face of impending doom, all she can do is laugh. Actresses like Bankhead succeeded by the sheer force of their personalities. They showed other women that they could be in control of their own destinies and that it was fine if they wanted to look or even touch.

Of course, Berger's claims about women being looked at applied to *young* women. The term 'Invisible Woman Syndrome' does not refer to a 1950s B-movie but to the phenomenon whereby women suddenly disappear from public view after turning forty. Older women appear much less in films, television and advertising, and in real life they may find it more difficult to get service in a shop, a spare seat on a train or a promotion at work. There is a sense of being 'looked through' in public places, which, in some contexts, might be welcome relief, but may also produce complex, ambivalent feelings, particularly if some kinds of attention had been a sign of validation. During the middle years of the twentieth century, Invisible Woman Syndrome became inextricably linked to camp as society grappled with this problematic identity. The decades after World War II saw accelerated social change – it was a period when women's rights came to the forefront, along with a conservative backlash that wanted women to stay in the bedroom and out of the boardroom. It was also a time when young people became seen as increasingly important. The new sexual openness meant that uptight conventions were torn down – the aim was a sense of freedom, although would sexual liberation result in a new hierarchy, advantaging some while excluding others?

The Stephen Sondheim musical *Follies* (1971) is an ode to ageing, loss and regret. It is set in a condemned Broadway theatre so there can be no doubt that what is to follow will be a camp tour de force, even by the standards of Sondheim. A desultory group of actors and chorus girls who performed in the musical revue *Weismann's Follies* between 1919 and 1941, have gathered at this once-grand location to attend what will be a bittersweet reunion. The Master of Ceremonies performs a song called 'Beautiful Girls' as a series of middle-aged (and upwards) former chorus girls, wearing sashes displaying their glory year on them, parade down a staircase and proceed on to the stage, while their younger 'ghosts' watch silently in the background. Even though it is an immensely silly number, and it occurs right at the start so there hasn't been time for the audience to develop any sort of investment in the characters, it chokes me up every time I see it performed.

But the highlight and essence of *Follies* is a song called 'I'm Still Here', a tour de force about female survival that is performed by showgirl Carlotta Campion, a relatively minor character (usually played by a comedy actress who knows how to belt it out, like Elaine Stritch, Carol Burnett or Patti LuPone). In the song, Carlotta recounts her life and career showing the mixture of humour and pathos that is Sondheim at his best. Elaine Stritch has opined that you can only get to sing 'I'm Still Here' when you have reached the age of eighty and she has reacted with annoyance to actresses in their forties to sixties who have sung it, asking, 'Where have they *been*?' One line in particular captures the three-stage trajectory of the female performer, with Carlotta telling the audience she has gone from being a sloe-eyed vamp, to someone's mother, to camp.

While roles for male actors have often tended to get more interesting as they get older, the scenario for women was pretty bleak. For much of the twentieth century, Bette Davis was the go-to camp actress, the one who all the drag queens impersonated, doing that strange tapping action with her cigarette, then rigidly holding it up with her elbow bent at ninety degrees. She excelled at 'bad girl' film roles like slatternly Mildred in *Of Human Bondage* (1934), spoiled Southern belle Julie Marsden in *Jezebel* (1938) and self-centred Fanny Trellis in *Mr Skeffington* (1944). By middle age, Bette's high-pitched reedy voice had matured into raspy imperiousness, apparently caused by her bursting a blood vessel in her throat as a result of screaming rows with her third husband, William Grant Sherry.

As Bette got older, there were still interesting roles to play – she was drawn to the character of Margo Channing in *All About Eve* (1950), a film about a middle-aged theatre actress who acquires a young, beautiful number-one fan who doesn't exactly have the best of intentions. Margo is cast in roles meant for much younger women and becomes increasingly obstreperous over the course of the film as she senses the threat of the younger woman. Of her husband, she says, 'Bill's thirty-two. He looks thirty-two. He looked it five years ago, he'll look it twenty years from now. I *hate* men.' If Bette isn't enough of a camp draw, *All About Eve* throws in George Sanders as a vinegary theatre critic, Marilyn Monroe as an ambitious ingenue, and Thelma Ritter as Margo's cynical maid – the dialogue sparkles with everyone tripping over themselves to say something witty. 'I detest cheap sentiment'; 'Fasten your seatbelts, it's going to be a bumpy night'; 'I'm still not to be had for the price of a cocktail, like a salted peanut'. It is rightly viewed as one of the best films of all time and won six Oscars.

In the 1950s former starlets were allowed to fret about losing their looks because there was dramatic potential in it, and the big names could still draw in audiences. *Sunset Boulevard* was released the same year as *All About Eve*, darkly ruminating on similar themes but centred around Hollywood rather than Broadway. Gloria Swanson, who had been a silent movie star, plays Norma Desmond, who had also been a silent movie star but was now hiding away in a decaying LA mansion, into which Joe Gillis (William Holden) a handsome struggling writer stumbles. Ms Desmond initially mistakes Joe for the undertaker who is about to bury her beloved pet chimp (we will get to see that Joe is almost as hairy) and the only other occupant of the mansion is a stony-faced manservant who drops several bombshells over the course of the film. 'It was all very queer,' Joe narrates. 'But queerer things were yet to come.' Swanson's performance is flawless camp noir. She conveys Norma Desmond as a woman who has never stopped acting in silent movies, communicating with massive gestures and manic facial expressions, accompanying lines such as, 'I am big. It's the pictures that got small.' She has the familiar mid-Atlantic accent with affected, hilarious pronunciations of *garage* (she pronounces it in the French manner), *pictures* (pick-chairs) and *dummy* (dumm-eh).

As with *All About Eve*, the film is driven by a horror of female ageing. Norma was once the biggest star in the world, but her roles have dried up and she's bored and lonely, yearning for a comeback (Norma: 'I hate that word, it's *return!*') to the screen. She hires Joe to improve a script of Salome she's written and – this is her flaw – she intends to play the star role of beautiful princess Salome, daughter of King Herod. Sad thing is, she's talented (in a comic highlight she entertains Joe with a fantastic Charlie Chaplin impersonation), but she's represented as hankering after roles that would work

Is that my camera? Norma Desmond (Gloria Swanson) finally gets her close-up in *Sunset Boulevard*.

better for a younger woman. Actually, though, why *shouldn't* Norma play Salome? Kim Cattrall has shown how older women can be both sexy and sexual in the series *Sex and the City* and onstage in *Antony and Cleopatra*. But this was 1950 when female desirability had a shelf-life of around twenty-eight.

Joe tries to get Norma to see sense: 'There's nothing tragic about being fifty. Not unless you try to be twenty-five.' But as *Sunset Boulevard* shows, the only way that a fifty-year-old woman can be a star of a film is to play a desperate, jealous fifty-year-old ageing actress who wants to be the star of a film. And also one who falls for unattainable men. 'Older woman who's well-to-do. Younger man who's not doing too well. Can you figure it out?' Joe asks. But we already know that it's going to end badly – the opening scene has Joe face down in a swimming pool, and the rest of the film occurs in flashback. At the end of the film, Norma gets her wish as the cameras are all turned on her once more, and she gets to descend a whiplash staircase, while everyone watches, frozen in time (gossip columnist Hedda Hopper, playing herself, looks genuinely terrified), although it's because Norma has achieved notoriety rather than fame.

Both *All About Eve* and *Sunset Boulevard* were hugely successful and critically celebrated, although they are especially appreciated by gay men of a certain age, who, on the one hand, love the wit, glamour and camp characterisations but also identify with the concerns of the ageing main characters. The tragi-comic song 'Nobody Loves a Fairy When She's Forty' was written in 1934 by Arthur Le Clerq and became a hit for Tessie O'Shea. The song's lyrics indicate that it's about a literal fairy, but the title could just as easily function as a damning indictment of the youth-obsessed gay scene. These days, a gay man reaches forty, shrugs, lets his facial hair grow and changes his Grindr profile to daddy or bear and all is well, but back in the mid-twentieth century there were fewer positive role models of any sort of gay man, let alone older ones. Margo and Norma addressed the anxiety that they would no longer be looked at but looked *through*.

This kind of gay ventriloquism was perfected in Tennessee Williams's *A Streetcar Named Desire* (1951), in which Vivien Leigh played Blanche DuBois (she says the name means 'White Woods'), a faded Southern belle, fallen on hard times. Williams was a gay man and in some of his scripts homosexuality is an off-screen insinuation, the secret that drives the plot along. In *Suddenly, Last Summer* (1959), for example, Sebastian uses his cousin Catherine (played by Elizabeth Taylor) as 'bait' to attract young Spanish men, while in *Cat on a Hot Tin Roof* (1958) Skipper commits suicide after he is rejected by his friend Brick. However, most of the on-screen relationships in Williams's works are heterosexual ones, though his female characters are ostensibly written as camp gay men. Blanche is the ultimate femme – she *floats* around, living in a world of illusion, fussing and exclaiming and clutching at herself. Although she presents herself as refined and chaste, it emerges that even the low-class Flamingo Hotel asked her to leave because of her sexual shenanigans: 'I have had many meetings with strangers!' she confesses. Fleeing her ruined reputation, Blanche comes to stay with her younger sister Stella, who has married a mumbling working-class brute called Stanley Kowalski, played by Marlon Brando. Blanche is appalled: 'He acts like an animal, has an animal's habits! Eats like one, moves like one, talks like one! There's even something – sub-human – something not quite to the stage of humanity yet!' But her repulsion is mixed with attraction. Williams endows her with the ageing queen's fear of her true age being revealed in daylight and she employs all of the familiar techniques that must be used to hide the truth. It ends horribly, but, even here, Williams cannot keep away from camp. Blanche's last line – 'Whoever you are, I have always depended on the kindness of strangers' – is one of those instant quotables and takes the edge off the shocking final ten minutes. Vivien's performance is so transcendental that it is not just parodied by gay men. In 1973, in the sci-fi comedy *Sleeper*, set 200 years in the future, Woody Allen and Diane Keaton respectively role-played as Blanche and Stanley during a bizarre deprogramming scene. The fact that anyone of any gender can have fun with these roles is a good indication of how exaggerated they were to begin with.

A decade later, Vivien was at it again as Karen Stone in *The Roman Spring of Mrs Stone* (1961), another Tennessee Williams adaption, which starts with a holiday-from-hell scenario on a plane to Italy when Karen's husband has a heart attack and dies mid-flight. Stuck in a weird life-limbo, she decides to stay in Italy and is befriended by a malevolent high-class madam called Contessa

Magda Terribili-Gonzales (played by Lotte Lenya). The Contessa introduces Karen to a gigolo, a much younger man played by Warren Beatty. However, it's a classic case of 'no fool like an old fool' and Karen eventually realises that he is only interested in her money. The Contessa cackles that Karen is a 'chicken-hawk', a term imported from the gay bars of the Castro. At the end of the film, it is implied that Karen is about to be murdered, having sunk so low as to let a sinister young homeless man into her apartment in her search for comfort. Wouldn't it have been nice if these films had presented their older women as desirable, well adjusted and confident in themselves, either as truly loved by men or simply not needing their validation in the first place? And, in casting older women as characters concerned about getting older, they are trivialised. Really, worrying about grey hair and crow's feet suggest an otherwise easy but inconsequential life. The level of anxiety over ageing is taken to such heights that it can only be seen as camp.

THE SEASON OF THE HAG

By the 1960s, even these roles were running out. Then, in 1962 a piece of stunt-casting changed everything. Two of Hollywood's greatest actresses, Joan Crawford and Bette Davis, teamed up to star in a psychological horror film called *Whatever Happened to Baby Jane?* It took the usual material – ageing actresses playing ageing actresses, decrepit mansion, delusional attempt at comeback – but everything was so grotesque that it spilled over into intentional camp. Bette played Jane, a child vaudeville star who'd enjoyed a brief spell of fame with a cloying song called 'I've Written a Letter to Daddy', but didn't have the talent to make it as an adult star. Her big sister, Blanche, *had* succeeded as a movie actress, resulting in nothing but jealousy from washed-up Jane. But tragedy ensues when Blanche loses the use of her legs after a car accident. When

'Butchya aah Blanche! Ya aah in that chair!'
Joan Crawford and Bette Davis in *Whatever Happened to Baby Jane?*

a TV channel starts playing Blanche's old movies, fan letters start to arrive in the post. This sends Jane, already a reclusive alcoholic, over the edge. Like many 1960s films, it could have done with a little judicious editing (it is two hours fourteen minutes *long*), but it has a killer final plot-twist and both actresses give memorable performances. Despite the fact that the characters have been parodied endlessly by drag queens, not everyone views it as camp. Critic Dan Schneider argues that the film has been ghettoized as a 'camp melodrama' rather than as a 'taut, if flawed, portrayal of sibling rivalry in extremis'.[83]

The story behind the film is even more fascinating. Bette played opposite long-term rival Joan Crawford, settling for a temporary cessation of hostilities, which were gradually resumed over the course of filming. The two women had been mutually jealous of one another for years – Davis hated Crawford because she was a proper 'star', with an enormous fan-club, while Crawford wished that she could be a real theatre-trained 'actress' like Davis.

Bette's daughter, BD had a small role in the film and Joan asked BD to keep away from her own twin daughters because 'they have been carefully brought up and shielded from the wicked side of the world and you obviously have not. I don't want your influence to corrupt them.' Miaow! Bette was livid. Joan kept bringing in gifts to win over crew and cast members and Bette asked her to stop doing so as she didn't have the time to go out and shop. As filming continued, the atmosphere became increasingly fractious. BD reported that Bette complained about Joan's breasts: '*Christ!* You never know what size boobs that broad has strapped on! She must have a different set for each day of the week! I keep running into them like the Hollywood Hills!'[84] Joan suggested that they should both appear in cages when the picture was promoted. There were claims that the rivalry spilled over into real violence, although this is most likely wishful thinking. In one scene Bette has to kick Joan, and rumour has it that she let loose and allegedly kicked Joan in the head, resulting in her needing stitches. 'That bitch could cry on demand!' Bette claimed.[85] As dramatic as it sounds, the actual contact takes place below frame, out of shot, so Crawford is unlikely to have even been present for the shot.[86] Another claim relates to a scene where Bette had to drag Joan across the room. Joan allegedly attempted to weigh herself down, knowing that Bette had back problems.[87] Whether this is true or not, it is the sense of older women overstepping boundaries that enables such acts of violence, whether on-screen or off, to be seen as camp. These women are meant to be serene, wise, non-violent, motherly – not kicking one another. Would we laugh as much if a couple of young male actors were described as behaving like this?

After shooting on *Baby Jane* had wrapped, Bette Davis placed a 'Situation Wanted' advert in *Variety* magazine.

> Mother of three – 10, 11 & 15 – Divorcee. American. Thirty years experience as an actress in motion pictures. Mobile still and more affable than rumor would have it. Wants steady employment in Hollywood (Has had Broadway). Bette Davis, c/o Martin Baum G.A.C. References upon request.

BD said she did it out of 'pure desperation'. Yet it was one of those tongue-in-cheek stunts that aims to both make fun of and draw serious attention to the ridiculousness of an unfair system. Not everyone realised that Bette was in on the joke, though, and while offers did start to come in, they weren't all for good parts in quality films.

Although a come-down from their usual roles, *Whatever Happened to Baby Jane?* earned both actresses a fair amount of critical acclaim *and* was successful at the box office. Bette even received an Oscar nomination, having the meatier acting role to contend with. Audiences wanted more – older actresses were now allowed to be looked at, as long as they were confined to these kinds of campy horror roles. And so it came to pass that a new genre was born – the Hag Film. The 1960s saw a slew of these kinds of movies as older actresses struggled to find serious work and resorted to increasingly ridiculous horror roles. What was most horrific about these films was the way that experienced actresses were reduced to taking parts that were well beneath their stature.

And these films didn't even bother to act as commentaries about the role of ageing women in society, they just had to pair older ladies with gruesome content. So, Bette and Joan agreed to appear in a mediocre follow-up to *Baby Jane*, a Southern Gothic called *Hush. . . Hush, Sweet Charlotte* (1964), which features a decapitation in an early scene. By this point relations between the pair had declined to the point of no return, so Joan pulled out and was replaced by Olivia de Havilland, who had played the nice girl in *Gone with the Wind* (eight Oscars) back in 1939. 'I'm glad she is taking my place,' said Joan. 'She needs the work.'

Olivia's reputation was to be degraded further when she appeared in *Lady in a Cage* (1964), as a woman who gets trapped in a cage-like elevator in her own home during a power cut, and then has to face the indignity of a home invasion by various petty criminals. Joan went on to make *Strait-Jacket* (1964), *I Saw What You Did* (1965), *Berserk!* (1967) and *Trog* (1970). The latter film's title really tells you all you need to know. It is never an edifying experience when your co-star is a professional wrestler wearing a monkey mask and you have to supply your own wardrobe. Joan's face acting is set to maximum throughout as, in desperation, she tries to upstage everyone, even the man in the monkey mask. No wonder that in the Ryan Murphy biopic series *Feud: Bette and Joan* (2017), a montage of Joan working on the set of *Trog* plays out over a soundtrack of Jim Morrison singing 'The End'. Its impact on the camp imagination is great, though, and the performance artist Miss Hope Springs (Ty Jeffries) has created a loving homage to *Trog*, with a song by the same name, which is well worth a listen.

Tallulah Bankhead got in on the hag act, cast well against type in *Die! Die! My Darling!* (1965) as a fanatically religious mother who is going to make sure her son's fiancée is punished for his death. But in the late 1960s and early 1970s, Shelley Winters, who had been Oscar-nominated for *A Place in the Sun* (1951), took up the hag mantle, appearing in *Bloody Mama* (1970), *What's the Matter with Helen?* (1971) and *Whoever Slew Auntie Roo?* (1972). Yet it is the dystopian musical comedy *Wild in the Streets* (1968) that contains her most out-there performance – she is the mother of revolutionary pop star Max Frost, who becomes President of the United States after the voting age is lowered to fourteen. Blaming the decisions of older people for all the ills of the world, Frost favours an extreme form of government, setting the mandatory retirement age at thirty and sending everybody over thirty-five to 're-education' camps where they are kept permanently high on LSD. In the final reel of the film, an off-her-head Shelley clutches at the barbed-wire fence of a prison camp, screaming, 'I am to be presented at the court of St James. The queen is receiving *me!* I need feathers, I have to have feathers! White feathers to be proper and respectable!' It is a commentary on the increasing dominance of youth culture and concomitant irrelevance of older people, but like the 1950s films about older women it also becomes the thing that it is trying to critique.

In the 1970s, hag films had to keep pushing the boundaries even further to get attention, and one of the last of the genre, *The Baby* (1973), is one of my favourites. It starred Ruth Roman as Mrs Wadsworth, the blowsy mother of an adult baby. Ruth Roman had previously been a glamour-girl, starring in the Hitchcock film *Strangers on a Train* (1951) as the hero's love-interest. Here, she is almost unrecognisable – in her first scene she appears to be wearing a maroon wigwam and her voice sounds like a cement mixer on a low setting. We are now intersecting hag films with camp horror, though, and must include films like *Rosemary's Baby* (1968), *Daughters of Darkness* (1971) and *Suspiria* (1977), all of which feature older women in sinister-comic roles. *Rosemary's Baby* had Ruth Gordon playing a pushy, talkative next-door neighbour with no boundaries. *Daughters of Darkness* had Delphine Seyrig as a sinister Hungarian countess who attaches herself to a honeymooning couple in an out-of-season hotel in Ostend. And *Suspiria* has two ominous ladies who run a ballet school, played by Alida Valli and Joan Bennett. In all three films, there is something suspicious about these women – they might be evil, they might have supernatural powers, they might want to kill you. All three are saturated in a colourfully camp atmosphere, being set in architecturally distinctive buildings, complete with heavily stylised lighting and music that make them feel like nightmarish adult fairy tales.

Not all of the ageing actresses went the hag route. Some announced that they wanted to be left alone and retired from the screen or went on to do other things. However, one woman simply decided to do what she had done all along – and that was to blithely ignore all of society's tedious rules about how women should act. For Mae West, it was a case of once a bombshell, always a bombshell – and God help anyone who dared to say otherwise. Bawdy, husky Mae had been camp from the very start, writing and appearing in scandalous plays in the 1920s and 1930s like *Sex*, *The Drag*, *The Wicked Age*, *Pleasure Man* and *The Constant Sinner*. She'd even gone to prison for 'corrupting the morals of youth' as a result of her plays, refusing to pay the fine that would have set her free, figuring it would be good publicity. Mae appeared in a series of films like *She Done Him Wrong* (1933) and *I'm No Angel* (1933), which were made in the short 'pre-Code' era of the early 1930s, meaning that they did not have censorship guidelines enforced. She played laconic, sexualised characters who relied on a steady stream of wisecrack and innuendo delivered with knowing insolence: 'When women go wrong, men go right after them'; 'It's not the men in my life that counts – it's the life in my men'; 'When I'm good I'm very good but when I'm bad, I'm better' – and so on, always punctuated with a little satisfied moan of pleasure.

As a woman who *really* loved men and revelled in the fact, Mae was always transgressive, particularly by early twentieth-century standards. And, as she got older, her shtick simply got more raucous – in the 1950s her Las Vegas show featured a bevy of muscle men, while her final two films, *Myra Breckinridge* (1970) and *Sextette* (1978) are almost unclassifiable – they push camp into a very strange place indeed and are not recommended for beginners. The former is based on a Gore Vidal novel (he disowned the film) about Myra Breckinridge, a trans woman who takes a position at her uncle's acting school and then seduces a couple of the students in order to destroy the patriarchy and reduce the world's population (a little ambitious perhaps, but I guess you have to start somewhere). Amid such questionable content, Mae West plays casting agent Leticia Van Allen who routinely seduces male actors. Introduced to one prospect who tells her that he is six feet seven inches, she quips, 'Well, never mind about the six feet, let's talk about the seven inches.' During one of the most remarkable set-pieces of a fairly unforgettable film, West's backing singers carry her onto a nightclub stage inside a palanquin. She emerges and sings a song called 'You Gotta Taste All the Fruit' while in the background Myra and her two student victims, Rusty, try to define normality. At the age of seventy-six, West puts in a game performance, although her voice struggles to reach some of the higher notes. Then the music goes up-tempo and she segues into a scary interpretation of Otis Redding's 'Hard to Handle'. She wisely talks her way through most of it.

But this is nothing compared to *Sextette*, where eighty-four-year-old Mae is Marlo Manners, a sexy, superannuated Cheshire cat who is on to her sixth husband, played by future James Bond star Timothy Dalton (fifty-three years her junior). All of the men in the film find West sexually irresistible – and why not? It was rumoured that West couldn't remember her lines and had to have them fed to her via an earpiece under her wig. The claim that it could pick up police frequencies, resulting in West giving the line, 'There's a 608', was, sadly, an exaggeration. The film's action occurs in a hotel where Marlo and her latest husband are honeymooning. There are shenanigans involving a compromising audio tape containing Marlo's memories of various lovers. Meanwhile, the hotel is hosting world leaders who are attending a conference at which world peace is at stake. A Russian delegate threatens to derail negotiations unless he can have sex with Marlo. Simultaneously, the (all-male) United States Athletic Team are training at the hotel and, in the film's high point, West staggers into the gym, clad in a black vampire dress with plunging neckline, and, after a bit of banter, sings a ditty entitled 'Happy Birthday 21' to a gap-toothed twink, while Tom of Finland models flex their muscles in the background. The film bombed and was critically panned. *Variety* called it a 'cruel, unnecessary and mostly unfunny musical comedy'[88] while the nastiest opinion went to Vincent Canby of the *New York Times*, who said that 'Granny should have her mouth washed out, along with her teeth'.[89] Ouch. Although, I doubt that Mae would have cared a jot.

THE DIVA DISAPPOINTS

Not only were the ageing stars demeaned by appearing in increasingly absurd films, their private lives were mined to yield even richer sources of camp. Daniel Harris wrote that camp was rooted in the gay man's profound disillusionment with celebrity culture, the fan's discovery that the carefully crafted image of the star was a lie – the diva was not a goddess but had a miserable life, and the press was there to record every misstep.[90] Fans therefore found camp in celebrating the fall of their idols, with reverence giving way to ridicule.

Both Bette and Joan had difficult relationships with their daughters who wrote tell-all exposés about them. In *My Mother's Keeper* (1985), BD painted Bette as a bullying, manipulative alcoholic, causing Bette to disown her. However, Bette got off relatively lightly compared to Joan. *Mommie Dearest* (1978) was written by Joan's adopted daughter, Christina, who was bitter after Joan had disinherited her and her brother Christopher for 'reasons which are well-known to them'. The book is a catalogue of physical and mental abuse – Christina claims that Joan slashed her favourite dress to bits, then made her wear it for a week, beat her with a tin of scouring powder, gave her Christmas presents away, tried to strangle her, sent her to a strict religious school and, bizarrely, stole Christina's limelight by standing in for her on a soap opera when she was recovering from an operation (there was doubtless trademark face acting involved too). The most notorious part of the book involves Joan beating Christina after discovering wire hangers in her closet (Joan had worked at a dry cleaner's before becoming a star and apparently the wire hangers triggered her – they were a reminder of her former poverty, so she preferred crochet ones).

A film of the same name came out in 1981, starring Faye Dunaway as Joan. Dunaway said that she'd hoped that the film would provide a 'window into a tortured soul, but it was made into camp'.[91] *Mommie Dearest* was critically panned, with Dunaway's performance seen as over-the-top Kabuki theatre. Joan actually beats Christina *with* the wire hangers when she discovers them in her closet. However, rather than simply being a complete flop, the film was an inadvertent camp hit – audiences responded by laughing, so Paramount adjusted its marketing campaign to exploit the film's unintended camp appeal. One post-release advert contained the quote: 'No wire hangers . . . EVER' above the words *Mommie Dearest*. A wire hanger is depicted hanging off the final 't', and the tag 'The biggest mother of them all' appears as a sign-off. The film became a cult favourite, with reports of audience members dressed as Joan chasing other audience members dressed as Christina down the aisles, while brandishing wire hangers.[92] Lines like, 'Tina! Bring me the axe!', 'I'm not mad at you, I'm mad at the *dirt*!', 'Don't fuck with me fellas, this ain't my first time at the rodeo', 'Don't you ever use that tone of voice with me, missy!' and 'I am not . . . one of your *fans*!' were screamed back at the screen.

Daniel Harris argues that reverence turns to ridicule because devotion always ends up consuming its object. Obsession demands

'Tina! Bring me the axe!' Faye Dunaway as Joan Crawford in *Mommie Dearest*.

greater and greater intimacy, which inevitably breaks down the distance required for idolatry.[93] In other words, never meet your heroes. However, I think that the feelings of gay men towards their divas are complex, with a camp perspective allowing them to simultaneously worship, identify with and laugh at these women. Certainly, the gay fans of Joan Crawford and Bette Davis I have spoken to are fully aware of the torrid backstories and reputations of these women. They make fun of their later films like *Beserk!* and *Madame Sin*, but they still admire the glamour, guts and acting chops they had when they were at their best. Fans know that the glamorous magazine profiles are public relations guff and when their idols can't live up to the fantasy image, it makes them more, rather than less, relatable. People may be less deferential than they used to be but they still love a good camp diva, and are usually happy to take the bad with the good. Although there are exceptions.

From the safety of an enclosure, I would like to introduce you to Fanny Cradock, a monstrous British television chef, who fellow presenter Esther Rantzen described as 'hell on wheels'.[94] Fanny's career began with a column in the *Daily Telegraph* newspaper in the 1950s under the pen name Bon Viveur. Like many camp British icons before her, Fanny drew inspiration from France, and she was a huge fan of the chef Auguste Escoffier, who ran his kitchens with military discipline and was the darling of the Ritz, the Savoy and the Carlton. In 1955, Fanny became the star of her own BBC cookery programme, a gig she held for two decades. Her French-inspired recipes looked fancy, but were surprisingly economical. They certainly got people talking – Fanny liked to zhoosh things up with garish food dyes or fancy piping. One of her signature dishes (Oeufs à la Riga) was hard-boiled eggs, dyed *blue*, decorated with anchovies and piped mayonnaise. If you didn't fancy that, how about green mashed potatoes or 'swans' sculpted out of boiled eggs and pipe cleaners. As Fanny got older, she became increasingly camp, wearing chiffon ballgowns and heels and taking her makeup to *Baby Jane* levels. Her eyebrows were drawn on about two inches above their original position and she started wearing outsize bows and ribbons in her hair. She looked terrifying.

Fanny's impatient and bossy shtick worked well when she was chiding her assistant/husband, Johnnie, who was implied to like a drink or two, but in 1976 it all went horribly wrong when she appeared on a television series called *The Big Time*, presented by Esther Rantzen. The programme was an early outing of reality television, with ordinary members of the public given the opportunity to live their professional dreams. One episode focused on an unassuming housewife from Devon called Gwen Troake, who had won a culinary contest called Cook of the Realm. Gwen subsequently appeared on the show, tasked with organising a three-course meal for a literary lunch at the Dorchester hotel, which was going to be attended by the British Prime Minister Edward Heath and Earl Mountbatten of Burma, both keen sailors. Fanny, being the nation's expert on such matters, was brought in to offer a bit of mentoring. She seems to have been in a particularly uptight mood that day, pronouncing all her favourite French phrases through clenched teeth while maintaining only the thinnest veneer of civility from the start.

Appropriately, Gwen had planned a meal with a nautical theme, deciding on a seafood cocktail as the first course, followed by duckling with a lemon jelly and corn-starch bramble sauce, finishing with a coffee cream dessert with rum. None of this was to Fanny's taste. She rolled her eyes as Gwen described the menu, repeatedly calling her choices sickly. 'A seafood starter and then straight into the duck?' Fanny's hand went to her temple, she turned her head away from Gwen, her eyes bulged in disgust and her cheeks puffed out as if she was holding in vomit. 'I wouldn't do it. I would never serve a seafood cocktail or crème farci aux fruits de mer before a duck. Never in a million years.' Gwen looked crest-fallen. 'What is the sauce of the duck?' asked Fanny, moving in for the kill. 'A bramble,' said Gwen. 'What *is* a bramble?' cut in Fanny. 'Blackberry,' offered Gwen. 'With duck?' Fanny pulled a face as if she'd smelt excrement. 'That's what I did for the Cook

Cooking up a storm: Fanny Cradock in trouser suit and headband.

of the Realm,' Gwen offered, grasping at straws. 'Yes, dear, but now you're among professionals,' said Fanny. When Gwen started talking about the lemon jelly, Fanny affected speechlessness, covering her face with her hand. 'All these jams. They are so *English!* . . . The English have never had a cuisine. There's nothing English. Yorkshire pudding came from Burgundy.'

To be fair, I think Gwen's meal sounds hideous, but this detail was, of course, overshadowed by Fanny's cruel critique. When the episode was broadcast, the public were outraged. The *Daily Telegraph* captured the mood, making an oblique Hitler comparison: 'Not since 1940 can the people of England have risen in such unified wrath.' Suitably chastened, Fanny wrote a letter of apology to Gwen, but the damage was irretrievably done. She never presented a cookery programme for the BBC again. The following year, to underline Fanny's expulsion, Gwen published the coffee cream dessert recipe in her own cookbook. Fanny and Johnnie retired to the south coast and became chat show regulars, with Fanny making her final television appearance in 1995 aged eighty-five on the *Parkinson* show, alongside the fabulous drag queen Danny La Rue, who happened to be dressed as Shirley Bassey. When Fanny realised that La Rue was a female impersonator she stormed out – a shame, I'm sure if she'd hung around she would have benefited *enormously* from his makeup tips. After she died, it emerged that, like Judy Garland, she had been addicted to amphetamines for most of her adult life. She kept a basket of dolls by her bed, which she called her 'hundreds and thousands'.[95] Perhaps if people had known that her difficult personality had been partly the result of drug addiction, they might have been more forgiving. But take heed of the lesson to be drawn from Fanny's error – camp barbs are only funny if your victim is also in on the joke or is at least able to defend themselves. Otherwise, it's just bullying.

Our final diva of this chapter is Donna Summer – the subject of another cautionary tale which shows that, no matter how camp someone is, if they are seen to reject those who love them, then those who love them may turn their backs. Summer became emblematic of the disco scene in the mid-1970s, with a string of hits that included 'Love to Love You Baby', 'Hot Stuff', 'Bad Girls', 'No More Tears', 'MacArthur Park' and 'I Feel Love'. Disco itself is a highly camp form of music – there's the frenetic bouncy beat, the glitter balls, the revealing colourful outfits and the stylised dance movements (the Hustle, the Bump, the Bus Stop, the Funky Chicken, the Lawnmower, the Sprinkler, the Electric Slide). One of the most well-known ones, the Disco Finger, made famous by John Travolta in the film *Saturday Night Fever*, involves thrusting your hips from side to side while pointing your right index finger up to the side of your head. Disco songs tended to have simple anthemic titles – 'We Are Family', 'Stayin' Alive', 'Disco Inferno', 'Boogie Wonderland', 'You Should Be Dancing', 'More, More, More', 'Rock Your Baby', etc. I particularly like two sub-genres: space disco, which is heavy on electronic sounds emulating laser guns and space-ships, and orchestral disco, which combines electronic and orchestral music, and sometimes even covers classical music, like the version of Beethoven's fifth symphony that appears in *Saturday Night Fever*.

Disco songs were highly sexualised, and Donna Summer's disco catalogue was no exception. 'Love to Love You Baby' had a soundtrack of Summer producing moans of pleasure that resulted in it being banned by the BBC and some American radio stations. 'I Feel Love' is perhaps her greatest achievement – with its droning synths and pulsing bassline it sounds like it comes from outer space *and* the future. It is deceptively simple, using only four chords and, although Summer makes use of seventeen words in the song, she apparently has seventeen orgasms during it (I'm not brave enough to count them). Initially a B side, it was re-released and became the gay anthem of 1977 – I imagine that the coloured squares of disco dance floors became rather difficult to navigate due to all the sweat and amyl nitrate that got spilled when it was played. In 2011, the Library of Congress added it to the National Recording Registry as 'culturally, historically, or aesthetically important'.

However, by the end of the 1970s Summer was having a bad time – relations with her record company were frosty, she'd lost several family members and was becoming hooked on anti-depressants and had considered suicide. So, Summer made a decision, perhaps one that saved her life, although it almost ruined her career – she asked God for help.

God responded, or at least, the prayer group she joined did. In 1980, Summer became a born-again Christian and decided to put the past behind her. She left her record company, sued her manager and in 1983 went on tour, performing in suburban, more conservative areas. Subsequently, there were reports that Summer no longer approved of her gay fans. *The Advocate* magazine quoted *Village Voice* journalist Jim Feldman who apparently reviewed a performance in Atlantic City. He claimed that Summer had repeated a statement by homophobic campaigner Anita Bryant:

'God created Adam and Eve, not Adam and Steve'.[96] There were reports that she said it jokingly, but rumours started to circulate about other concerts, with people saying she had told her gay fans, 'I'll pray for you tonight', 'God loves you. But not the way you are now' and 'AIDS is your sin'. An article in *Gay Times* in 1984 claimed she had said, 'Homosexuals brought AIDS on themselves as a divine retribution from God for their sinful ways' on an (unnamed) American chat show.[97] Did she really say these things? Despite the claims, I have not been able to find actual proof. However, the stories went round and round, making many of her gay fans livid.

Subsequently, Summer's music was banned from London gay nightclub Heaven and there were calls to boycott her. When the gay group Bronski Beat collaborated with Marc Almond to produce a cover of 'I Feel Love', *Gay Times* reported how disgusted they were to learn of Summer's alleged views, proclaiming her dead to them.[98] Initially, requests from the gay press to interview Summer went unanswered. However, when she volunteered to perform at an AIDS benefit in New York in 1984, she was rejected. She issued a statement to *The Advocate* that recognised her support and friendship from the gay community and said it was a source of concern that anything she may have said cast her as homophobic. She said that as a Christian she loved everyone and it was not her place to judge others. In her statement she did not embrace her gay fans, which some might interpret as not going far enough.[99] But subsequently Summer tried repeatedly to quash the claims – putting an advert in a programme for an AIDS benefit on Fire Island in 1987, and then writing to the activist group ACT UP (AIDS Coalition to Unleash Power) in 1989, denying having made anti-gay remarks.[100] She also sued *New York Magazine* in 1991 for repeating the rumours as fact,[101] with the case being settled out of court for an undisclosed sum.

What this episode reveals is the potential for camp to turn serious, not because of its content but due to its creator. For many, camp cannot be enjoyed if its representative is believed to be against the very people who the camp is aimed at. It becomes impossible to separate the product from the producer, in other words. It is a reminder that behind every camp creation there is a human being, and a flawed one at that. While sometimes those flaws can be incorporated into a camp narrative, this is not always the case. It also tells us that we shouldn't view fans of camp as a set of frivolous, shrieking hedonists who only care about a good laugh or a dance. Putting aside the question of whether the fans who turned on Donna Summer were acting on faulty intel, they showed that you can love camp and simultaneously be driven by strong political views. As a counter-balance, consider Bette Midler – also much loved by gay audiences. In 1970 she began performing at the Continental Baths, a gay bath house in the basement of 2109 Broadway, accompanied by Barry Manilow on the piano. To empty the steam room your brand of camp would have to be *ultra*, and Bette made sure that between her songs her jokes were on-message. How's this:

> Zsa Zsa Gabor and her hairdresser checked into a hotel in Cleveland Ohio. And they went up the stairs up to the room to see what the room looked like. And Miss Gabor opened the door and there were two naked men in the bed. Well, she fled in panic. But the hairdresser *stayed*.[102]

She was so popular that she was named 'Bathhouse Bette'. Her humour had a hard edge and Bette didn't shy away from joking about her gay fans, but she stayed true to them, and not just because they gave her that big break. Years later, in 2022 when the US Supreme Court ruled that there was no constitutional right to abortion, Midler tweeted a call to arms in her characteristically direct way: 'GET READY GAYS. YOU'RE NEXT.'

In the middle of the twentieth century, camp was what a woman became when society decreed that she was past her sell-by date, but *she* had not. At least later decades were a little gentler to their 'hags'. In the 1980s, the sitcom *The Golden Girls* took four old lady stereotypes, set them up in the same household, clad everything in pastel and allowed the women to be kind, funny, bitchy, complicated and sexual. It was ground-breaking and the jokes are still fresh today. The sketch show *Victoria Wood: As Seen On TV* (1985–7), featured numerous older ladies in comedy roles – the forthright Kitty (Patricia Routledge), rickety char lady Mrs Overall (Julie Walters) and the ancient, beaming 'two soups' waitress (also Julie Walters). These sketches were regularly shown in British gay pubs and clubs in the 1990s. And, in 1992, Meryl Streep and Goldie Hawn had a lot of fun with the ageing star trope in the campy, cartoonish film *Death Becomes Her*, figuring out that the fountain of youth causes more problems than it solves. My current favourite camp lady of a certain age is Jennifer Coolidge, who has a talent for playing larger-than-life characters with little self-awareness. But at least she knows which side her bread is buttered. 'The gays just know how to do stuff, you know. They're survivors. For some reason, they're always obsessed with me. I don't know why. But I like it', she observes in the romcom *Single All the Way* (2021). For me, this speech was momentous, at last an acknowledgement of our 'special relationship', although, hilariously, in the second series of *The White Lotus*, her character, Tanya, observes, 'These gays, they're trying to murder me.'

Of course, the films discussed in this chapter had special resonance for gay men because they warned what would happen to them as they became older and, by implication, less attractive. But this wasn't only about vicarious identification for gay men – with liberation beckoning from around the corner, they were about to have their own reckoning with camp, and it was not always going to be pretty-pretty, as the following chapter will reveal.

CHAPTER 5

Clenched Fists on Limp Wrists

It is 2010 and I'm in a taxi that's driving through the Campest City on Earth, Las Vegas, gawping at all the ostentatious hotels on the Strip. Just like Lord Redesdale's daughters two chapters ago, each hotel is sillier than the last. Finally, we reach New York-New York, a hotel that replicates the skyline of Manhattan, complete with its own Statue of Liberty. The interior is made to look like outside, with paving and lamp-lit streets, although with the air conditioning and absence of litter or daylight the effect is oddly theatrical, like being permanently on stage.

'Can I take you guys to a titty bar?' drawls the taxi driver suddenly. 'No thank you,' my husband replies, in brisk, British tones. Although it would have provided an excellent explanation, he doesn't elaborate that we have other plans – later on we are going to the Liberace Museum to pay homage to one of the greatest camp acts of all time. Liberace was an accomplished pianist with a cosy, relatable line in patter and a reputation for outfits that involved ridiculous amounts of fur, feathers, sequins and glitter. No trip to Vegas would be complete without a pilgrimage.

The museum is out of town so we have to get a minibus that has been specially laid on. All of the other passengers are elderly ladies, who remind me of the actresses Ruth Gordon and Elaine Stritch. They sigh in chorus when a recording of Liberace's distinctive voice comes on over the intercom, welcoming everyone. They are having the time of their lives and so are we, but I am not sure they are having the *same* experience as us. Once we get to the museum, the ladies coo solemnly over Liberace's flamboyant costumes on display, almost as if they are in the presence of a collection of religious icons. I want to be respectful so I have to repress the urge to bellow with laughter and spoil the mood. After half an hour, too much is too much, and we decide to leave. There isn't a bus for ages so we foolishly decide to walk back to New York-New York – a grave mistake and we are forced to return to the museum, suffering from sunburn, dehydration and heatstroke. We couldn't have lasted much longer than thirty minutes in the unforgiving Vegas climate, although it would have been a delightful epitaph to have died as a result of a visit to the Liberace Museum.

Don't libel me, bitches! – Liberace camps in a cape.

I think Liberace would have approved of us not telling the taxi driver that we were going to his museum. Despite the fact that he was camper than Cher singing a Christmas medley while disguised as Carol Channing, he lived in a glass closet that was fortified with barbed wire. In 1956, a *Daily Mirror* columnist wrote that Liberace was:

> . . . the pinnacle of Masculine, Feminine and Neuter. Everything that He, She and It can ever want . . . a deadly, winking, sniggering, snuggling, chromium-plated, scent-impregnated, luminous, quivering, giggling, fruit-flavoured, mincing, ice-covered heap of mother love.[103]

Tucked in among that overdose of adjectives, is the word *fruit* – American slang for homosexual, and Liberace sued the newspaper for libel, claiming that he was not homosexual. He *won* the case and was awarded £8,000 in damages. In July 1957, he also won a similar case against *Confidential* magazine, which claimed that his theme song should be Noël Coward's 'Mad About the Boy'. It was all a big lie, obviously – his chauffeur and lover, Scott Thorson, sued for palimony in 1982 after being dismissed, and in 2011 *Golden Girl* Betty White told interviewer Joy Behar that Liberace's manager had her accompany him to premieres, although he was not always the most gallant of dates. One windy night they were getting out of a car, Betty reached out her hand, thinking Liberace would help her, but instead he was holding onto his hair because he didn't want it to move.[104]

In a world where male homosexuality was largely illegal, and thus dangerous, many gay men kept quiet about it in public, affecting either a muted or exaggerated distracting form of masculinity (that was sometimes depressingly expressed as flamboyant homophobia). But a few men didn't hide it, either because they were extraordinarily brave and headstrong and/or because it was near-impossible to suppress how fabulous they were. As a result, the visible gay men were the ones who ticked nearly all of the boxes on a list of stereotypes – showy wardrobe choices, mincing gait, exaggerated gestures, pursed lips, lisping voice, sweeping pitch, dragged out vowels, catty sense of humour, feminine interests and excessive displays of emotion. Perhaps surprisingly for such a homophobic world, they were enormously popular. Looking at footage of Liberace's performances, it seems fantastical that he could be seen as anything but gay. But this was a more sexually naïve and repressed time – you *could* be as camp as you liked, as long as you disavowed homosexuality.

The 1960s and 1970s were a flashpoint for this kind of camp male identity, because, in both the UK and US, social attitudes around homosexuality were starting to relax a little, and with that came changes to laws, which decriminalised them, to an extent. It was a time of rapid social change and during those two decades there was a period of intense self-reflection on the roles of gay men and their relationship to wider society. There were a range of stances to take – some that involved loudly asserting difference, others that involved assimilation and acceptance. Some simply wanted to be allowed to quietly continue as they were. Caught up in the middle of all of this was the issue of camp, a political hot potato, albeit one that had been chopped up into a delicious fricassee then sprinkled with liberal helpings of rosemary. Gay men were starting to show up on film and television, but they were often cast in humorous or villainous roles, which relied on the instant recognition of camp stereotypes. In real life, such men had long borne the brunt of society's homophobia, but now they were going to find a new enemy – from within. As a camp horror film called *Black Christmas* (1974), would put it: 'Jess, the caller is in the house. The calls are coming from the house!'

FUN UNCLES

As Vito Russo has described, the camp man or *sissy* had been a long-standing staple of comedy, often appearing in supporting or cameo roles as shop assistants, clerks or hairdressers.[105] In the silent film *A Wanderer of the West* (1927), Clarence the Clerk is described as 'one of nature's mistakes' and flirts (unsuccessfully) with the film's hero. Other peripheral sissies appeared in *The Broadway Melody* (1929), *Call Her Savage* (1932), *Myrt and Marge* (1933) and *Top Secret* (1952). An exception that put such men front and centre appeared on the BBC radio sketch series *Round the Horne* (1965–8), which featured a recurring pair of out-of-work West End actors called Julian and Sandy, played by Hugh Paddick and Kenneth Williams. Back in 1892, Oscar Wilde's boyfriend Lord Alfred Douglas published a poem called 'Two Loves'. He referred to homosexuality euphemistically as the love that dare not speak its name, and indeed, for much of the century to follow, homosexuality was alluded to rather than openly mentioned. However, in the 1960s and 1970s you could often spot the gay characters because they would never shut up, like Julian and Sandy. They have so much to say that the third character in their sketches, Mr Horne, barely gets a word in.

A couple of outrageous, screaming queens, Jules and Sandy bitched and gossiped their way through each sketch, drawing heavily on euphemism and innuendo, so that the young and sheltered listeners among their Sunday afternoon audience were kept in the dark. As a typical exchange, in one sketch, the pair have opened a holiday agency called Bona Tours Ltd and Sandy eagerly makes suggestions to Mr Horne when he comes a-knocking: 'Why don't you try camping. It's all the rage in Europe . . . let's see, you could go cruising . . . We often go cruising, don't we, Jules.' 'You speak for yourself,' Julian replies. As a further form of subterfuge, the subcultural language Polari was sprinkled around the sketches like confetti at a gay wedding. Sometimes this was fairly innocuous – so, for example the catchphrase 'how bona to vada your dolly old eke' simply meant 'how nice to see your pretty old face'. But at other times, the Polari enabled much ruder jokes. In one sketch, where the pair are domestic cleaners, Julian exclaims, 'We can't wash up in here, all the dishes are dirty.' It is Sandy who retorts,

'Speak for yourself' this time, alluding to the fact that, in Polari, dish meant bum. The sketches also contain references to old flames and friends – Jock, a sailor; Gordon, a biker and steam-room attendant; Reynard LaSpoon, a choreographer; Pando Wildebeeste, a film director – suggesting that the characters inhabited a rich social scene, one that most of the audience could only guess at. The camp humour was so coded that the sketches escaped criticism from morals campaigner Mary Whitehouse, who instead went after another character on *Round the Horne* – the folk singer Rambling Syd Rumpo, whose lyrics were less camp but more obviously suggestive.

Julian and Sandy were not politically minded, although they did occasionally make the odd comment about the illegal status of gay men. In a sketch called 'Bona Law' they claim to be solicitors saying, 'We've got a criminal practice that takes up most of our time' while in 'Bona Nature Clinic' they are 'homeopathic practitioners', a pun on the legal term 'practising homosexuals', and they say that they're 'not recognised by doctors', a nod to the unsympathetic stance taken by the medical profession. Their cheerful refusal to obey the law suggests that they could be seen as subversive, indeed, their existence was at least a form of representation, even if they were stereotypes. For mainstream audiences, camp was the spoonful of sugar that made them palatable.

Julian and Sandy were typical of a generation of increasingly popular comedy gay personalities. In the US, the role was filled by Paul Lynde who came to prominence in the comedy musical *Bye Bye Birdie* both on Broadway (1960) and on film (1963). He went on to guest star in numerous sitcoms, although he is most well remembered for the role of Uncle Arthur in the series *Bewitched* (1964–72), a family-oriented comedy about a witch living in modern times. Wearing loud check shirts, turtlenecks or snazzy ascots, Uncle Arthur would pop up in the most unexpected locations – inside Samantha's oven, or on her television, 'Oh, Sammy, you turn me on!' he'd coo ambiguously. Uncle Arthur sometimes teamed up with Samantha's haggish mother, Endora (played by Agnes Moorehead), a kind of supernatural Bette Davis, or her mischievous cousin, Serena. Samantha's supernatural relatives all conveyed a sense of regal camp – they were omnipotent, condescending and terminally bored. In one of my favourite episodes, Uncle Arthur and Serena lose their powers and have to take mortal jobs on a production line, making frozen chocolate-covered bananas. It starts well, but the conveyor belt speeds up and everything descends into chocolate-covered chaos. 'Serena, there's no time for the trays, they're starting to melt, just throw them to me here, honey,' Uncle Arthur shouts. By the end everything is covered in melted chocolate. 'Well, that was a good day's work,' Uncle Arthur surmises sarcastically.

Between 1966 and 1979, Paul Lynde appeared 707 times on the gameshow *The Hollywood Squares* (a human noughts and crosses or tic-tac-toe game), taking up the privileged centre square. His jokes regularly verged on the risqué. When asked why a chef pounds his meat, Lynde answered 'loneliness'. To the question, 'Does anything bring tears to a monkey's eye?' Lynde replied, 'Learning that Tarzan swings both ways.' And how about this for queering a question about *The Wizard of Oz*? 'The tin man wanted a heart, and the lion wanted courage. What did the straw man want?' Lynde responded, 'He wanted the tin man to *notice* him.'

What surprises me again and again is how family-friendly, even child-friendly, the gay comedians of the 1960s and 1970s were. This was during a time when social attitudes towards homosexuality were pretty dire, and gay people were depicted in the news as child molesters or proselytisers. The way had already been paved, to an extent, by pantomime, a camp form of live entertainment developed in the UK from Italian and French *commedia dell'arte*. British pantos were usually performed over the Christmas period and were based on traditional children's stories like *Cinderella* or *Aladdin*. Cross-dressing was in pantomime's DNA, as the leading male character was usually played by a young woman, while the main comedy figure, the pantomime dame, was played by a middle-aged man. The dame made little effort to disguise the fact that she was a man in drag – makeup was exuberantly, if cartoonishly, applied (there was no attempt at face contouring), padding was aimed at making the dame look portly rather than accentuating feminine curves, and voices were gravelly. But, as with all drag queens, the defining feature was camp. Children loved the dames, and the long-standing success of panto helps to explain why female impersonators were well-established acts in the UK, with the 1960s and 1970s seeing comedians like Stanley Baxter, Dick Emery and Les Dawson regularly dragging up for television sketches, as well as full-on female impersonators like Danny La Rue, Hinge and Bracket, and Dame Edna Everage being popular.

Even out of drag, camp comics were seen as suitable for children's entertainment. Both Kenneth Williams and Paul Lynde voiced characters in animations aimed at children. Williams voiced all the characters for a cartoon series called *Willo the Wisp* (1981), including a fairy called Mavis, a witch (in the shape of a television) called Evil Edna and a cat called Carwash, based on Noël Coward. Lynde was the voice of a greedy rat in *Charlotte's Web* and played Mildew Wolf in a cartoon series called *It's the Wolf* (1969–70). However, his most famous voice work put the arch into archvillain, in the role of Sylvester Sneekly aka the Hooded Claw, in *The Perils of Penelope Pitstop* (1969–70), a homage to cliff-hanger movie serials of the silent movie era. The premise of the cartoon is somewhat incredible for a children's animation series – Penelope is the heiress to a huge fortune and the Hooded Claw is trying to *murder* her.

Penelope, with her blonde tresses, pink racing outfit, white go-go boots, balletic running motions and deep-South accent was inspiration for future drag queens, although despite her cries of 'Hay-elp!' she proved to be remarkably resourceful and was often able to rescue herself. An example of her deep commitment to camp is the fact that she is depicted wearing a purple racing helmet with goggles attached but she doesn't seem to put the goggles on –

they're just an accessory. Several times in each episode the Hooded Claw would capture Penelope, taking great delight in describing in detail how each of his over-complicated, theatrical plots to kill her would work.

> As you know, Pitstop, you're tied up snuggly inside that batch of fortune-cookie batter. When the batter reaches the roller, it will flatten you. Then the automatic cookie cookers will cut you to cookie size. Then, my dear, you will be baked, into about twenty-three crispy, crunchy, little bitty fortune cookies. Hahahhahaha!

During these sequences the cherry on the cake is the 1960s rinky-dink music playing in the background. Lynde's gleefully camp voice sends children the message that they should be laughing at this pantomime villain, rather than being scared of him, and Pitstop usually responds to his threats with a laconic comeback, indicating that she never really believes that she is in any serious danger: 'You fiend! At least you could have made it an even two dozen!' Exchanges like these constitute a nice example of camp being deployed to defeat camp. The Hooded Claw never succeeds in his plans, but he is unvanquished and at the end of each episode he often shakes his fist and makes the sniggering threat, 'I'll get you next time, Penelope Pitstop!' Camp and villainy have long gone hand-in-hand: Servalan from the BBC sci-fi series *Blake's 7*, Ursula in *The Little Mermaid*, King Candy in *Wreck-It Ralph*, Vincent Price in just about anything. They don't necessarily make villains more relatable, but they certainly make them more entertaining and fun-scary as opposed to real-scary. However, as with the camp characters in earlier twentieth-century fiction, there's still a sense of relegation to the margins.

But there were signs that this was about to change. A more homely version of the camp gay man was found in the UK when, from 1978 to 1982, Larry Grayson regularly attracted viewing figures of more than eighteen million people while hosting the Saturday night gameshow *Larry Grayson's Generation Game*. Fame came to Grayson late – he was in his mid-fifties and had spent three decades touring the UK in male revues, variety and drag shows, appearing in regional theatres and working men's clubs. When he came to television, he had a wealth of material to fall back on, including tales of his friends Slack Alice, Everard, Apricot Lil and Pop-it-in Pete the Postman. As a gameshow host, Grayson relied on the British tradition of muddling through in the face of chaos. He would often purposefully make mistakes when reading information about contestants from cue-cards, and he would join in with some of the gameshow challenges, usually making a mess of things. During a 1979 episode, there was a malfunction with a door that was used in one of the games and Larry made camp out of trying to get it to open, close and stay upright. Doors appeared to have dogged his performances – while onstage at a seafront theatre in the seaside town of Redcar, his act was repeatedly interrupted by a door that kept blowing open in the wind.[106] 'Shut that door!' he shouted and such was the audience reaction that it became a regular catchphrase of his, along with, 'Look at the muck in 'ere!' (while inspecting the edge of a chair with his finger), 'I've got the worms!' (while rubbing his nose), and 'You need to cut your hair' (to show general disapproval towards someone). Other catchphrases – 'What a gay day!' and 'Seems like a nice boy!' – clearly implied his sexuality, but he never spoke openly about it. He accepted the boundaries of the time and gave audiences camp without the threat of sex – he was never going to confuse anyone's husband. During his final performance at *The Royal Variety Performance* in 1994, a month before his death, the audience hung on his every word, although once he had left the stage and the applause had died down, there was the definite sense of the end of an era.

The existence of personalities like Larry Grayson and Paul Lynde begs the question, can a masculine lesbian be camp? I have always thought that Beryl Reid in *The Killing of Sister George* (1968) turns out a wonderfully camp performance. Beryl plays actress June 'George' Buckridge, who is district nurse 'Sister George' in a fictional and well-observed BBC rural soap opera called *Applehurst.* While Sister George is the kindly, lovable star of the show, 'off-screen' June tells bawdy jokes, smokes cigars, drinks to excess and gets into a jealous rage if anyone pays attention to her pretty girlfriend. She is not the easiest person to work with and, after a row on set with an Australian colleague whom she calls a 'cow', she storms off, gets drunk, climbs into a taxi occupied by a pair of novitiate nuns and proceeds to interfere with them. George fails to perform as a stereotypical 'nice' feminine woman because she acts in ways that are normally associated with boorish men or naughty schoolboys. When chastised for her behaviour, she can't help sniggering immaturely, and when she does make a genuine apology it is to say, 'I'm sorry, you know, if I've been a bad boy.' Despite being a tragedy, a camp sensibility runs through the film.

Killing it. Beryl Reid and Susannah York mucking around in Laurel and Hardy drag.

When George loses her job, she is introduced to a woman called Mrs Coote who works in children's television and wants George to provide the voice of a flawed, credible cow in a cartoon. Paul Lynde might have jumped at the chance, but George views it as an insult, gets drunk and ends up wrecking the set of *Applehurst*, mournfully calling out 'moo!' It might be a career low but it is a pretty camp one all the same. And George herself is played for laughs – Beryl Reid was an excellent comedy actress and she gives George a twinkle in her eye, making what could have been a monster into an entertaining, complex character that you root for. At times I feel angry at George, or sorry for her, but I mostly laugh along *with* her, rather than *at* her. However, I wonder about the extent to which mainstream audiences of the time were laughing with or at their camp comedians. They were loved but they played court jester roles and confirmed many of the narrow stereotypes about gay people. As we will see later in this chapter, towards the end of the 1970s there would be voices speaking out against them. But let's take a detour first, to consider some of the more subversive ways that gay men used camp in the mid-twentieth century.

FUCKED BY MONTY

In 1959, playwright Joe Orton and his boyfriend, Kenneth Halliwell, had just moved into a small flat at 25 Noel Road in Islington, London. They had met at the drama school RADA and been in a relationship for eight years. During this time, they had worked occasionally but there had also been long periods of unemployment where they had collaborated on a number of novels, which had all been rejected by publishers. It is likely that boredom, frustration and a general inclination to make mischief led them to carry out various forms of guerrilla camp on members of the public and institutions.

In 1962, unimpressed by the less-than-inspiring range on offer at their local library on Essex Road, which they viewed as endless rubbish, they stole seventy-two books and defaced them at their flat, returning them back to the shelves to outrage unsuspecting librarians and lenders. This was no ordinary case of scribbling rude words in the margins though. They skilfully altered the synopses of some of the books, so Dorothy L Sayers' *Gaudy Nights* was changed to read: 'At her most queer, and needless to say, at her most crude.' Readers were advised to read another of her books, *Clouds of Witness*, behind closed doors 'and have a good shit while you are reading'. The pair also employed the artistic technique of collage, carefully cutting and pasting pictures out of magazines, to alter the book covers, in surreal, shocking and hilarious ways. Some of the books got off more lightly than others. Agatha Christie's *The Secret of Chimneys* was doctored so that several gigantic cats stared out at the reader above the background of a country house. The *Collins Guide to Roses* had a baboon's face superimposed onto a rose. A biography of John Betjeman contained a picture of an elderly tattooed man in trunks, while romance novel *Queen's Favourite* by Phyllis Hambledon wound up with a couple of hunky men wrestling on its front cover. *The Collected Plays of Emlyn Williams* were retitled as 'Olivia Prude', 'Up the Front', 'Up the Back', 'Mr Winifred', 'He was Born Grey', 'Knickers Must Fall' and 'Fucked by Monty'. As well as containing the word *fucked*, the latter title was especially subversive as it was most likely a reference to Field Marshal Bernard Law Montgomery, a bastion of masculinity and homophobia, who had commanded the British Eighth Army from the Second Battle of El Alamein to the final Allied victory in Tunisia. Despite Monty's violent opposition to homosexuality, in 1976 the biographer Lord Chalfont noted that his subject had a 'predilection for the company of young men', while in 2011 another biographer, Nigel Hamilton, went further, claiming that Monty had had 'quasi love affairs' with boys and men.[107]

There is something delightfully British in the serious response and dogged tactics that the library authorities took to apprehend these criminal masterminds, making the story worthy of an Agatha Christie mystery. First, undercover staff were brought in from other libraries, but this was not successful. Then a senior law clerk, Sydney Porrett, suspected that Orton and Halliwell might be behind the book defacing, so he devised a plan, writing to them claiming that they had illegally parked their car and asking them to remove it. It was the sort of bait that Halliwell couldn't resist. They didn't even *have* a car, he wrote back, using the letter as an opportunity to complain about the pettiness of the council. But it was a trap – Halliwell had typed his response and the print matched that on some of the defaced book covers.[108] The police were called out to their flat, where the most damning evidence of all was found – book jackets in the process of being tampered with, and missing art plates from some of the other books hung on the walls. The two men were arrested and pleaded guilty at Old Street Magistrates, being sentenced to six months in prison each. Orton later commented that their sentences were draconian 'because we were queers'. When the *Daily Express* reported the trial, on the same page it also mentioned a news story about a drunk driver who had killed his passenger and who had also received a sentence of the same length as Orton and Halliwell.[109]

The pair were sent to separate prisons – which proved to be a turning point for both of them in different ways. Orton enjoyed the experience; it inspired him creatively and brought detachment to his writing – afterwards he wrote the plays that brought him fame and success, *Loot* and *Entertaining Mr Sloane*. But Halliwell hated his time in prison, attempting suicide; he never really recovered from the experience.

Another of their long-running camp pranks involved a letter-writing campaign carried out by Joe, under the guise of Edna Welthorpe (Mrs). They had been inspired by reading a preface that the dramatist Terence Rattigan had written in volume two of his collected plays. Rattigan imagines a theatre-goer called Aunt Edna who is 'nice, respectable, middle-class, middle-aged . . . with time on her hands and the money to help pass it'. Aunt Edna is also a 'hopeless lowbrow' who disapproves of Kafka – 'so obscure my dear, and why does he always look on the dark side of things' – and Picasso – 'those dreadful reds, my dear, and why three noses?' Rattigan advises playwrights that, while Aunt Edna should not be mocked, she ought not to be pandered to either: 'the old dear rather enjoys a little teasing and even, at times, bullying.'

Joe loved the idea of Aunt Edna and decided to bring her to life. So, in the guise of Edna, he wrote to a range of businesses and institutions, offering her many opinions, parodying the style of a certain type of self-assured, reactionary woman. Some of the letters appeared to be simply intended to waste the time of venues that represented the establishment. For example, Edna wrote to the Ritz claiming that:

> During our brief stay at your hotel I lost a brown Moroccan handbag with the initials E.W. stamped on the flap. The contents of the bag weren't valuable – they consisted of a purse containing a few loose coins, a Boots folder with snapshots of members of my family and a pair of gloves made of some hairy material.

The manager of the Ritz wrote back that an exhaustive search had failed to locate the bag and Edna replied in an accusing tone: 'I feel you are not being open with me. If you have found this bag and are secretly enjoying its contents, I can only say that your behaviour is reprehensible. Why don't you come out into the open and admit that your curiosity has got the better of you.'

Edna also had an exchange with Orton's local vicar, which became increasingly surreal. She claimed to be secretary of a drama group who wanted to present a controversial play about homosexuality called 'Nelson is a Nance' at the church hall. The vicar tried to fob her off, replying that the church elders who agreed on lettings of the hall only met once a year and they had just recently met. He added that he did not approve of the lampooning of national heroes. Joe replied as Edna's mother, informing the vicar that Edna had died and she had found Edna's letters and other correspondence relating to her drama activities in a cupboard under the stairs. She urged the vicar to permit the group to use the church for the play. The vicar then responded to say he was deeply grieved to hear of Edna's death but 'I can't help feeling she had got into the wrong set'.[110] Edna clearly had a talent for drawing out the camp in those whom she wrote to. A similar letter to Rev G W Sherry of Heath Baptist Church asked if the Phallus Players could put on a production of a play called 'The Pansy' at the church hall. Rev Sherry did not reply, resulting in a second letter from Edna complaining about his lack of 'common courtesy', to which the reverend did reply, criticising Edna for not including a self-addressed envelope. Ewan King, who displayed the letters in 2012 at the church, said, 'The funny thing about the letters is just how very very English they are. The Rev Sherry is not bothered about the homosexuality but the fact that someone could have the cheek to reproach him for not replying when someone did not attach a self-addressed envelope.'[111]

When Orton found fame with his plays, Edna was used to whip up controversy around them. The writer and theatre director David Benedictus had criticised the judges of the *Evening Standard* for giving Joe's play, *Loot*, an award. Joe first wrote to the theatre magazine *Plays and Players* as Donald H Hartley, who disagreed with Benedictus, saying, 'If every pip squeak circus pony were to give awards for Horse of the Year, goodness knows where we should be.' Then Edna had her say, disagreeing with Hartley:

> I agree that no one could seriously nominate as the play of the year a piece of indecent tomfoolery like LOOT. Drama

> should be uplifting. The plays of Joe Orton have the most unpleasant effect on me. I was plunged into the dumps for weeks after seeing ENTERTAINING MR SLOANE. I saw LOOT with my young niece. We both fled from the theatre in horror and amazement well before the end. I could see no humour in it. Yet it is advertised widely as a rib-tickler. Surely this is wrong?

For me, the camp is in the detail, the use of phrases like 'Boots folder', 'hairy material', 'plunged into the dumps' and 'fled from the theatre'. It's the specificity of the fact that Edna wants the reader to know that this is not just any old folder, it's one from Boots the chemist, a piece of information that is hardly relevant. And the shortened phrasing 'Boots folder' implies that Edna expects whoever reads the letter to inhabit the same social world as her, a sign of her limited worldview. It's a technique that British comedian Victoria Wood also used in her scripts. For example, in a playlet she wrote called *The Library*, a character called Margaret struggles to get her keys from her bag, which are under a book, saying, 'Hang on, my Yale's under my Wincey Willis.'

This isn't a story with a happy ending. In 1967, Halliwell and Orton were visited by their friend Kenneth Williams (who was playing Sandy in the Julian and Sandy sketches). They discussed the new legislation that was intended to decriminalise homosexuality to an extent. The three of them somewhat pessimistically concluded that the new law would accomplish very little (Williams also noted in his diary that it didn't apply to Scotland, 'So it won't do any good for the queens of Dundee & the like.'[112]) Two weeks later Halliwell killed Orton with a hammer, then took a fatal overdose of pills. While impossible to fully understand his reasons, it has been argued that Halliwell was either envious of Orton's success and/or afraid that Orton was going to leave him.

Years later, their camp pranks are celebrated. In 2016, Islington Museum paid £8,000 for a screen collage made by

Halliwell that featured numerous pictures of cats – it went on display alongside some of the defaced books.[113] And in 2017, Joe's Edna Welthorpe (Mrs) letters inspired an annual letter-writing competition to teach school children about Joe Orton and satire. Their story indicates that for some gay men in the 1960s, rather than being laughed at, they were turning the tables and laughing back at the camp they saw everywhere in society. And as we're about to see, across the Atlantic that attitude would be taken to a whole other level.

CAMP KICKS BACK

In America, camp wouldn't just be used for pranking the establishment, but as part of violent protest. This portion of our story begins with a police raid on a gay bar in the early hours of 28 June 1969 in New York City, where, as with the rest of the US, it was illegal to solicit for any form of same-sex relationship. Despite this, there was a thriving network of gay bars and clubs, particularly in cities around America – although until 1966 in New York it was illegal to serve alcohol to gay people as they were viewed as disorderly. A protest at a bar called Julius brought attention to the issue and the city's human rights commission overturned this form of discrimination. However, gay bars and clubs were still subject to raids.

The Stonewall Inn was one of many such bars that was located in Greenwich Village. It had been purchased in 1966 by the Genovese family, one of the Mafia families that ran crime-based activities in New York City, and it had been opened as a gay bar. It didn't need a liquor licence as, in theory, patrons were meant to bring their own alcohol and sign their names in a book on entry. The family bribed the police (envelopes of cash were known as 'gayola') to stay away from the bar, and, without any sort of official scrutiny, the Stonewall's attitude to health and safety left a lot to be desired. There was no fire exit or running water to wash glasses, the toilets were disgusting and drinks were often watered-down. Did I mention that the owners were blackmailing some of the more well-heeled clientele who worked in the Financial District? Some of these patrons were cajoled into stealing negotiable bonds and handing them over.

There was corruption and exploitation at the Stonewall Inn, but also a sense of community among its racially diverse patrons. The bar was popular with feminine men who wore makeup, as well as homeless young people and runaways who tried to get older customers to buy them drinks. *Occasionally*, drag queens were allowed in. There were still monthly raids, but the police usually tipped off the owners in advance, so alcohol could be hidden away first.

But, in the early hours of 28 June, the raid happened without warning. At 1:20am, the Stonewall was buzzing, with over 200 customers. Police burst in, found alcohol, arrested thirteen people and manhandled the patrons. Normally, people would have to line up and produce identification, while those suspected of being dressed in 'gender-inappropriate' clothing would be taken off to the bathroom by a female officer to be examined. However, this time things happened differently – the patrons refused to co-operate. Around 100 to 150 people gathered outside the bar, some who were patrons who had escaped arrest, others who had been attracted by the raid. The crowd became increasingly unhappy as they watched how the police were treating the patrons. A butch young woman, possibly the entertainer Stormé DeLarverie, was hit on the head by an officer as she was forced into one of the vans. Bleeding from a head wound she shouted to the crowd, 'Why don't you guys do something?' And so they did. Suddenly people started throwing things at the police – pennies and stones and beer bottles. There were shouts of 'pigs' and 'faggot cops'. It is claimed that Stormé threw the first punch.[114] By this point the crowd had grown to around 500 to 600 people. Michael Fader, who was present, later said:

> We all had a collective feeling like we'd had enough of this kind of shit. It wasn't anything tangible anybody said to anyone else, it was just kind of like everything over the years had come to a head on that one particular night in the one particular place and it was not an organized demonstration.[115]

These queens mean business.
A crowd attempts to stop police arrests outside the Stonewall Inn.

Sylvia Rivera, a homeless Latina drag queen who engaged in survival sex, remembered her attitude towards the police: 'You've been treating us like shit all these years? Uh-uh. Now it's our turn! . . . It was one of the greatest moments in my life.'[116]

The gathering escalated into a riot, with garbage cans and bricks being hurled at the windows of the Stonewall, first by those who were the most outcast – the camp queens, the hustlers and the homeless kids. Eyewitness accounts differ over who threw the first brick. Some claim it was Marsha P Johnson, a Black drag queen who arrived some time after the riot had started. Johnson could not afford to purchase drag items from expensive stores and she slept under tables used for sorting flowers in Manhattan's Flower District. She would make crowns of leftover fresh flowers and dress in flowing robes, red plastic heels and bright wigs. However, others have claimed that the first brick was thrown by another Black drag queen called Zazu Nova Queen of Sex, or a homeless sex worker with blonde hair called Jackie Hormona who wore subtle makeup but was not a drag queen.

Garbage was lit on fire and thrown through the broken windows of the Stonewall. The police grabbed a fire hose, thinking they could put out the flames and use the water to disperse the crowd, but there was no water pressure. They called for back-up and the Tactical Police Force arrived, in their helmets, carrying nightsticks. They formed a line trying to push the rioters back, but the crowd were having none of it. They started their own line, an impromptu chorus line at that, with synchronised kicking like the Rockettes of Radio City Music Hall and singing a song to the tune of 'Ta-Ra-Ra Boom-De-Ay': 'We are the Stonewall girls. We wear our hair in curls. We don't wear underwear. We show our pubic hair.' This was something new – weaponised camp as part of a violent, disorganised, political uprising.

One of the protesters said:

> I just can't ever get that one sight out of my mind. The cops with the [nightsticks] and the kick line on the other side. It was the most amazing thing . . . And all the sudden that kick line, which I guess was a spoof on the machismo . . . I think that's when I felt rage. Because people were getting smashed with bats. And for what? A kick line.[117]

The numbers of protesters kept growing – at one point the police were chasing them down the street, the next minute they were overpowered and being chased themselves, with people screaming, 'Catch them!' By around 4am, the riot appeared to have ended and the streets were relatively quiet, with people gathering in groups to discuss what had happened. But this was just an interlude. The protest had gathered momentum and was now impossible to stop.

In the hours that followed, graffiti was daubed on the walls of the Stonewall Inn – 'Drag power', 'Support gay power', 'Legalize gay bars'. One of the pieces of graffiti read: 'We are open' and, by the following evening, thousands of people had gathered outside the bar. Emboldened by the events of the previous night, there were now open displays of same-sex affection. More fires were started and again the Tactical Police Force were called in. There were further kick lines and police chases. Craig Rodwell, who had founded the Oscar Wilde Memorial Bookshop in 1967, described how Marsha P Johnson climbed up a lamppost and dropped a bag containing a brick onto a police car, shattering its windshield.[118] The riots went on from the early hours of that first Saturday morning to the Wednesday night, with protesters gathering outside the offices of the *Village Voice* on the last night, threatening to burn it down after the *Voice* had published articles about the protests referring to 'forces of faggotry' and 'limp wrists'.

Those nights had a dramatic impact on the way that gay political campaigning would be conducted from that point. Up until then, groups like the Mattachine Society had advocated a respectable form of activism, with members wearing suits and ties, and no displays of same-sex affection. However, after the Stonewall riots, a new organisation, the Gay Liberation Front, was formed, using methods associated with Black and anti-war movements. A year after the riots, the first Gay Pride marches took place in the US.

Not everyone in the new gay equality movements wanted to include trans people, despite the fact they often needed support the most. Marsha and Sylvia formed the organisation STAR (Street Transvestite Action Revolutionaries), which focused on helping queer homeless young people with food and shelter. For a time, they rented a four-bedroom apartment and paid for the rent with money they made through sex work. In 1973, Sylvia gave an impassioned address to the Gay Pride Rally in New York City – she had to fight to get her spot on the stage, a fight that took the best part of the day. When she took to the stage, amid boos, she chastised the crowd, 'Ya'll better quiet down!' going on to talk about the gay men and lesbians who were in jail, being beaten up and raped and how nobody was doing anything for them. At the end of her speech, Sylvia said, 'The people are trying to do something for all of us and not men and women that belong to a white middle-class, white club, and that's what you all belong to! Revolution NOW!' She got the audience to spell out the initials of the slogan Gay Power and then screamed it back to the crowd, overcome with emotion. As she left the stage, she dropped the microphone to the ground.

The crowd's reaction to Sylvia had devastated her.

> I was hurt and I felt that the movement had completely betrayed the drag queens and the street people. And I felt that the years that I had already given them had been a waste. I went home, locked up the house. If it wasn't for Marsha I wouldn't be here now . . . She came home and found me bleeding to death.

Sylvia left the movement and moved to the suburbs in Westchester where she set about educating a new set of people. 'Of course, you get the first strange looks. Ain't bothering me. Next thing, you become friends with everybody. I feel that I have liberated a lot of people just by living here in the suburbs. Just by being myself. Just by being a campy queen.'[119]

Sylvia campaigned to include trans people and drag culture in New York City's gay rights bill, producing a petition to one meeting. The councillor who led the meeting refused to even look at the petition, so Sylvia marched up to the front of the meeting and hit her over the head with it.[120] The eventual bill, which passed in 1986, did not mention drag queens, trans people or non-binary people. Sylvia's response was, 'Hell hath no fury like a drag queen scorned.'[121] She campaigned throughout her life, dying aged fifty as a result of complications from liver cancer.

Marsha continued to work as an activist, becoming involved in activism related to AIDS, joining the group ACT-UP. She also worked with Hot Peaches, a drag theatre group whose work has been described by the *New York Times* as 'political camp, dominated by drag, but surprisingly clean'.[122] But, in 1992, Marsha's body was discovered in the Hudson River – she was just forty-six. Although police viewed her death as a suicide, she had a large head wound. She had been campaigning against violence towards LGBTQ+ people and police bias, and some of her friends suspected foul play. Additionally, Johnson had been harassed by local criminals, one of whom had apparently boasted about killing her. Johnson's death was changed to 'unclassified' in 2002 and, in 2012, Mariah Lopez successfully had her case re-opened as a possible homicide.

In 2005, two blocks from the Stonewall Inn, the corner of Christopher and Hudson streets was renamed Sylvia Rivera Way, and, in 2020, Marsha had a state park in New York named after her. There have also been several murals dedicated to them. For me, the Stonewall riots put to bed the claims that camp isn't political. It's all in the context – and in certain circumstances, being camp is the ultimate political statement, where simply walking down the street or opening your mouth to speak is an act of rebellion. As Richard Dyer asks, 'You know those clenched fists you get on political badges (including women's liberation and GLF)? Well, why shouldn't it be a clenched fist on a limp wrist? Divine.'

NOT ON CHRISTMAS!

In the 1950s, you had to get your camp where you could find it, locating it through mainstream sources like Hollywood films that were, to all intents and purposes, heteronormative stories. Gay men might have identified with Bette Davis as Margo Channing in

All About Eve or Joan Crawford in *Mildred Pierce*, or they may have thrilled at the gratuitously displayed muscular bodies in Biblical Epics like *The Ten Commandments* (1956) but they were not particularly the intended audiences of these films. Until the 1960s hardly anything was produced that was aimed squarely at a gay audience. Photographers and artists like Bob Mizer, Quaintance and Tom of Finland had produced erotic films, photographs and drawings, which depicted a homoerotic, hyper-masculine world and these works could also be interpreted as having a camp sensibility. Mizer sometimes posed his models using props to frame them as classical statues or dressed them in cowboy hats, motorcycle jackets or construction equipment to further exaggerate their masculinity, and there is a playful sense of humour in the images. However, despite the huge muscles, there is something feminine about the models too – perhaps because, typically, it is women who are looked at. Mizer's models normally had shaved chests and carefully pomaded hairstyles – like Beau Brummell, they look like they have engaged in a lot of work to look attractive, both in and out of the gym. The men drawn by Tom of Finland have the bodies of superheroes and, like them, they are usually dressed in tight clothing and are placed in cartoonish situations. During a period where homosexuality was criminalised and stigmatised, these men were pictured as *happy*, grinning knowingly, as if they are thinking, 'Isn't this a lark!' A camp sensibility suffuses the gay erotica of the 1950s and 1960s, arguably making it more subversive than the more serious-minded and explicit stuff that was to follow in later decades. Richard Dyer has described how Tom of Finland's art shows the ambiguity of camp – at one level the pictures are over-the-top camp, but they are also a turn-on. He goes on to say that camp helps us to demystify art – we are meant to be solemn in the presence of art and even to see the worlds that are depicted on television and in films as real. But, if we take a camp perspective, we can focus on the artifices employed by artists, reminding us that depictions like the exaggerated bodies of the Tom of Finland men are fabrications.[123]

Another case of camp in the mid-twentieth century was through the concept of the 'so-bad-it's-good film'. The sci-fi genre was particularly prone to bad movie making, due to the fact that special effects were often laughably unrealistic, scientific explanations unconvincing and the actors who starred in these films tended not to be of the highest calibre. The driving concepts of such films were often silly, sometimes consisting of barely disguised sexual fantasies. Planets filled with beautiful women tended to crop up repeatedly – *Cat Women of the Moon* (1953), *Queen of Outer Space* (1958), *Fire Maidens from Outer Space* (1956), *Voyage to the Planet of Prehistoric Women* (1968). *Queen of Outer Space* was notable for its casting of Hungarian-American legend Zsa Zsa Gabor, who utters the immortal line: 'I hate dot qveen!' Monsters from outer space also provided material for cheesy sci-fi – the killer cucumber from Venus in *It Conquered the World* (1956), robot gorillas in *Robot Monster* (1953), a massive turkey in *The Giant Claw* (1957) and murderous jelly in *The Green Slime* (1968).

Perhaps the most famous 'bad' filmmaker was Ed Wood, who directed a number of risible low-budget movies including *Glen or Glenda* (1953), *Jail Bait* (1954), *Bride of the Monster* (1955) *Plan 9 from Outer Space* (1957) and *Night of the Ghouls* (1959). Wood played the starring role in *Glen or Glenda*, a semi-autobiographical docudrama which was a plea for tolerance about cross-dressing. In one of the final scenes, Glen tells his girlfriend, Barbara, that he has a female identity as Glenda. Barbara initially reacts with distress, but decides to stay with him, taking off her angora sweater then holding it out to him as a sign of her acceptance. It is meant to be a touching, serious moment, although the stilted acting and melodramatic orchestral soundtrack take the film into camp territory, and it has been viewed as one of the worst movies ever made.[124]

Plan 9 from Outer Space is often seen as Wood's magnum opus. The film starred Bela Lugosi, who unfortunately died before production began – so Wood used some previously shot footage of Lugosi and also employed his wife's chiropractor, Tom Mason, as a stand-in for some of Lugosi's scenes. Another actor in the film, Maila Nurmi, was known as Vampira for her signature pale skin and tight black dress; she had hosted her own television series, *The Vampira Show*, from 1954 to 1955. The film's plot involved aliens who had unsuccessfully made eight attempts to invade Earth and had now hit upon Plan 9, which involved raising the dead to cause chaos. The alien spaceship consisted of a plastic model kit of a flying saucer. During a scene in an airplane cockpit, an actor is seen reading his lines from a script on his lap, and the shadow of the boom microphone is visible. In other scenes, chalk-marked Xs can be seen on the ground, intended to show the actors where to stand.

The film was narrated by a flamboyant psychic called Criswell, who was notorious, both for claiming to sleep in a coffin and for his inaccurate predictions. He begins the film with the following statement: 'Greetings, my friend. We are all interested in the future, for that is where you and I are going to spend the rest of our lives. And remember, my friend, future events such as these will affect you in the future.' This was not the only case of verbal redundancy in the film. In a later scene, Lieutenant Harper says, 'One thing's sure. Inspector Clay is dead. Murdered. And somebody's responsible!'

These films were not intentionally bad – they were just incompetently made and had budgets that were nowhere near large enough to do justice to the imagination of the scriptwriter. Obviously, they were not critically acclaimed when they came out, but neither did they receive a great deal of attention; they often had short releases and appeared as B-movies, screened alongside higher-budget films. Reviewers paid scant attention to them and the mostly young audiences are unlikely to have had the ironic distance to view them as camp masterpieces at the time. This didn't happen until the late 1970s, when such films were reappraised. Brothers Harry and Michael Medved published a series of books with titles like *The Fifty Worst Movies of All Time* (1978) and *The Golden Turkey Awards* (1980) – the latter presented *Plan 9 from Outer Space* with the award for the 'worst film ever made'.

However, the camp potential of these kinds of films had not gone unnoticed by everyone. One such person was John Waters, a young filmmaker in Baltimore who was one of the first people to create movies that were *intentionally* camp. Waters had seen Vampira in films when he was a child: 'Vampira was the first exaggerated woman I ever yearned to meet. As a child, she never looked scary to me; I thought she was pretty.'[125] Waters also loved the Wicked Witch of the West in *The Wizard of Oz*, describing her as:

> . . . the jolie laide heroine of every bad little boy's and girl's dream of notoriety and style, whose twelve minutes of screen time in *The Wizard of Oz* can never be topped. And her outfit! The Wicked Witch inspired my lifetime obsession with wearing weirdly striped socks.[126]

Waters assembled a small troupe of local actors, which included David Lochary, Mink Stole, Edith Massey, Mary Vivian Pearce, Divine, Pat Moran, Cookie Mueller and Channing Wilroy, using them in movies that he wrote, directed, produced, filmed and edited. His films in the 1960s and 1970s were of the low-budget variety, featuring outlandish characters screaming outrageous dialogue at one another. Take, for example, *Female Trouble* (1974), which tells the story of 'bad girl' Dawn Davenport, played by drag actor Divine, who ends up being sentenced to death in the electric chair. In an early scene, Dawn goes ballistic when her parents buy her the wrong type of shoes for Christmas. 'What are *these*?' she yells, on opening her present. 'Those aren't the right kind, I told you cha-cha heels. Black ones!' She snatches back the presents she gave to her parents and throws them on the floor, stamping on them. When Dawn's mother tries to intervene, crying, 'Please, Dawn, not on Christmas!' Dawn shouts 'Get off me, you ugly witch!' pushing her into the Christmas tree, which then falls on top of her. The sequence was inspired by an incident in Waters's childhood when a Christmas tree fell on his grandmother and he

Go ahead – put me in your electric chair. The cast of *Female Trouble*.

started singing 'O Christmas Tree' in an 'insane fit of childhood hyperventilation'.[127]

Waters's early films initially had a small cult following but were not widely viewed as camp at the time of their release. Instead, he describes how they were seen as pornographic or obscene, and the films received bad reviews. However, Waters celebrated these reviews, and even included quotes from them on the posters advertising his films. It is a tactic that he says wouldn't work today as critics are too hip to give quotes that could be used in that way.[128]

In the 1980s, Waters's films became increasingly popular, with growing numbers of fans appreciating their cult appeal. His later films were larger-budget affairs, featuring established actors, with a more polished look. While they continued to have a camp sensibility, the trashier aspects were toned down and the celebration of amorality was sometimes replaced with moral messaging. *Hairspray* (1988), involved a 1960s TV show that featured Baltimore teenagers dancing to popular music, based on *The Buddy Deane Show* (1957–64). The film's protagonist is Tracy

Turnblad, a teenage girl who becomes the star of the show. As the film progresses, the story focuses on Tracy's campaign to integrate Black teenagers into the TV show. *Hairspray* was one of Waters's most popular films, inspiring a musical theatre version, then remade in 2007. Its anti-racist message was different to Waters's earlier themes, such as 'crime is beauty', although latterly *Hairspray* has been criticised for having a white-saviour narrative.[129] One of my favourite Waters films is *Serial Mom* (1994), which starred A-list actor Kathleen Turner as Beverly Sutphin, a suburban mother who starts harassing and even killing her friends and neighbours for minor misdemeanours, such as taking a parking space or not recycling. Beverly is eventually apprehended and brought to trial, and the film shows how she becomes a media celebrity. Amid the camp, *Serial Mom* has a point to make about the public's morbid fascination with crime and how its fictionalisation can create a sense of distance from it. In one scene, a couple of teenage horror film fans discover one of Beverly's victims and are traumatised, noting that the blood doesn't look like special-effects blood in films.

Waters's films were ahead of their time and many of them are now viewed as classics. It's a recurring theme with camp movies across this book. However, while the films like *Plan 9 from Outer Space*, *Valley of the Dolls* and *Mommie Dearest* gradually won over fans because they were unintentionally camp and thus hilarious, Waters always knew exactly what he was doing and he found it all the more amusing when audiences responded to his films with outrage or disgust as opposed to finding them funny – 'If someone vomits watching one of my films, it's like getting a standing ovation.'[130] Waters's role in the story of camp is a crucial one: he was one of the first to make the shift from unintentionality into intentionality – and he was incredibly gracious while he patiently waited for the rest of the world to catch up. When I recently saw the film *M3GAN* (2022), about a camp killer robot doll who comes out with lines like, 'This is the part where you run' and 'You ungrateful little bitch', I immediately thought of John Waters.

Waters's films often featured queer characters and occasionally he would give characters lines that subverted traditional views on sexuality. In *Female Trouble*, a character called Aunt Ida, played by Edith Massey in a black leather S&M outfit, tells her resolutely heterosexual nephew:

> Oh, honey, I'd be so happy if you'd turn nelly . . . Queers are just better. I'd be so proud of you as a fag . . . I'd never have to worry . . . I worry that you'll work in an office, have children, celebrate wedding anniversaries. The world of [the] heterosexual is a sick and boring life.

Ida's concerned speech parodies the popular view of the time that homosexuality was a form of mental illness and has since been read as an early form of queering or challenging heteronormativity.[131] However, Waters's perspective was pretty rare for the 1970s, and in the final section of this chapter we will see a very different kind of reaction from gay men towards camp.

CRIPPLING DISTORTIONS

The Golden Age of British sitcom camp was largely due to three men – David Croft, Jimmy Perry and Jeremy Lloyd, who between them were responsible for a series of hugely popular ensemble sitcoms, including *Dad's Army* (1968–77), *Are You Being Served?* (1972–85), *It Ain't Half Hot Mum* (1974–81), *Hi-de-Hi!* (1980-8) and *'Allo 'Allo* (1982–92). Apart from *Dad's Army*, all of these sitcoms featured at least one regular camp male character who, it was hinted, was gay.

In *'Allo 'Allo*, set in a French town under German occupation during World War II, Guy Siner was cast as German officer Lieutenant Gruber, who occasionally performed in the local café, singing 'Mad About the Boy' or 'Can't Help Lovin' Dat Man'. The war was also the backdrop for *It Ain't Half Hot Mum*, based around a British Royal Artillery concert party during the last months of World War II in India and, later, Burma. Melvyn Hayes played Gunner Beaumont, an excitable drag queen called Gloria. Sergeant Major Williams, who presided over the troupe, was a bigoted ball of toxic masculinity, frequently referring to the other men as 'puffs'. *Hi-de-Hi!* was set in a holiday camp at the start of the 1960s, and Barry Howard played effete dancing instructor Barry Stuart-Hargreaves. Barry and his wife, Yvonne, were frightful snobs who felt that they were too good for the holiday camp and they walked around disdainfully, looking as if they were sucking on lemons. It was implied that Barry had been in trouble with the police and was ineligible to join the army. The marriage seems to have been loveless and Barry mysteriously left Yvonne before the series ended.

None of these characters were particularly well-rounded, and they were laughed at for their camp mannerisms or the allusions to their homosexuality. So, when Lieutenant Gruber flirted with heterosexual café owner René, audiences found it funny simply because it made René uncomfortable.

Arguably, the most famous, popular and perhaps most rounded of these camp characters was Mr Humphries in *Are You Being Served?* Set on the clothing floor of a large department store, the sitcom had an addictively busy theme tune with a female lift operator announcing what was available on each floor, 'Ground floor: perfumery, stationery and leather goods, wigs and haberdashery, kitchenware and food. Going up!' I always have to restrain myself from saying these words whenever I get in a lift. The show was full of camp staples, not least of which being Mrs Slocombe, played by Mollie Sugden, who dyed her hair in outrageous colours and made unintentional innuendos about her pet cat, Tiddles: 'I've got to get home. If my pussy isn't attended to by eight o'clock, I shall be stroking it for the rest of the evening.' Mr Humphries, played by John Inman, worked in menswear, and was comfortable in his own shoes. His catchphrase, 'I'm free!' when called upon to serve a customer, had a hint of suggestiveness about it. In one episode, when it is announced that everyone is going to be sacked, Mr Humphries says, 'My horoscope said I was going to get a new position. But I interpreted it quite differently.' With his fruity, lyrical voice, light-footed mincing gait and wry one-liners, Mr Humphries's camp demeanour didn't detract from the fact he was more grounded and self-aware than any of his co-workers. He quickly became the star of the show, appearing in increasingly flamboyant outfits and equally ridiculous storylines – being involved in a wrestling match, directing a Punch and Judy show, contracting a tropical disease and running a gossip column.

There was a coyness around Mr Humphries's sexuality – in one episode he claims to be too busy to serve a customer but then drops everything when he realises the customer is a sailor, and when a fire alarm goes off he pretends to faint so that he can be given a fireman's lift. However, in another episode he rejects the flirtatious advances of a camp cameraman. That isn't too surprising – many camp men in this period wanted butch lovers. The character was almost written out after five episodes, when a senior executive at the BBC told David Croft 'get rid of the poof'. Croft refused, threatening to walk as well, so Mr Humphries got to stay.[132] Perhaps to pre-empt outright homophobia, both writer Jeremy Lloyd and Inman himself claimed that Mr Humphries wasn't gay, but a 'mummy's boy'. Audiences weren't convinced, though; not that they minded – the series ran for ten seasons and attracted twenty million viewers.

The fact that people loved unapologetically camp men like John Inman and Larry Grayson was perhaps a sign that attitudes were changing. After all, homosexuality had been partially decriminalised in the UK since 1967 (although not for the queens of Dundee and the like). Decriminalisation allowed LGBTQ+ people to organise and congregate without (as much) fear of arrest. In particular, some younger people, who had not experienced decades of having to hide their relationships, were keen to campaign for further social change. They viewed being gay as a source of pride and saw coming out as the best way of improving society's treatment of them. Movements like the Gay Liberation Front (GLF) and the Campaign for Homosexual Equality (CHE) became popular and during this time there was increased sensitivity around portrayals of gay people, especially by the mainstream media, which was seen as stereotyping and harmful. When the BBC released an album of Julian and Sandy sketches in 1979, a decade after the show had ended, the journalist Peter Burton reviewed them negatively, describing them as 'dull and dated . . . Years on it is all very very tired'.[133]

Around the same time, film studies academic Richard Dyer appraised camp sensibility as a product of the oppression of gay men, arguing that, like women, gay men have been kept out of powerful 'male' positions, like chairman of the board. However, while women can marry these kinds of influential men, have their babies and look attractive by their side, gay men are even further down the pecking order, reduced to creating the styles and services to make women and their homes look nice – fashion designer, hair stylist or interior decorator. These jobs aren't seen as serious or as having much practical use. They position gay men in a somewhat parasitical, subordinate role. Dyer describes how this kind of relegation to the world of camp puts these men on the edges of society and involves them in the objectification of women for the benefit of heterosexual men. He also argues that, for such men, the continual emphasis on surface and style can become obsessive, meaning that it is difficult for them to view anything seriously.

Despite these concerns, Dyer is rather a fan of camp, noting how he greets male friends with phrases like, 'It's Miss Jones.' A rather less compromising late-1970s appraisal of camp was provided by film critic Andrew Britton, writing in the magazine *Gay Left*. Britton's essay is a response to Susan Sontag, using her numbered *Notes on "Camp"* formula. He starts by sniffily observing that 'It almost seems at times to have become a matter of common acceptance that camp is radical', and then goes on to argue that it is actually not.[134] Instead, he characterises gay camp as 'little more than a kind of anaesthetic, allowing one to remain inside oppressive relations while enjoying the illusory confidence that one is flouting them'. His essay ends:

> . . . we should not, *pace* Richard Dyer, feel it incumbent on us to defend camp, on charges of 'letting the side down' or wanting to be John Wayne. Camp is simply one way in which gay men have recuperated their oppression, and it needs to be criticised as such.

It is interesting that, in the same issue of *Gay Left*, there is also an article called 'Happy Families? Paedophilia examined', which argues that 'socialists and gay groups must support the freedom of speech and the right of paedophiles to associate and organise to raise social awareness about the issue'. From today's perspective, and for many at the time, it is a disgracefully shocking article and, although there is no direct connection between it and the one on camp by Andrew Britton, both of them demonstrate shifts in thinking within certain gay circles between the late-1970s and the present day.

Julian and Sandy had been creatures of the 1960s and were already fading memories, but Mr Humphries was right there, week after week, mincing across the shop floor of Grace Brothers and delivering suggestive punchlines every few minutes, showing that what was supposed to be 'very, very tired' was still vibrantly funny for many. John Inman was in demand, making public appearances in entertainment venues around the country. However, his shtick wasn't always seen as funny. In 1979, a TV comedy sketch show called *End of Part One* aired a parody of the sitcom. *Are You Being Stereotyped?* updated the lyrics of the theme tune as follows: 'Ground floor: poofters, always taking inside legs, mincing round with silver hair and camping up like fairies, going up!'[135] But this was nothing compared to how some members of the CHE and other gay rights groups found Mr Humphries. During the late 1970s, Inman was regularly picketed by gay groups who protested that he was playing a harmful stereotype. People wrote letters and telephoned the BBC, demanding that the writers remove Mr Humphries from the series.[136] The *Daily Express* reported that members of the CHE had handed out leaflets at the Brighton Dome during one of Inman's concert performances. 'He is just too free with his exaggerated gestures and his "camp" clowning,' a CHE spokesman said.[137] When Inman appeared at the Wembley Conference Centre a demonstration organised by ALGG (All London Gay Groups) passed out leaflets that read:

> Tonight you are going to laugh at an act which many homosexuals think is no joke. No joke to lose your job, family or custody of your children. No joke to be attacked and ridiculed. Many gays have been physically attacked – three brutal murders in London this year.[138]

The protests even stretched to the other side of the world – when Inman went on tour to New Zealand, he was picketed by the Auckland Gay Activists Organization, which called him 'the latest in a long line of ignoble entertainers to make a very good living from holding up a caricature of the homosexual for the rest of society to mock and denigrate'.[139] Robin Hughes, in *Gay News*, wrote that by laughing at Inman and those like him 'we're laughing at ourselves – which may or may not be healthy – and we're forgetting that the rest of society is laughing at us too, but for wholly different reasons'. The article ended with: 'If we have any pride or anger or love we must rage now against the crippling distortions of our lives. If we don't, the future is infinitely bleak.'[140] Inman attempted a rapprochement, meeting with members of the CHE on the evening of a performance he was giving at Lewisham's Concert Hall. A 'genuine exchange of views' took place but, afterwards, John Foot, the Lewisham CHE convenor, ventured that Mr Inman would not be joining the CHE.[141]

Poor old Mr Humphries – there were a handful of portrayals of gay men on mainstream television in the 1970s and those like him were expected to do a lot of heavy lifting, standing in for *all* gay men *everywhere*. I suspect that there may have been a tiny smidgen of internalised homophobia driving the criticisms of him, with some gay men hating the idea that they might be perceived in the same way. It is no surprise that around the same time, the 'clone' look came into fashion, with gay men appropriating the style of Tom of Finland models en masse and discos suddenly full of fancy-dress lumberjacks and motorcycle gangs. Gay men didn't just want to be seen as masculine, they wanted to be even more masculine than the average heterosexual man. And, of course, in turning the dial up to eleven, the over-application breaks the needle, causing it to swing right back over to camp territory, particularly because not everyone could convincingly pull the act off. You may put on a black leather jacket, grow a handlebar moustache, tease your hair into a pompadour quiff and scowl like a hoodlum, but the image is ruined if your conversation runs to whether 'Ding-a-dong' should have been the winner of the 1975 Eurovision Song Contest, Princess Margaret's affair with Roddy Llewellyn (seventeen years her junior!), and the quality of the soft furnishings at Biba's flagship store on Kensington High Street. Oh, darling, nobody thinks you're butch in that get-up anyway, and we're back to camp as unintentional failure.

Not all gay people disapproved of Inman. *Gay News* reported that the Wembley Conference Centre picket was poorly attended, with some activists feeling either that Inman should be left alone or that the public would not appreciate the arguments against him. A letter to *Gay News* in June 1978 argued that Larry Grayson and John Inman were a 'boon to us, not a derogation of homosexuality'.[142] And an article by C P Lusher acknowledged the potential harm of the stereotypes, but argued against banning them, instead encouraging the use of acceptable comic alternatives, as well as representations that show homosexuals as ordinary people.[143] As we'll see, in the 1980s and 1990s that advice was taken *very* seriously, with non-camp gay representations like Colin in *EastEnders*, Stephen in *Dynasty* or Matt in *Melrose Place*. After that, the sensitivity died away somewhat. Sitcoms like *Will & Grace* (1998–2020), *Gimme Gimme Gimme* (1999–2001), *Vicious* (2013–16) and *Q-Force* (2021) continued to make use of the camp comedy queen, but at least had the decency to put him centre stage. And nobody got picketed either.

Andy Medhurst, looking back on the 1970s backlash, provided a note of optimism. 'Camp . . . was weaned on surviving disdain – she's a tenacious old tigress of a discourse well versed in defending her corner. If decades of homophobic pressure had failed to defeat camp, what chance did a mere reorganization of subcultural priorities stand?'[144] It's a statement that's worth remembering when we encounter claims that camp has died, later on in the book.

So, the 1960s and 1970s were a prickly time for camp, particularly where gay men were concerned. Some camp gay men insisted on remaining in absurd closets, others used camp to win over mainstream audiences, while others deployed camp as a weapon, to fight for their rights, to disrupt the system or cause chaos. And, among all of this, camp gay men were typically viewed as cuddly and hilarious – they were even used to entertain children. But, despite this, some of the more earnest gay equality campaigners thought that camp characters were harmful stereotypes – and they wanted to shut them down. However, the joke was to be on the whole of society as within twenty-five years *every single person* who was alive in the 1970s would be viewed as hideously, hilariously camp themselves. That part of our story is two chapters away, though, and before we get to it we need to consider the period in between – which saw camp return to its roots of lavish excess and start challenging mainstream audiences in a way they had never been challenged before.

CHAPTER 6

Camp in a Cold Climate

BURN, BABY, BURN!

As far as camp is concerned, the 1970s are the Golden Years – a kind of tipping point where mainstream style and culture reached peak levels of silliness with a blurring of unintentional camp and intentional campiness. In the last chapter we saw how some gay activists campaigned against camp stereotypes, believing them to be irreconcilable with equality. However, there was an even more concerted backlash against camp towards the end of the decade. To paraphrase one of my favourite movie stars, Angela Arden from *Die, Mommie, Die*, when did it start? When did it all go *wrong*? For me, it is the summer of 1979. One feels the memory lingering, like fog over a canyon. In the UK, on 3 May, the British electorate decided it wanted to be steered by Margaret Thatcher, who favoured starboard over port and took the country off in a very different direction socially and economically. In America, the political tide was about to turn too, and a key night that summer was 12 July, when a Chicago DJ called Steve Dahl started a Disco Inferno, effectively bringing the camp extravaganza of the 1970s to a devastating finish. The decade to follow is subsequently fascinating to write about, despite being much less colourful, in my opinion.

Disco was one of the key cultural artefacts of the 1970s, and while straight male groups like the Bee Gees had helped it to go mainstream, its heart was in an amalgamation of gay, Latin American and Black culture. Disco divas like Cheryl Lynn, Evelyn Champagne King, Thelma Houston, Donna Summer and Gloria Gaynor ruled the dancefloors, with gay men taking them to their hearts. Gaynor's 'I Will Survive' is a classic example of a gay anthem, with a piano flourish as an introduction, followed by lyrics that outline the history of a toxic relationship and the singer's determination to never be hurt again. Then there were openly gay disco groups like the Village People, with hits including 'YMCA' and 'In the Navy' – essentially homages to cruising. Perhaps the campest disco artist of all time was Sylvester, a Black gay man who wore drag and sang a falsetto cover of 'You Make Me Feel Mighty Real'. The video for the song has Sylvester first descending a staircase with flashing steps, then sporting a fabulous fan for the rest of the song, while managing several costume changes. However, disco's popularity resulted in over-supply, then a kind of disco-washing where any old song could be zhooshed up with a funky backtrack. Highlights of this doubling down on camp included 'Disco Lucy' by the Wilton Place Street Band (a disco version of the theme tune to 1950s sitcom *I Love Lucy*) and *The Ethel Merman Disco Album*, now a collector's item. In her early seventies by this point, Merman, who was allegedly the inspiration for Helen Lawson in *Valley of the Dolls*, seems to have belted out a set of her standards in one take and a disco backtrack was added later. There were disco covers by other artists of 'Bridge Over Troubled Water', 'Whole Lotta Love', 'California Dreamin'', 'I Heard it Through the Grapevine' and 'Day Tripper'. Even a disco diehard like me would have opted for a dancefloor break if they came on.

Twenty-four-year-old DJ Steve Dahl *hated* disco, viewing it as shallow and annoying. Worse still, it had cost him his job when his radio station, WDAI, decided to switch from rock to disco. Fortunately, for him, he was able to get a position at a rival rock station called WLUP, and he decided to get revenge on WDAI by mocking its 'Disco DAI' slogan, referring to the station as 'Disco DIE'. Dahl attracted a following, who he referred to as the Insane Coho Lips, and he urged his fans to gatecrash various discos, inevitably ending in the police having to break up fights. Dahl didn't care, he was on a roll and he even recorded his own song, a parody of Rod Stewart's 'Do You Think I'm Sexy?' called 'Do You Think I'm Disco?' which painted disco dancers as vain and superficial, with blow-dried hair and a sock stuffed into their underwear for erotic effect (it reached number fifty-eight on the Billboard Hot 100). When Black artist Van McCoy died suddenly on 6 July 1979, Dahl marked the occasion by destroying one of McCoy's most famous disco records, 'The Hustle', on air. Not. A. Good. Look.

What could be more anti-disco than organised sports? Dahl and his co-host sidekick, Garry Meier, got together with Bill Veeck who owned a baseball team, the Chicago White Sox. Along with other employees at WLUP, they came up with a promotion to attract fans. A game between the White Sox and the Detroit Tigers at Comiskey Park on 2 May had to be postponed due to rain. As a result, it was rescheduled to occur as part of a 'doubleheader' – two games played back-to-back – on 12 July. To promote the radio station, it was suggested that WLUP organise an anti-disco night, marketed as 'Disco Demolition Night'. During the brief period between the two games, Dahl aimed to blow up a massive collection of disco records, on the pitch. Anyone who brought along a disco record would be admitted to the ballpark for ninety-eight cents (as the radio frequency of WLUP was 97.9). The evening proved to be very popular, with attendance officially reported as 47,795, slightly above capacity – although other estimates suggest that up to 55,000 people turned up. Word had spread and people tried to get in without tickets, so security guards were sent to stop them, leaving the field unattended. Meanwhile, the atmosphere on the stand began to get heated, with some fans drinking liquor and smoking marijuana. People began throwing their disco records onto the pitch, along with firecrackers, bottles and lighters. As the records sliced through the air like frisbees, the game had to be stopped several times and players were advised to put on their batting helmets to avoid decapitation.

The donated disco records were eventually gathered into a large box, rigged with explosives and, after the first game ended, Dahl, Meier and a model called Lorelei (who did public appearances for WLUP) circled the field in a jeep, encouraging the crowd to chant, 'Disco sucks!' Dahl told them, 'This is now officially the world's largest anti-disco rally! Now, listen – we took all the disco records you brought tonight, we got 'em in a giant box, and we're gonna blow 'em up reeeeeeal goooood.' Dahl then set off the explosives, destroying the records and ripping a hole in the grass. With levels of excitement peaking, around 5,000 to 7,000 fans stormed onto the pitch, causing mayhem – starting fires and damaging both the grass and baseball equipment. Eventually, the police arrived, dispersing the crowd and arresting thirty-nine people. The field was so badly damaged that the second game was deemed unplayable, so had to be forfeited, due to the White Sox having failed to provide acceptable playing conditions.

There was a harsh reaction from members of the music press, many of whom viewed Disco Demolition Night as a mass display of only slightly supressed homophobia and racism. Later that year, in *Rolling Stone* magazine, Dave Marsh wrote that:

> . . . white males, eighteen to thirty-four are the most likely to see disco as the product of homosexuals, blacks, and Latins, and therefore they're the most likely to respond to appeals to wipe out such threats to their security. It goes almost without saying that such appeals are racist and sexist, but broadcasting has never been an especially civil-libertarian medium.[145]

Nile Rodgers, guitarist for the band Chic said that the event was like a Nazi book burning, while in 2011 academic Tim Lawrence called the 'disco sucks' campaign homophobic.[146]

Dahl denied the accusations of homophobia and racism, saying that the event had been reframed as prejudiced. Other disco stars have also given different takes on what happened – Gloria Gaynor believed that the 'disco sucks' campaign was motivated by economics,[147] while Harry Wayne Casey of KC and the Sunshine Band viewed Dahl as nothing more than an idiot.[148] Whatever the underlying motivations, the backlash against disco looks to me like a mainstream reaction against camp, which was in keeping with a cultural and political shift at the start of the 1980s. The fact that this all occurred on a sports pitch feels highly significant. While sports matches can be a fruitful source of unintentional camp (the cheerleaders, the mascots, the National Anthem, the exaggerated displays of emotion from fans and players), they are not usually places where intentional camp occurs. And one thing that usually unites camp people is their dislike of sports. The British author Ronald Firbank wrote eight novels that were described as part of the 'canon of camp' by Susan Sontag. Firbank studied at Cambridge in 1905, where he was spotted by Oscar Wilde's son, Vyvyan Holland, dressed 'in the costume of sport'. Holland asked him what he had been doing and Firbank replied that he had been playing football. Holland asked whether it was rugby or soccer. In one version of the story, Firbank responds, 'Oh, I can't remember' – although in another he says that he hadn't been able to get close enough to the ball to find out. So, it feels fitting that the baseball pitch at Comiskey Park was turned into a scene of camp martyrdom in the ongoing battle between the forces of camp and anti-camp. Camp had always had its detractors but Disco Demolition Night represents the first widespread movement against it. Ironically, of course, the complete over-reaction, which spilled over into violence, casts the whole event as more camp than the disco music that it wished to eviscerate.

BURNT CHAMPAGNE

Disco may well have died that night (actually it threw on a new wig and morphed into high-energy dance music), but that is not to say that the 1980s were a camp-free zone. With a Republican (Ronald Reagan) in the White House and a Conservative in 10 Downing Street (Margaret Thatcher), the decade saw a return to moral puritanism, along with a homophobic backlash ushered in by the discovery of the HIV virus that caused AIDS and disproportionally affected gay men. This was also a decade when Milton Friedman, an economist from the 'Chicago school' became hugely influential in both the UK and the US. Friedman advocated free trade, open markets, privatisation, deregulation and a reduced public sector – a set of policies that are sometimes collectively referred to as neo-liberalism. Their implementation resulted in a widening gap between rich and poor, with the winners being able to indulge in ostentatious displays of wealth. It is within that context, that life at Versailles would be televisually reimagined, transported to the American city of Denver, where, in place of Louis XIV, there is Blake Carrington, a blue-haired billionaire oil baron with the manner of easy-listening singer Perry Como in a testy mood.

Excessive inequality literally brings to mind the camp epitaph 'Too much!' Sometimes, when narcissistic people have excessive money or power, they try to impress others with their importance through ostentatious displays of wealth. They mistakenly believe that 'bigger is better' when actually 'bigger is vulgar'. A sign of being too rich is not even bothering to have any taste of your own but outsourcing it to other people. The ostentatious homes of the ultra-rich, are nearly always, by their very nature, camp, because everything, from the letterbox to the ceiling roses, screams 'Look at *me* and BE IMPRESSED!' Despite efforts to make such homes appear stylish and sophisticated, there can be a child-like fairy-tale aspect to them, particularly when everyday objects or furnishings are clad in gold. When the wealth is amassed in the context of inequality, it can provoke disgusted laughter. Iraqi dictator Saddam Hussein's palaces had gold taps, dishes, sinks, wastebaskets, bidets and toilets, during a period when as many as one in three Iraqis had no plumbing and had to relieve themselves in buckets.[149]

From 1981 to 1989 every Saturday evening, my family would congregate in our sitting room to watch *Dynasty*. As a treat, my mother would buy everyone a small bottle of lemonade and a packet of Smiths Crispy Tubes crisps (which we viewed as 'posh' because they were advertised on television by a tennis umpire who referred to them as 'rather elegant'). *Dynasty*'s opening credits featured a cast roll-call, with each character portrayed against a different signifier of glamour (skyscrapers, fountains, roulette tables, jewellery, brandy balloons). As we watched Adam Carrington superimposed next to a suggestively spurting bottle of champagne, we all opened our little 10p bottles of lemonade, without commenting on the ironic juxtaposition. *Dynasty* was watched in rapt silence, with only conversation that was *about Dynasty* being permitted, during it. My mother would sometimes say, 'See, money doesn't bring you happiness' after Krystle Carrington got kidnapped and replaced with a trashy lookalike actress, or Alexis Carrington Colby Dexter Rowan Morell got sent to prison for suspected murder.

Alexis, played by breakthrough British B-movie actress Joan Collins, was the star of the show. The 1970s had not been kind to Joan, and she had gone from low-budget horror films like *Tales from the Crypt* (1972) and *Empire of the Ants* (1977) to playing Fontaine Khaled, a callous, bored nightclub owner in *The Stud* (1978) and its sequel, *The Bitch* (1979). These latter two films are so delectably awful that I was able to get the AI chatbot ChatGPT to come up with the script to an imaginary sequel called *The Cougar*, which had a more coherent plot, better-rounded characters and sassier dialogue.

As colourfully camp as Joan's '70s films are, her previous roles were simply groundwork for Alexis, who burst into *Dynasty*, instantly ensuring its global success. Alexis had a haughty British accent (lots of her dialogue seemed to be written in italics *and* underlined), a killer wardrobe and an inexhaustible supply of bitchy one-liners. She was every Bette Davis and Joan Crawford character rolled into one, initially appearing as a mystery witness in a veil when her ex-husband, Blake, was tried for murder at the end of the season one finale. After that, she dominated the show, causing mayhem in her quest to destroy Blake and his anodyne new wife, Krystle. She was a super-bitch who fired a shotgun that caused Krystle to fall off her horse and have a miscarriage, she lived in a penthouse with a lift that opened up into her living room, and she got to sleep with Dex Dexter, the manliest stud on the show. Alexis was often given other bitchy female characters to sharpen her claws on, including Blake's half-sister, Dominique Deveraux, played by Diahann Carroll. In one scene, Dominique accuses Alexis of serving 'burnt' champagne – 'This champagne was obviously frozen in the bottle at some point' – and then informs her that she is also serving the wrong kind of caviar – 'This is Ostetrova and I prefer Petrossian Beluga.' I remember watching that scene, aged thirteen, feeling as if I was witnessing something in a foreign language set on an alien planet.

Krystle and Alexis famously brawled in a lily pond in season three, but my favourite Alexis moment was the season six finale when she took possession of Blake's mansion. As Blake and Krystle arrive home, they are surprised to find a pile of luggage in the entrance hall. Blake's evil brother, Ben, appears, announcing that Blake is broke. Then they notice Alexis on the balcony that adjoins the double staircase. 'You heard him, Blake! You're finished. You've lost everything and I now own this house!' 'This house! Are you insane?' Blake says. 'Perfectly sane,' Alexis replies, holding up a fur coat of Krystle's in each hand. 'So, take this *junk*' (she throws the coats over the balcony) 'and your blonde *tramp!*' (she gestures at Krystle) 'and get out of my home.' In a quick gesture she pulls a piece of paper out from under her dress and gloatingly announces, 'It's all mine, Blake. And I have the papers to prove it.' (This is accentuated with a sassy little head bob.) 'And there's absolutely nothing you can do about it.' 'Damn you, Alexis!' cries Blake, running up the staircase. 'I'm gonna kill you!' He grabs her by the neck and, for a single second, in a wide shot we see that Alexis has been replaced by a stuntman wearing a wig and a dress – a surreal moment which pushes the scene into a rare exospheric level of camp. Then, it is back to Joan Collins, and we see Blake start to throttle her. For a series to end its *sixth* year on such a high note (and I haven't even mentioned that the rest of the cast were trapped in a hotel – called La Mirage because French equals elegance – that was burning down while all this was going on) is pretty admirable.

'Damn you, Alexis!' The camp of *Dynasty* summed up in a single image.

Like all the best villains, Alexis was sometimes painted sympathetically – she (mostly) loved her children and secretly still loved Blake. In the following season, Blake had amnesia after an oil rig explosion and somehow thought it was 1964 and that he and

Alexis were still married (such a *relatable* storyline). Alexis decided to play along, in order to get some South China Sea leases back from him. She whisked him off to a villa in Singapore to recuperate, but ripped up the papers once Blake had signed them because all she really wanted was to have him back. 'I love you!' Blake told her. 'Oh, Blake,' she replied, 'I love you too. I always have and I always will.' It is a touching scene and heart-breaking when Krystle shows up in the next episode and Blake gets his memory back and leaves with her. But, usually, Alexis would do anything to get her way. In another legendary episode she charms an oil-well owner into selling his assets to her by performing a perfect country and western line dance while wearing tight brown pants with a huge silver belt buckle. Using a chair as a prop, she follows up with an impromptu country and western performance of the Marlene Dietrich standard 'The Boys in the Backroom'. Despite a couple of bum notes, the look of pure joy on Joan's face during this camp divertissement is delightful.

Dynasty and its spiritual successor *Melrose Place* (discussed in the following chapter) both had gay male characters (Stephen and Matt, respectively), although they were a different breed from the gossipy queens of earlier decades. But for the fact that they had the occasional relationship with a man, you wouldn't clock that these guys were gay. They were handsome and straight-presenting, but also portrayed as sensitive and a bit goody-two-shoes. Crucially, they had none of the qualities of toxic masculinity associated with many of the heterosexual men in these soaps. It says a lot that the campest output of the 1980s completely disassociated its camp from homosexuality. Perhaps those protests against John Inman a few years earlier had taken effect.

Dynasty and its contemporaries, *Dallas*, *Falcon Crest* and *Knots Landing* were big-budget night-time soaps that traced camp back to its roots in Versailles, with more than a nod to the 1950s 'Women's Films' along the way. *Dynasty* also made a star out of Denver, not exactly a tourist destination up until that point, with a local travel agency reporting how Europeans were flocking in, while a local gay bar, Garbo's, set up three televisions for mass-viewing nights. Bartender Mike Gambino reported that patrons would dress up as characters from the show and buy champagne (hopefully not burnt) to toast Alexis with. 'It gets very campy in here,' he observed.[150] I can well imagine.

SCREAM, QUEEN!

During the 1970s and 1980s, children were still expected to be seen and not heard. They were sometimes called the latch-key generation, as both sets of parents were now required to work in order to meet living costs, while the relaxation of taboos around divorce resulted in increasing numbers of single-parent families. Left to their own devices, this was one of the last periods when children experienced the freedom of unsupervised outdoor play and exploration. There were, of course, concerns that they may get into danger whilst outside, and while today this is no longer a problem due to the mass TikTok addiction of everyone aged under eighteen, earlier attempts at child protection involved the use of camp horror. The British Central Office of Information created a series of campaigns that used fear-based messaging to gratuitously scare children into being sensible, hazard-averse and self-sufficient. Several times a year during primary school, my class would be herded into the library, an enormous television was wheeled out and we would be shown around an hour's worth of terrifying short films that would always reduce even the most hyperactive pupils to subdued silence.

Sometimes these films could be quaintly camp, such as the 1976 road safety advert that featured glam rock pop star Alvin Stardust, decked out in a black leather jacket and huge bouffant hair, wagging his finger in disgust at two girls who blithely walk into traffic. 'Just look at them. They must be *crackers!* A double decker bus could be right on top of them and they'd never even see it.' Confronting the girls, he says, 'Hey! You must be out of your tiny minds!' Other adverts were more overtly sinister. *Lonely Water* (1973) had a character dressed as the grim reaper who hung around ponds and rivers. A voiceover by the horror actor Donald Pleasence announced, 'I am the spirit of dark and lonely water. Ready to trap the unwary, the show-off, the fool.' The camera then showed a group of children using a stick to retrieve a football from a small pool. 'The pool is deep. The boy is showing off. The bank is slippery,' observed the robed figure with interest. The boy fell in the water and the grim reaper figure was shown approaching to claim another victim.

If you grew up during this period it felt like death, or at least a severe maiming, was waiting around every corner. Children were warned about talking to strangers, playing with fireworks, climbing inside old fridges and going near power lines or electric substations. There was also a flood of adverts aimed at stopping kids from smoking or using heroin, as well as terrifying messaging campaigns about HIV/AIDS. And over all of this was the constant threat of nuclear war, with the realistically devastating film *Threads* (1984) being shown on the BBC when I was twelve, providing sombre discussion during playtime the following day – my friends and I calculated whether we lived close enough to school to run home if a warning alarm sounded. Unsurprisingly, many of the children who survived these existential threats coped by developing a cynical love of irony, which will come to the fore in the following chapter.

Camp horror wasn't limited to public information films, though. A device called a VCR (videocassette recorder) had recently brought the cinema into living rooms and video rental shops quickly sprang up everywhere. In my town, a 'video van' patrolled the streets, run by one of my neighbours. The van's interior always had a sweaty smell and you had to crouch in it to peruse its wares – mostly low-budget trash where the imaginative cover artwork bore little resemblance to the actual film. There was always a lot of horror on offer. American movies like *Halloween*

(1978) and *Friday the 13th* (1980) had kick-started a trend for 'slasher' films that involved teenagers being stalked and brutally murdered by a silent, unstoppable killer. Influenced by the camp, colourful films of the Italian Giallo era – like *The Bird with the Crystal Plumage* (1970), *The Case of the Bloody Iris* (1972) and *What Have You Done to Solange?* (1972) – the slashers were even bloodier and less elegantly made. A media panic ensued, with claims that the VCR era made 'video nasties' accessible to children and, as a result, seventy-two of the most notorious ones were banned in the UK.

The *Nightmare on Elm Street* series is arguably one of the campest examples of the 1980s horror craze. It was centred around a child-killer called Freddy Krueger who had been freed on a technicality and was subsequently burnt alive by vigilante parents. However, magically, Freddy began appearing in the dreams of teenagers who lived on Elm Street, and if he killed you in your dream then you died in real life. Freddy had some odd sartorial choices – he dressed in a red-and-black striped sweater, wore a brown fedora hat and had a metal-clawed glove on his right hand. Unlike the silent stalkers of other slasher films, who never seemed to enjoy their killings, Freddy revelled in his evil and had a *lot* to say, much of which was in the form of camp repartee. When killing a girl with a television he cackled, 'Welcome to primetime, bitch!' When one character confronted him, calling out, 'Krueger!' Freddy responded with 'Well, it ain't Dr Seuss.' At one point he even paraphrased the Wicked Witch of the West in *The Wizard of Oz*: 'I'll get you, my pretty, and your little soul too!'

In 1991, I attended an all-night showing of the *Nightmare on Elm Street* film series at a cinema in Newcastle-upon-Tyne. The event started at midnight and I remember being a little taken aback by the army of surly security staff positioned strategically around the auditorium. All was explained when the first film began – the audience was beyond rowdy and the atmosphere felt on the verge of full-scale riot, making what was happening in the theatre more threatening than anything on the screen. It was impossible to hear the dialogue of the first film due to the constant screaming and shouting. During the second film, energy levels were dropping and the yelling was limited to a few groups who entertained everyone else by calling insults at one another, and by the third film people were starting to doze off. Afraid of what might happen if I did fall asleep, I tried to stay awake, much like the teenage victims in the *Elm Street* films. In the morning, I stumbled, bleary-eyed into daylight, with a renewed respect for the characters who had battled Freddy.

I had been especially worried about how the audience would react to *A Nightmare on Elm Street 2: Freddy's Revenge* (1985), due to its rather unusual plot for the period. The story involved a slightly feminine teenage boy called Jesse, whose body is repeatedly possessed by Freddy Krueger. What made the film remarkable was the insinuation that Jesse was gay. 'Daddy can't help you now! Shhhh! I need you, Jesse,' Krueger tells him, caressing Jesse's brow with his claw fingers. 'We've got special work to do here, you and me. You've got the body. I've got the brain.'

Screamer! Mark Patton in the shower in *A Nightmare on Elm Street II*.

In these kinds of films, it was unusual to have a male protagonist – during this period, young male audiences would be unlikely to identify with a man who showed the required amount of terror to make the film scary. So, the surviving character would usually be female, dubbed the 'final girl'. Such girls would usually be characterised as morally superior to their friends, in that they wouldn't have sex or use drugs and they usually had short hair, were demure and might have a unisex name like Avery, Chris or Sydney. Carol Clover, who coined the term, noted that the final girl would often survive by taking a knife or chainsaw to the killer, becoming masculine so that the male audience could identify with her to an extent.[151] Consequently, Jesse is a 'final boy' and, like the final girls, he doesn't act in a way that is typical of his sex. At the start of the film, he wakes up from a nightmare, giving a remarkably girly scream, and twenty minutes in there is a scene where he performs a suggestive dance routine while tidying up his room, wiggling his backside to close the drawers on his dresser, bouncing around on his bed and playing with a bicycle pump as if it is a phallus.

The film also features several sequences that are highly homoerotic, mostly centred around sports fields and locker rooms. As with any depiction of desirable, partially clothed men, the resulting sexualisation can easily loop into camp. During a baseball game, Jesse gets into a tussle with his handsome jock friend, Grady, who pulls down his sweatpants, revealing Jesse's backside. The two then wrestle on the ground until they are pulled apart by their sadistic coach who tells them to 'assume the position' (they are made to perform the plank exercise). And later, in the film's strangest sequence, Jesse dreamily walks through a thunderstorm late at night, with his shirt open. Soaking wet, he enters a crowded bar called Don's Place, which has a muscle-man poster on the wall and patrons who are dressed in BDSM clothing. One male patron licks the face of another man. Jesse orders a beer from the bartender, who is wearing spiked leather gloves. Then the coach appears, clad in a revealing black vest with leather panels, gripping

Jesse's wrist and staring into his eyes. Suddenly, the two are back at the school, and Jesse is running laps around the sports hall. 'Hit the shower!' the coach tells him. While Jesse showers, the coach grabs some skipping ropes from an equipment cabinet, with the implication that he is going to tie Jesse up and presumably have sex with him. However, he is disturbed by a noise and watches as the sports equipment in his office starts to come to life – balls begin bouncing everywhere (ahem) and the coach has to drop to the ground to avoid being hit. The skipping ropes then magically fix themselves to his wrists and he is dragged into the shower room, his clothing is stripped from him and then his backside is whipped by demonically possessed towels, while Jesse, also naked, watches. Jesse then turns into Freddy and kills the coach.

Towards the end of the film, Jesse visits Grady in his bedroom, jumping on top of him, then asking to spend the night with him. 'Something is trying to get inside my body,' he cries. However, during the night Jesse turns into Freddy and kills Grady who is wearing nothing but a pair of tight-fitting shorts. The film appears to end happily, with Jesse reunited with his girlfriend, Lisa, who gives him the strength to fight Freddy. But in the final scene it is implied that Freddy has not been vanquished and has captured the few surviving cast members by commandeering the school bus. It is all very strange and sums up the 1980s perfectly.

At the time that the film was made, the media panic around HIV/AIDS was beginning to reach a peak, and one way of reading the film was that it acted as a very long version of a public information scare film, with the warning that homosexuality would lead to death. Jesse's struggle against Freddy could be seen as him trying to repress his gay desires, hence the killing of the coach and his friend Grady. On the other hand, the film could be seen as appealing to gay audiences, with its use of male nudity, sexually ambiguous characters and a shamelessly camp sensibility. It was certainly a film that made me brave the acrid-smelling video van in order to rent it more than once. David Chaskin, the writer, initially denied that the film had a gay subtext and blamed actor Mark Patton for playing the part of Jesse as 'too gay'. Patton himself was gay but closeted at the time – his manager had lectured him on the kinds of clothes he should be wearing and had told him to be seen in public with a girl (the same advice we saw given to Liberace back in the 1950s).[152] While working on the film, Patton had noticed changes being made to the script, which made the film even queerer.

> It just became undeniable. I mean, when you're looking at dailies and I'm lying in bed and I'm a pietà and the candles are dripping and they're bending like phalluses and white wax is dripping all over . . . It's like I'm the center of a what do they call it? – a bukkake. Like I'm a bukkake video.

Louis Peitzman, who interviewed Patton, notes, 'This wasn't just unsubtle; it was completely in-your-face. It was *camp*.' With fear around HIV/AIDS causing stigma, gay actors had been frog-marched into the closet. Patton's boyfriend, the actor Timothy Patrick Murphy, who had a role in the soap opera *Dallas*, was outed by a tabloid and died of an AIDS-related illness in 1988. So, the film was a case of art imitating life, with both Jesse and Mark Patton facing a crisis around their true sexual identity, which played out amid a horrific backdrop of dying men. Patton's experience of working on the film was so traumatising that afterwards he quit acting and became an interior designer.

Chaskin later admitted that the gay themes had been deliberate, saying, 'Homophobia was skyrocketing and I began to think about our core audience – adolescent boys – and how all of this stuff might be trickling down into their psyches . . . My thought was that tapping into that angst would give an extra edge to the horror.' Some who were involved in the film, like director Jack Sholder, have denied that they saw the gay subtext at the time it was being made. Others, however, definitely saw it. The gay magazine *The Advocate* apparently dubbed the film the gayest horror film ever made. With that said, the barely controllable audience at my Newcastle cinema were not cinematically or sexually literate enough to decode the film, so nobody responded by screaming homophobic slurs at the screen. They fell strangely quiet during the homoerotic scenes, as if they couldn't make sense of them, instead reserving their ire to shout 'moose!' repeatedly whenever Jesse's girlfriend appeared (moose was a local 1980s slur for an unattractive woman). Like the 1950s Women's Films described in Chapter 4, the camp was there, hiding in plain sight to some but completely invisible to others.

In 2019, a documentary called *Scream, Queen! My Nightmare on Elm Street*, co-produced by Patton, gave his perspective on the making of the film and its effect on his life. The film is difficult to watch at times, showing the devastating effect of HIV/AIDS and the homophobic climate of the time on male actors. The documentary also charts the initial polarising reaction to the film to its more recent status as a cult classic. Indeed, while researching this book, I would often sidle up to people and ask them, 'What's the campest thing you know?' *A Nightmare on Elm Street 2* came up several times, with one person telling me that later that week he was attending a fancy-dress party as Freddy Krueger. The film shows one of the most unusual and ambivalent uses of camp horror during a period when fear of homosexuality was rampant and highly visible. And in the following sections we will see what happened when gay people fought back, using camp to subvert the narrative.

NORMAN LAMONT'S RED BOX

While Larry Grayson and John Inman had been embraced by earlier audiences because they were relatable, chummy and sexually unthreatening, in the 1980s a new generation of gay comedians took a different approach, using camp in a much spikier way – to respond to the malevolent politics of the era. In 1978, Paul O'Grady created a character called Lily Savage, based on various working-class female relatives from his home-town, Birkenhead. Glaring and snarling in a giant blonde hair-do with black roots showing through, lots of jewellery and a cigarette perpetually hanging out of her mouth, Lily was a scary drag queen with a quick, sharp sense of humour who suffered no fools and had a no-nonsense working-class worldview. O'Grady performed in gay venues around London, eventually working in Vauxhall, first at the Elephant and Castle pub where he compered an amateur drag night, then at the Royal Vauxhall Tavern. Police raids of gay venues are a recurring theme in this book, and we haven't had one yet in this chapter, so let's travel to a cold evening in January 1987, when the RVT was raided by thirty-five policemen, who used the excuse that the customers were drunk.

It wasn't the first time that the pub had been raided – a month earlier, police had seized bottles of amyl nitrate from the pub and charged the landlord with 'conspiracy to administer noxious substances with intent to injure'. This time, around forty patrons were lined up outside and a police doctor looked at them one by one and declared them drunk. They were then herded into vans that were waiting to take them to the local police station. Meanwhile, O'Grady was onstage, in full drag, noticing that the police were wearing rubber gloves, so they didn't have to touch anyone they arrested. The raid itself was bad enough, with the venue being targeted because it was a gay club, but the use of gloves was exceptionally offensive, not to mention ignorant. So, Savage had the perfect comeback, calling from the stage, 'Well, well, it looks like we've got help with the washing-up!' Lily herself was then carted off to a police station and ordered to give her name to the desk sergeant. She told him 'Lily Savage', to which the officer demanded that she give a 'real name'. She shot back, 'Lily Veronika Mae Savage'. Eventually everyone who was arrested was released without charge and it was business as usual the following night.[153]

For gay audiences, drag queens had always been bawdy and shocking but, during the 1980s, mainstream comedy saw a sea-change, with younger comics keen to break from the established ways of making people laugh – no longer relying on sexism, racism and homophobia, or lazily drawing on stereotypes like the battle-axe mother-in-law. In the UK, the new 'alternative comedy' was typified by Ben Elton, Rik Mayall, Dawn French, Jennifer Saunders, Harry Enfield, Keith Allen and Jo Brand. Their humour was loud and confrontational and it was often critical of Conservative politics. In Canada, a sketch show called *The Kids in the Hall* (1988–1995) featured a regular monologue by cast regular Scott Thompson, a gay man, who played Buddy Hall – an effeminate, opinionated older gay man. Buddy was based upon a man whom Thompson had gone on a brief date with, but the character also reflected some of his own insecurities: 'He was a very flamboyant, very sexual, powerful, effeminate gay man and I was so full of self-loathing at the time over my own non-classically masculine behaviour.'[154] Thompson notes that 'A lot of gay men think they don't read gay, but they do. So Buddy's accepting of all of it – he's accepting of who he is, where he stands in the world.'[155] With his R-rated reminiscences, Buddy had the potential to offend everyone. Describing how he fell in love at first sight when he was living in Baghdad, he said, 'it was a sexy, sunny Iraqi day. Mmmm. And I was lounging about the pool at the Danish consulate wearing next to nothing. Oooh. In fact, at one point, all I was wearing was a diplomat's hand.' He made fun of straight people, claiming that whenever he mentions anything anal they always rush out to vacuum their cars. But in contributing towards the camp sissy stereotype, he was also criticised by the gay community. Thompson said:

> A guy being like that was pretty hilarious, and you could laugh at him from a point of superiority. For all of the advances we have made against homophobia, the effeminate, older gay male is still pretty low down in the pecking order, and I made sure that Buddy reflected that awareness and threw it right back.[156]

In one sketch he says, 'People make fun of me because I lisp. Really! Such a lot of fuss over a few extra s's!' Thompson lisped while growing up and had speech therapy for years. So doing Buddy was him subconsciously becoming the lisp. Despite being an openly gay man on television, Thompson says he has not been acknowledged by the gay community and never mentioned by GLAAD (Gay & Lesbian Alliance Against Defamation), something which he says speaks to the self-loathing of gay men.[157] An argument could be made that Thompson was ahead of his time – and I'm a Buddy fan; many of the lines in his sketches have seared themselves into my memory.

Thompson's experiences indicate that it was hard work being a gay comedian in the late 1980s as society struggled to reconcile camp with homosexuality. In the UK, a comedy series called *Friday Night Live* ran from 1985 to 1988, partly modelled on the long-running American series *Saturday Night Live*, although it tended to rely on stand-up routines as opposed to sketches. One of the regular comics to appear on the programme was Julian Clary, who was billed as 'The Joan Collins Fan Club' (Miss Collins was not initially impressed but years later they became friends and Clary even saved her life, plucking her out of a swimming pool in St Tropez when she became trapped under an inflatable armchair[158]). Tall and slender, clad in leather and PVC, usually with a studded collar, and heavy makeup, Clary looked like a gay nightmare conceived by the tabloid press – the stranger danger your parents warned you to keep away from. Clary was softly spoken, although unlike Larry Grayson and John Inman, he spoke laconically and deliberately, in short utterances, with an air of bored majesty, using silence to make people wait for the punchlines. He lulled audiences into thinking he was polite, but would then go on to insult them with withering put-downs. 'What's your name, any idea?'; 'Hello. How old are you? Twenty-one, really? Quelle surprise.' Like the camp comics before him, Clary relied on innuendo, although tended to push the boundaries further: 'What's that punter there doing, mincing in at this late hour? I'm afraid you've missed my spectacular opening'; 'Huge this stage huge – biggest erection I've ever worked on.'

In 1980s UK, Conservative politicians, religious leaders and tabloid columnists railed against gay people, whipping up fear about HIV/AIDS and believing that children needed to be protected from educational campaigns that tried to present positive images of homosexuality. In 1986 in the House of Lords, Lord Halsbury claimed that there were 'sick' homosexuals who could be identified through promiscuity, exhibitionism and proselytising and 'they act as reservoirs of venereal diseases of all kinds'. In 1988, a notorious law, referred to as Section 28, proclaimed that local authorities should not 'intentionally promote homosexuality' or 'the acceptability of homosexuality as a pretended family relationship'. When a gay character called Colin appeared in the soap opera *EastEnders*, tabloid journalists printed the actor's address, resulting in him having a brick put through his window. In this atmosphere of homophobia, Clary mocked the negative gay stereotypes by appearing to inhabit all of them at once. His brand of camp was much more challenging to mainstream audiences – it was in-your-face, unapologetic and insulting. Audiences were ready for it, though, and Clary was given his own late-night gameshow, *Sticky Moments* (1989–90). The programme had a colourful, cartoonish set and functioned as a parody of gameshows, with Clary arbitrarily giving points to contestants based on whether he liked them.

Clary's popularity grew in the early 1990s, and he was asked to read the nominations for the top comedy personality at the British Comedy Awards in 1993, a mainstream event that was televised live and watched by thirteen million viewers. Earlier in the programme, the UK Chancellor of the Exchequer Norman Lamont came onstage to announce one of the winners, earning boos from the audience. The Conservative Party, having held on to power for fourteen years, was becoming increasingly unpopular. Despite mounting a 'Back to Basics' initiative, which was meant to revive traditional British family values, the party had been weakened by a number of sex scandals, such as Alan Amos (MP for Hexham) being arrested at a London cruising area, Hampstead Heath.

It was a difficult time for Julian Clary. His boyfriend, Christopher, had died in 1991 from an AIDS-related illness and since then he had been having panic attacks and was using Valium to get through the day and Rohypnol to sleep at night. On top of that, Conservative policy, including the message conveyed by Section 28, had contributed towards a nationwide climate of homophobia. Clary had noticed Norman Lamont backstage at the Comedy Awards, and his hackles rose. So, when he came onstage, wearing a dinner jacket with an elegant brooch, he didn't pull any punches, deciding he would 'very graphically' explain 'what gay men do to each other'.[159]

'It's very nice of you to re-create Hampstead Heath for me here,' he told the host, Jonathan Ross, referring to the way that the set was incongruously decorated with fake trees. The audience applauded. Then Julian made an off-the-cuff reference to the Chancellor of the Exchequer, which would go down as one of the most shocking moments ever in the Camp Hall of Fame. 'As a matter of fact, I've just been fisting Norman Lamont. Talk about a red box!' The audience exploded with laughter. For those who are not familiar with the intricacies of British politics, the Chancellor of the Exchequer traditionally carries his Budget speech to the House of Commons in a red leather-clad Despatch Box, similar in appearance to a briefcase. Clary's reference to Lamont's 'red box' was a particularly rude innuendo, and it is the only time I can recall hearing a reference to 'fisting' on national television. Jonathan Ross joined in, asking, 'So how did you jump to the front of the queue then?' Julian beamingly replied, 'Just clawed my way through.' Ross acknowledged the remark and then seemed to remember that he was hosting an awards show. 'Are we still on?' he asked, implying that the live feed may have been cut, resulting in further audience laughter.

Although the joke was made around forty minutes after the nine-o'clock watershed, after which more adult content was possible, because the programme had begun at 8pm, it was believed likely that it would have retained a family audience. So the network, London Weekend Television, was required to broadcast a peak-time apology after seventeen viewers complained. In the *Mail*, columnist Lynda Lee-Potter wrote that Clary 'was offensive, coarse and unpleasant. He described a disgusting, violent and dangerous homosexual practice, and attempted to turn it into a joke'. She called for punishment of performers if they choose to be lewd and said that television was not the place for the perverted and the sick.[160] *Sun* journalist Garry Bushell accused Clary of dragging British comedy into the sewer and called for Clary to be banned from live TV. Work didn't exactly dry up but there were consequences – at the eleventh hour, Clary was removed from the guest list at the British Comedy Awards ceremony in 1998, due to concerns that he might repeat his performance of 1993.[161] Clary later spoke about how, after the 1993 appearance, he went a bit 'doolally' and considered suicide, booking himself into the Intercontinental Hotel in Hyde Park, intending to take an overdose. Even this event was subjected to camp humour, with Clary choosing to laugh at himself. 'When I got to the hotel it was all rather sumptuous, with room service and CNN, so I thought: "I'll wait until morning." That's the thing with camp people – we're all desperately shallow.'[162] Over the years, Clary's camp became a bit less shocking while audiences grew less shockable – in other words, there was a definite meeting halfway, and Clary went on to become a National Treasure, winning the television gameshow *Celebrity Big Brother* in 2012. As for Norman Lamont's red box – I suspect that a good application of rubbing alcohol would have restored it back to its former glory with no lasting damage done.

CATEGORY IS . . . APPROPRIATION!

In 1990, an American documentary film called *Paris Is Burning* shone a spotlight on a hitherto underground ball culture of Black,

Latino, gay and trans people in New York. Filmed over the course of six years, the film interspersed footage of the balls with interviews with participants, who belonged to Houses made up of chosen family members, a tradition dating all the way back to the House of Swann, formed a century earlier. The Houses competed at the balls, which featured drag competitions where contestants had to adhere to a particular theme or category, dancing and walking across the ballroom floor like a runway model. Like old-fashioned ballroom dancing, a panel of judges held up numbered cards to indicate scores out of ten. Contestants were judged according to their dancing abilities, fashion and the realness (ability to convincingly blend in) of their drag, with the winning contestants awarded trophies and much coveted 'legendary' status.

The balls had evolved since the 1960s when they featured drag queens who dressed as Vegas showgirls with feather headdresses and beads – a documentary film called *The Queen* (1968) catalogues one of these early contests, which were more like a traditional beauty pageant, but with more shade. During *The Queen*, one entrant in the 1967 Miss All-America Camp Beauty Contest, Pepper LaBeija, describes receiving a draft notice and being turned away due to her feminine appearance and manner, despite wanting to serve in the army. The film is narrated by the contest's winner, an androgynously beautiful twenty-four-year-old whose drag name is Flawless Sabrina. After she receives her crown, there is a scene of high drama when fourth-placed contestant, Crystal LaBeija, who had stormed off the stage earlier, confronts Sabrina, protesting that the contest was fixed. Crystal would go on to form the House of LaBeija.

In *Paris Is Burning*, one of the queens, Dorian Corey, explains that during the 1970s the contests changed, with participants emulating film stars like Marilyn Monroe or Elizabeth Taylor, while in the 1980s the remit was widened to include models like Christie Brinkley and Maud Adams. The number of categories was also increased, to enable more people to participate – not everyone was able to look like a showgirl. Many of the categories were aspirational, but not all of them involved men dressing as women, for example, 'Banjee Realness' involved gay men dressing in stereotypically macho-straight guises as sailors, soldiers and hoodlums, while 'School' had contestants dress as if they were college students, wearing cardigans and spectacles while flicking through textbooks. 'High Fashion Parisian' had contestants sashay across the ballroom to the instruction *shantay* (a shortened form of the French word enchanté). 'Town and Country' saw contestants wielding riding crops and galloping across the stage as if on horseback, while 'Executive Realness' involved business suits. Dorian Corey said:

> In real life, you can't get a job as an executive unless you have the educational background and the opportunity. Now the fact that you are not an executive is merely because of the social standing of life . . . Black people have a hard time getting anywhere. And those that do are usually straight. In a ballroom, you can be anything you want. You are not really an executive but you are looking like an executive and therefore you are showing the straight world that 'I can be an executive. If I had the opportunity, I could be one.'

Pepper LaBeija said: 'Those balls are more or less our fantasy of being a superstar. Like the Oscars or whatever. Or being on a runway as a model. A lot of those kids in the balls they don't have two of nothing. Some of them don't even eat. They come to the balls starving.'

The soap opera *Dynasty* was singled out for inspiration, with another interviewee explaining:

> I would always see the way that rich people lived. And I'd feel it more, you know. It would slap me in the face. I'd say, 'I have to have that'. Because I never felt comfortable

> being poor. I just don't. Or even middle-class doesn't suit me. Seeing the riches. Seeing the way people on *Dynasty* lived. These huge houses. And I would think, these people had forty-two rooms in the house, oh my God, what kind of a house is that, and we'd got three. So why is it that they could have it and I didn't? And I always felt cheated.

Some of the balls even had *Dynasty* as a category, with queens dressing as Alexis or Krystle. A young softly spoken contestant called Venus Xtravaganza said, 'I would like to be a spoiled, rich white girl. They get what they want . . . They don't have to really struggle with finances.' Some of the people in the documentary had been rejected by their families and many lived in poverty or were homeless, saving the little money they had for sex-confirmation surgery. Venus had become a sex worker to survive and, towards the end of the film, her House Mother, Angie Xtravaganza, was shown receiving the news that Venus had been found strangled to death, possibly by a client. Once again, camp and tragedy are interweaved.

There are clear parallels between the nineteenth-century cakewalks and the twentieth-century balls in that both involved Black people emulating more socially privileged identities in a competitive context for entertainment, although while the cakewalks emphasised parody the balls were a more complicated mixture of parody and realness – there is a tension between the contestants both performing conventional gender roles and challenging them. Camp seems to get more and more complicated the further into this book that we go.

One aspect of ball culture was an energetic and graceful dance style called voguing, where the competitors posed in glamorous positions as if they were modelling for a photoshoot for the fashion magazine *Vogue*. Arm and leg movements were angular, linear and rigid, moving quickly from one fixed position to another.[163] Voguing grew out of shade, a way of insulting other contestants to impress judges. But rather than physically fighting, contestants would use dance competitively towards one another – whoever did the better moves would be seen as throwing the best shade. For example, in the film one contestant described how he would pretend to be holding a compact mirror in his hand and he would start doing his makeup with his other hand. Then he would turn the compact around, to face his contestant, and start doing *their* face, implying that they needed a makeup job.

Paris Is Burning received mostly critical acclaim, with Michelle Parkerson, in *The Black Film Review*, describing it as 'a politically astute, historically important document of our precarious times'.[164] But not everyone liked it – the writer bell hooks (who uses lowercase letters in her name) said the film showed the balls as a spectacle to pleasure white spectators[165] and she questioned whether the balls themselves had political, artistic or social significance. She describes the contestants as obsessed with 'an idealized fetishized vision of femininity that is white',[166] and is critical of the way that the sadness of Venus's murder is upstaged by spectacle, with nobody shown as mourning her.[167] Despite criticisms, the film won a large number of awards on its release, including the Grand Jury Prize for Documentary at the Sundance Film Festival (1991) and Outstanding Film (Documentary) at the GLAAD Media Awards (1992). With that said, a documentary film about queer culture was never going to break box-office records in 1990. And that was a shame, the world deserved to know about Pepper, Venus, Dorian and their friends.

However, by 1990, voguing had become a worldwide phenomenon. A chain of consequences had been set in motion twelve years earlier when a remarkably determined twenty-year-old woman called Madonna Louise Ciccone dropped out of college and moved to New York City with just $35 in her pocket. She worked with dance troupes and supplemented her income with a job at Dunkin' Donuts. And she also attended dance clubs where she learned about voguing. When Madonna released 'Like a Virgin' in 1984 she became a star overnight and, although her appearances in films were not always received enthusiastically, she produced hit after hit throughout the 1980s. In 1990, inspired by members of the House of Xtravaganza, Madonna released the pop song 'Vogue'. It was an instant hit, topping the music charts in more than thirty countries and going on to be the best-selling single of the year. The accompanying video was filmed in black and white, featuring an Art Deco set design and backing dancers who included Jose Gutierez Xtravaganza. The song's lyrics offer one of camp's key messages – with voguing viewed as a form of escapism from the pain and heartache of everyday life. I was eighteen when the song was released, and it is the one I associate most with my coming out as gay. I must have danced to it upwards of a hundred times in the decade that followed, without realising where voguing actually came from.

And that was the problem. 'Vogue' was such a huge hit that it brought a little-known aspect of an underground culture right into the mainstream, but as there was so little focus on the provenance of 'Vogue', the actual creators of voguing were side-lined. As Ricky Tucker points out, even the song lyrics didn't acknowledge voguing's origins. In the bridge of the song, Madonna names sixteen stars, many of them from Hollywood's Golden Age, including Marlene Dietrich and Bette Davis, as well as the baseball star Joe DiMaggio. Tucker highlights that 'white names and sensibilities are used as lube for the ears and sensibilities of white audiences dying to be penetrated by Black experience'.[168] Worse still, Tucker continues, apart from being married to Marilyn Monroe for a time, what on earth has Joe DiMaggio got to do with queerness or Blackness or dance or anything? He's not even run-of-the-mill glamour!

Madonna benefited from her discovery and, to be fair, she used two members of the Xtravaganza family to choreograph the dancing in her *Blonde Ambition* tour. But there were accusations of appropriation – with a straight white woman getting the credit and cash for something that had not been invented by her. Some

None of these people are Joe DiMaggio.
Some of the cast of *Paris Is Burning*.

have argued that this was more of a case of appreciation, that Madonna wanted to embrace the culture and respect it. She was certainly a strong advocate for LGBTQ+ rights during a period in American history when few other voices spoke up, and she also publicised a safe-sex message around HIV/AIDS, helping to remove stigma around talking about sex. As a queer teen, I always felt that Madonna was on my side, her image on a poster above my bed, watching my development with wry interest. I don't want to think that Madonna intended to exploit the queer people of the ballroom culture, but, sadly, they continued to be disenfranchised, with few of them truly benefiting from the world's love of voguing.

It wasn't until 2018 that Ryan Murphy's television series *Pose* brought awareness of the ball culture into the mainstream, starring Billy Porter as Pray Tell, the emcee of the Balls, Dominique

Jackson as Elektra Evangelista and Michaela Jaé Rodriguez as Mother Blanca Rodriguez-Evangelista. Murphy (whose work is discussed in more detail in Chapter 8), was inspired by *Paris Is Burning*, and based several of his characters on people who had been in the documentary. Madonna gamely gave the series the rights to use 'Vogue' and the controversy is addressed in *Pose*'s second series, with central character Mother Blanca initially saying optimistically, 'Madonna is shining a bright spotlight on us . . . Everything is changing.' And some of the characters do experience opportunities – one teaches a voguing class while another gets a modelling contract, but the series also shows 'what it feels like to be part of a disenfranchised community that gets quickly swept up in a trend and then dumped unceremoniously'.[169] *Pose* didn't aim to 'bash' Madonna but instead wanted to highlight the complexities that resulted when aspects of the ball culture went mainstream.

As far as camp is concerned, the 1980s were a difficult decade. We have gone from the death of disco to voguing in just a few years. Despite, or perhaps because of, the Conservative dominance of the era, camp became more important than ever. But we are now approaching the end of the twentieth century – I hope you've got your finest feathers on for our Millennium Party. And as we count down those final seconds it's time to pause a little, take a breath and look back. Retro-camp here we come.

CHAPTER 7

Just Little Bits of History

In my school days I had a partner-in-camp called Kathryn. It was one of those gay-boy-straight-girl friendships that we mistakenly thought was much more unique than it actually was. Aged seven, we were both super-nerds, placed on 'top table', reigning over the class in a mostly benevolent way. But the following year we were separated into different classes and lost contact. Several years later, out of the blue, I received a phone call. 'It's me,' Kathryn announced. And, just like that, we were best friends again.

We bonded over many things, none of which were popular at the time. Neither of us was 'cool', we were out of step with 1980s youth culture and too disaffected to be seen as liking anything mainstream. Then we found inspiration. During one of her phone calls in 1988 Kathryn told me, 'Come over! Look what I've found in my sister's record collection!' It was a *Reader's Digest* album box set called *The Sensational '70s*. We shrieked at how awful the music was, although I secretly quite liked the more psychedelic-inspired hits from the start of the decade and the bouncy disco ones towards the end. So, while our contemporaries were bellowing 'Acid!' and dancing mindlessly in smiley-faced T-shirts to a computerised drum rhythm, we had a camp old time laughing over the hits of yesteryear by the Bay City Rollers,

Abba, the Dooleys and the Three Degrees. This led to a series of 1970s parties where we attired ourselves in forgotten items from the back of our parents' wardrobes, covered the walls in homemade peace symbols, turned on my newly purchased lava lamp and danced the night away with a few like-minded friends. One Friday in 1989 we took one of these parties on a late-night excursion to our local town centre, posing for photos with an abandoned shopping trolley as a prop. I was wearing my dad's wedding suit from 1971 and had blow-dried my hair, then brushed it forwards into a bowl-cut. To our contemporaries, coming out of our town's only nightclub, we looked ridiculous. But that was the point.

Kathryn is my longest-standing friend. We might be middle-aged now, rather than sulky teenagers, but our love of finding camp in the past is hard to shake. During a recent visit to Kathryn and her husband, we decided to make fun of the 1980s, the era that we had absolutely no interest in when we lived through it. We bought food and drinks that were popular at the time – Babycham, Findus Crispy Pancakes and Viennetta, a chocolate ice-cream dessert. Kathryn made a 1980s music quiz and afterwards we lapsed into slightly drunken role-play, banging on about the 1984 miners' strike and Margaret Thatcher. Good times. I suspect that in twenty years we will be having parties that make fun of the 2020s.

This chapter is about the last years of the twentieth century, an unusually self-conscious and reflective period by which time camp was sufficiently recognised, even by mainstream audiences, and therefore it had fallen into short supply. To get their fix, connoisseurs of camp ransacked the past, and camp began to increasingly morph into campy – the intentional form. Not everyone got the joke, though – and, as we'll see, the film *Showgirls* is about to go down in history as one of the most misunderstood and maligned forms of camp ever. But we'll start with another way that camp's profile was raised, as a bona fide subject of academic inquiry.

ACTIVISTS MAKE CAMP, ACADEMICS BREAK CAMP

For queer people in UK, the 1990s did not get off to a great start. Years of homophobic newspaper columns by journalists like George Gale, Jean Rook, John Junor and Garry Bushell had fanned the flames of hatred, and moralising around HIV/AIDS had been rife. In 1986, George Gale wrote in the *Sunday Mirror* that 'Aids should be made a notifiable disease and buggery, almost certainly the main way of transmitting it, should once more become a criminal offence'[170] while in the *Sunday Express* John Junor wrote: 'Isn't it time the Government either stopped pretending that the fairies who started this disease, and the even filthier fairies who keep spreading it, are the fairies at the bottom of the garden.'[171] A public attitudes survey from 1987 had found that three quarters of the British public thought that homosexuality was wrong,[172] while Section 28 in 1988, which banned 'promotion of homosexuality' by local education authorities, hammered the message home.

However, the government had made a grave miscalculation. The irony of Section 28 was that it galvanised the LGBTQ+ community into fighting back, politicising large numbers of people who demonstrated against the legislation in a range of ways, from political lobbying to organised marches and creative acts of non-violent direct action. The House of Lords, the *Ideal Home* Exhibition and a live news broadcast at the BBC were subjected to shockingly camp 'invasions' by resourceful female protesters. The Shakespearian actor Ian McKellen outed himself on national radio, when he debated Section 28 with Peregrine Worsthorne, the editor of the *Sunday Telegraph* who had written a piece that referred to the 'bold and brazen, proselytising cult' of homosexuals of which many members had 'positively flaunted their aberrant sexual tastes'.[173] McKellen spoke eloquently about the dangers of Section 28, as well as helping to organise gala benefits and marches. He was also one of the co-founders of the lobbying group Stonewall, which aimed to achieve LGBTQ+ equality through dialogue with political, religious and cultural leaders. Sincere and articulate, McKellen debated with politicians in a way that was calming and disarming, and, although he had been concerned that speaking out would damage his career, he was knighted in 1991, ironically alongside Peregrine Worsthorne.

The fact that McKellen accepted his knighthood produced criticism from some quarters. The filmmaker Derek Jarman wrote an angry article in the *Guardian*, which stated: 'As a queer artist, I find it impossible to react with anything but dismay to his acceptance of this honour from a government which has stigmatized homosexuality through Section 28.'[174] Jarman said that McKellen's acceptance of the knighthood diminished him as it allowed people to argue that the Conservative government wasn't really anti-gay. Despite McKellen receiving a letter of support signed by eighteen prominent people in the arts, the decision indicated a split between those who wanted to work with the government and those who had decided to take a more combative stance. Another group, formed around the same time as Stonewall, called OutRage! protested through public stunts. For example, they held mass kiss-ins in public and handed out educational material about gay sex outside schools. They also engaged in 'outing' figures of authority who had advocated homophobic policies but were secretly gay.

One group who were more aligned with the values of OutRage! than Stonewall were the Sisters of Perpetual Indulgence. It was an organisation that had begun in America in the 1970s and involved men who dressed as nuns. The sisters used camp humour and drag to reclaim traditional notions of virtue and bring a sense of spirituality to the LGBTQ+ community. There was also a strong political intent behind the Sisters: they were one of the first groups to address HIV/AIDS, distributing information leaflets about safer sex in the Castro area of San Francisco. They also created inclusive ceremonies for LGBTQ+ people, like partnership ceremonies or house-blessings, which helped to highlight the intolerance and exclusionary practices of mainstream religious movements. In the

UK, the London branch of the Sisters of Perpetual Indulgence had heard about Jarman's disappointment at Ian McKellen's knighthood, and they decided that they would go one better, making Jarman a living saint. On 22 September 1991 they visited Jarman at his cottage in Dungeness, on the coast of Kent, and conducted a ceremony where he was canonised.

The ceremony was conducted in the 'dead' theatrical language Polari, which had been adopted by gay men and popularised in the 1960s by Julian and Sandy in the radio series *Round the Horne*. However, since then it had been subject to a mass 'forgetting' by gay communities in the UK. Concerned that Polari was being lost, its adoption by the Sisters was a way of drawing attention to queer history and was also designed to provide an exotic feel to the ceremonies, as it was reasoned that Polari was to gay men as Latin was to Catholics. The transcript of the ceremony certainly reads as camp.

> Sissies and Omies and palonies of the Gathered Faithful, we're now getting to the kernel, the nub, the very thrust of why we're gathered here today at Derek's bona bijou lattie. The reason being that Dezzie, bless his heart-face, is very dear to our heart. Look at him, his little lallies trembling with anticipation, heart of gold, feet of lead, and a knob of butter. So, perhaps we could take a little time to reach out and touch, to handle for a moment Dezzie's collective parts.

Jarman died of an AIDS-related illness in 1994, and the ceremony used camp in a way to challenge the stigma around people who were HIV+ but also, as is so often the case with camp, to mock the seriousness of the situation. Jarman's body was revered but it was also the object of ridicule, and the ceremony made him both sacred and profane. During the ceremony he was crowned with a 'bona helment on his riah' and a necklace made of cock-rings and pornographic pictures.[175] Jarman enjoyed his canonisation, viewing it as one of the happiest days of his life.[176]

Ian Lucas, one of the Sisters, published an account of the canonisation in a collection of papers on queer linguistics. His paper was one of a number published in the 1990s that indicated a burgeoning academic interest in camp. David Bergman published a book called *Camp Grounds: Style and Homosexuality* in 1993, while Moe Meyer published *The Politics and Poetics of Camp* a year later. Then, in 1999, Fabio Cleto published *Camp: Queer Aesthetics and the Performing Subject*. Many of these essays dealt with the camp canon – Oscar Wilde, seventeenth-century royalty, Liberace, John Waters films, all of which were interpreted under Queer Theory, a theory that had arisen from a new academic discipline called Queer Studies, which was designed to disrupt the view of heterosexuality as normal. Queer Theory was heavily influenced by a new form of philosophy called postmodernism (more on that later). And, my goodness, the essays in these books took camp oh so *seriously*. Andrew Ross, who had an essay in David Bergman's book, wrote that camp can be seen as a cultural economy. 'It challenged . . . legitimate definitions of taste and sexuality. But we must also remember to what extent this cultural economy was tied to the capitalist logic of development that governed the mass culture industries.'[177] Another of the Bergman essayists, Scott Long, called camp a 'moral activity', noting that it helps gay men to parody the forces of oppression.[178] Meanwhile, Moe Meyer defined camp as 'the total body of performative practices and strategies used to enact a queer identity, with enactment defined as the production of social visibility'.[179] He says camp is 'solely queer discourse'. While most of this writing about camp was self-consciously earnest, Andy Medhurst, writing about camp in 1997, was one of the few academics who took a less high-falutin' tone. He noted 'Meyer's excessive claims for camp as always-and-only-radical cannot convince anyone who has spent time among camp queens, whose turns of phrase and ideological outlook can be frighteningly reactionary'.[180]

The Queen of Queer Theory was Judith Butler, who came up with a concept called gender performativity in the early 1990s. This was the view that being born male or female doesn't determine how we behave but rather we learn the appropriate ways to perform as a man or woman by internalising the messages we get from society. Camp can occur when people do not, for whatever reason, obey those messages. Cleto's book on camp contains a reprint of one of Judith Butler's essays from her book *Gender Trouble*, which outlines gender performativity theory. Here's an excerpt, don't worry – there won't be a test later.

> The redescription of intrapsychic processes in terms of the surface politics of the body implies a corollary redescription of gender as the disciplinary production of the figures of fantasy through the play of presence and absence on the body's surface, the construction of the gendered body through a series of exclusions and denials, signifying absences.[181]

The irony, of course, is that this kind of writing style can't help but be seen as a prime example of unintentional camp in itself. And it was prose like this that won Butler first prize in a Bad Writing contest run by the journal *Philosophy and Literature* in 1998. Not everyone saw the funny side, though. The philosopher Martha Nussbaum was having none of it, claiming that Butler's ideas were thin. 'When Butler's notions are stated clearly and succinctly, one sees that, without a lot more distinctions and arguments, they don't go far, and they are not especially new.' She argues that Butler 'prefers a verbosity that causes the reader to expend so much effort in deciphering her prose that little energy is left for assessing the truth of the claim'.[182] A similar point was made, rather more forcefully, by female drag queen Holestar in 2017: 'Academia's got its place, but the thing is, it's so snooty. It's not inclusive. It's saying: "Oh, you don't understand because you've not read Judith Butler." Bollocks!'[183]

In the 1990s, as a struggling acolyte of Queer Theory, I asked one of my academic mentors why almost everyone in the field wrote in such an impenetrable way, which to my mind was something of an own goal if the whole point was to question and subvert power hierarchies. My mentor told me that the field was new and it had a bit of an inferiority complex, so the people in it were trying ever so hard to impress and be taken seriously. Maybe that held true thirty years ago, but sadly the writing style hasn't changed much since then. What we should be taking away from this, however, is that the 1990s saw camp turn into a respectable topic of academic inquiry, where it was theorised, debated, dissected and ultimately drained of fun. And, due to camp's slippery, indefinable quality, its potential to produce a lot of conference papers and thus zhoosh up the careers of academics was enormous. On the one hand, we can argue that this is a good thing, as it gives camp a wider reach. The more people who can appreciate Dolly Parton's 'Jolene' or Bobbie Gentry's 'Fancy' as camp, the better. But, on the other hand, well, it's taking something that was hugely pleasurable and making it a bit of a chore, really. Unlike my conversations with friends, whose breathless enthusiasm inspired me to seek out their favourite camp lodestones, I was never inclined to go off and find out more about the books, films and songs discussed in those academic papers. And that's a shame.

NOSTALGIA CAMP

Susan Sontag was onto something when she remarked in 'Note 30', that:

> . . . the canon of Camp can change. Time has a great deal to do with it. Time may enhance what seems simply dogged or lacking in fantasy now because we are too close to it, because it resembles too closely our own everyday

> fantasies, the fantastic nature of which we don't perceive. We are better able to enjoy a fantasy as fantasy when it is not our own.

'Note 30' appears to be specifically written for the 1990s. Fashion is sometimes viewed as having a five-stage life cycle: introduction, rise, peak, decline and obsolescence. However, I prefer Laver's Law – a view of fashion put forward by critic and museum curator James Laver, which takes the long view. In 1937, he wrote that the same costume will be Indecent ten years before its time, Shameless five years before its time, Outré (daring) one year before its time, Smart – (in the present day), Dowdy one year after its time, Hideous ten years after its time, Ridiculous twenty years after its time, Amusing thirty years after its time, Quaint 50 years after its time, Charming 70 years after its time, Romantic 100 years after its time, Beautiful 150 years after its time.[184] Laver's view of the cycle goes beyond obsolescence, then, to allow for rediscovery and reappraisal. And it is that sweet spot between Hideous and Amusing where the campest spokes on the fashion cycle are located.

In the twentieth century the wheels of fashion had been spinning like never before. People in 1900 looked very different to those in 2000 and between those years there had been so many fashion shifts that it was difficult to keep up – phrases like 'so last season' exemplified neo-liberalism's imperative to keep buying new things. And, by the 1990s, there is a sense of something – exhaustion, frustration, perhaps. The idea that it was getting harder to come up with new ideas. Even for her most ardent fans, it is a stretch to refer to Australian soap-star-turned-pop-star Kylie Minogue as a prophet, but in 1990 she captured the flavour of the coming decade with a mildly disposable pop song called 'Step Back in Time'. The song advocated a return to 'the old days' because 'nothing is new'. Camp legend Shirley Bassey also captured the retro zeitgeist. Bassey was best known for recording the theme songs to three James Bond films and, in 1997, she released a song called 'History Repeating' with the group Propellerheads. In the song's video, a 1960s jazz music programme is invaded by DJs playing scratch music and members of the television crew start spontaneously body popping while Shirley sings that she's seen it all before and it's a case of history repeating itself.

There was a feeling of finality about that decade – after all, it was the end of the millennium. There were bizarre claims that a computer bug would break the world's computers and bring about some sort of apocalypse that would result in planes falling out of the sky. It didn't. Less dramatic, though more real, was a sense of political closure. The Berlin Wall had come down and the Soviet Union had dissolved. In 1992, Francis Fukuyama wrote that history had ended, claiming that liberal democracy was the final form of human government. Since then, history has had its revenge, proving itself to be brazenly alive and full of its usual surprises (hello 9/11, Trump, Brexit, Putin and COVID), but at the turn of the millennium, there was a sense of completion. Instead of moving forward, it was time to pause awhile, and look back.

The word *nostalgia*, meaning a sentimental yearning for the past, is formed from the Greek words *nóstos* (return home) and *álgos* (pain). It is a concept that has been popular since the Romantic era, which began towards the end of the eighteenth century and was found in the neo-Gothic architecture that was inspired by the Middle Ages. Nostalgia doesn't have to be camp and, up until the 1990s, it was often simply fond. The British television programme *The Good Old Days* (1953–83) recreated the nineteenth-century Music Hall, with the entire theatre audience kitted out in period drag, while entertainers like Larry Grayson, Ken Dodd, Barbara Windsor and Eartha Kitt performed old-fashioned acts, singing half-forgotten songs that brought tears both of laughter and of nostalgia to the eye.

In recent decades, nostalgia has often centred on what was happening twenty to thirty years ago, perhaps because middle-aged people are especially interested in looking back to more hopeful times in their lives when their bodies looked and worked better. In the 1980s, I recall a lot of television programmes about how great the 1960s were – endless retrospectives about the Beatles and series like *The Rock 'n' Roll Years* (1985–94) which played music from the 1950s onwards over old news clips. The films *Back to the Future* (1985) and *Peggy Sue Got Married* (1986) had their protagonists travel back in time to 1955 and 1960, respectively, with the past represented in an idealised form – pure unironic nostalgia. These kinds of entertainment were aimed at the Baby Boomer generation (born between 1946 and 1964). I remember being shocked at seeing photos of my Boomer parents in their late teens – they were so cool. My father had shoulder-length hair and managed a pop group. He was always getting stopped by the police because the van they toured in was painted in psychedelic whiplash swirls that screamed, 'We are all on LSD!' (they weren't). My mother wore mini-skirts and even had bells in her hair for a while. Who *were* these people? And how depressing for them that their own children would never be as cool as them. It was certainly a sentiment experienced by Patsy and Edina, two heavy-drinking, fashion-obsessed middle-aged hipsters, in the camp BBC sitcom *Absolutely Fabulous* (1992–2012). Edina's teenage daughter, Saffron, was introverted, studious and much more sensible than her mother, to Edina's everlasting shame. Patsy and Edina don't just have nostalgia for the 1960s and 1970s, they never really left the era, and the two women are often shown in flashbacks to their misspent youth, where the clothes, language and attitudes were much sillier than the buttoned-down '90s.

The children of the Baby Boomers were known as Generation X (born between 1965 and 1980), and they were stereotypically portrayed as cynical and apathetic. They were defined by their love of irony, which Bruce LaBruce argued had become so widespread by this point that it was normalised and generalised into the default sensibility of the entirety of popular culture.[185] And so the last years of the 1980s represent a kind of tipping point as more people became aware of camp. For example, in 1987, the Sunday evening religious television programme *Highway* began with an extraordinary musical sequence set in a newly opened shopping mall in Ipswich called Tower Ramparts. Around thirty ordinary, middle-aged women, in their smartest clothes, performed the song 'Who Will Buy', from the musical *Oliver*. As they sang, they rode escalators and marched purposefully around the mall, using public telephones as props. At one point, one of the ladies holds up a wad of cash. The effect was wonderfully camp and the comedian Victoria Wood said it was her favourite television clip, which she watched every Christmas with her family.[186] It is a clip I love too, but I always watch it with a sense of sadness, because, after that point, it becomes harder to find such lovingly oblivious examples of camp television. *Highway* in 1987 feels like the end of High Camp, or at least the beginning of the end. And by the 1990s, awareness of camp had become so common that it was getting difficult to identify contemporary cases of unintentional camp – so many people were in on the joke that a lot of the camp output of the time was on purpose – campy, rather than camp. As we'll see later, campy shows like *Melrose Place* can be a massive source of fun, but the decade was low on proper camp.

If you can't find something around you, you have to look elsewhere. Compared to some of the earlier decades of the twentieth century, the 1990s were fairly buttoned-down, style-wise, and when Generation X looked back in time, it discovered a smorgasbord of outrageous styles. Suddenly, the entire period from World War II to 1990 was seen as a huge camp resource – with the 1970s being singled out for special attention. From my perspective, it is hard not to see the 1970s as the campest decade of them all. But did the people who lived through it view it that way at the time? I suspect most of them didn't – I was too young to know any better; the 1970s were my normal. But it certainly was a decade of excess, where unintentional camp and on-purpose campy were found in abundance and in almost equal measure. Part of this goes back to the mid-to-late 1960s psychedelic drug culture, which, as the word implies, involves changes in perceptions. People who took hallucinogens like LSD and mescalin sometimes reported seeing colours that they had never seen before and psychedelic art used surreal images, swirls, kaleidoscopes and paisley patterns along with bright and highly contrasting colours, which would act as mind-bending stimuli to those who took the drugs. By 1976, colour television sets outnumbered black-and-white ones for the first time in the UK, and programmers exploited the technological possibilities, showing viewers a funky, futuristic, fashionable new world. The word *multi-coloured* was suddenly popular – a UK Saturday morning children's series that began in 1976 was called *Multi-Coloured Swap Shop*. Music shows like *Top of the Pops* became full of saturated limes, browns, oranges and golds. Home decorating styles were equally outré, with colour-blocking or the use of contrasting colours becoming fashionable. In the 1970s, my parents' living room had a chartreuse sofa while the carpet boasted a vibrant fractal shell pattern that contained *all* the colours – I think the design was called 'mystic crystal revelations'. All of this is a long way from the fashions of the early 2020s – when I last tried to buy new kitchen units, there were lots to choose from, as long as your colour palette taste ranged from muted grey to off-white.

When I need a quick camp fix, it is always late 1960s or 1970s YouTube videos that I turn to. Something like Julie Driscoll's 'Season of the Witch' (1968) or Gwen Verdon dancing to 'Mexican Breakfast' (choreographed by Bob Fosse, and later inspiring Beyoncé) on *The Ed Sullivan Show* in 1969. That was a good year – it also gave us the Johnny Harris Orchestra performing a surreal version of 'Satisfaction' with its emotional 'Twelve Days of Christmas' crescendo on German television show *Pop Goes the Sixties*, and it's the year Dusty Springfield was trapped in a cartoon-strip room singing 'Ain't No Sun Since You've Been Gone' on her TV show, *Dusty*. Rounding off, I might watch Cliff Richard and Una Stubbs giving it their all in an energetic routine to Hank

Marvin's 'Foot Tapper', the cast of *Promises, Promises* performing the neck-breaking song 'Turkey Lurkey Time', also on *The Ed Sullivan Show* (both in 1970), or the animated version of Cher's 'Dark Lady' (1974). If I require something more sustaining, I might devote an evening to *The Marti Caine Show*, which began in 1979, or watch one of the 1970s Eurovision Song Contests. It is always difficult to decide which year has the campest material – Belgium's 'Baby Baby' (1973) by Nicole and Hugo in their sparkly black trouser suits, or 1975's philosophical 'Ding-a-dong' by Netherlands group Teach In. Or how about Fredi & The Friends with their appropriately titled 'Pump-pump' in 1976, or Germany's 1979 strange disco hit 'Dschinghis Khan' by the band of the same name? Viewing these Eurovision hits is even camper now as, in this period, audience members were restrained, rather elderly and wore full dinner suits. The contrast with the music is hilarious. It was only in the 1990s that the audiences became full of gay men who rightly loved Eurovision for its camp and danced the night away.

By the end of the 1980s, even the cultural output of a decade earlier was starting to be reinterpreted as camp. In the UK, soap operas had been popular since the 1960s, having grown out of 'kitchen-sink' dramas that were centred around working-class communities. The women in soaps like *Coronation Street* and *EastEnders* were all camp, suffering magnificently with their true grit, big hair and regional accents (all the men, by contrast, were disappointing losers). By the 1990s, soap camp had become self-aware, with comedic storylines on *Coronation Street* like sensible Ken Barlow teaching dippy barmaid Raquel how to speak French, which has become legendary ('Bonjour, Ken, je m'appelle Raquel. Voulez-vous coucher avec moi, ce soir?') When Deirdre Barlow got involved with a con man and was wrongly imprisoned for fraud, in 1998, mock outrage from fans was so marked that Prime Minister Tony Blair said that he would get the Home Secretary to look into the case, as 'anyone with eyes in their head' could see she was innocent.[187] Australian soap operas were becoming increasingly popular too – first *The Sullivans* and *Sons and Daughters*, then shows aimed at younger audiences like *Neighbours* and *Home & Away*. Then, in the late 1980s, the British television channel ITV started showing *Prisoner Cell Block H*, a soap set in a women's prison called Wentworth Detention Centre, which had run in Australia from 1979 to 1986 over 692 episodes. The original run of the programme had been viewed seriously, as a hard-hitting adult drama that dealt with topics like homosexuality, abortion, feminism and social reform. The soap regularly won Australian drama series awards and developing storylines were breathlessly covered in magazines like *The Australian Women's Weekly*, which also interviewed and profiled the actors. In praising *Prisoner* for winning TV's most popular drama series for the third year in a row, *TV Week* reported that:

> The *Prisoner* formula is a unique one which Australia has given the TV world. Other series and movies have portrayed women as appendages of men thrown into groups by suddenly losing those men, but *Prisoner* has as its base characters a group of women who are all individual people fighting for their own place in the world.[188]

Upon reading these articles I don't get the sense that the show was viewed as camp. Exciting, yes. A source of national pride even. But not camp. Yet, there was an amateurish and low-budget quality to the soap – walls occasionally wobbled,[189] overhead microphones were sometimes visible, sets were minimalist, and the prison corridors and cells were poorly lit and often indistinguishable. There was a bit of a 'school play' feel to it all, especially as Australia did not have a wide stock of actors to draw upon, so the same faces kept cropping up in different roles as the soap progressed.

Watching the first episode in 1988, aged sixteen, I laughed at how deliciously dated everyone's clothes and hair were, even though the show was just under a decade old. Some of the characters looked as if they were from the *1950s*, especially Erica Davidson, the prison governess, who had a photograph of Queen Elizabeth II on her office wall and behaved just like her, or Lizzie Birdsworth, the alcoholic old lag who had been in prison forever. The storylines were often outlandish – prisoners went on the run dressed as nuns, Nazis invaded the prison to kill a Jewish prisoner, one villain escaped by clinging onto a helicopter (although it looked as if the budget didn't stretch to a stunt double so viewers saw a dummy dressed in prison clothes lashed to the landing skids). In the first episode, pretty new prisoner Lynn Warner kept screaming that she had been falsely convicted of kidnapping and burying a baby. A tough prisoner called Bea Smith, who lorded it over the prison laundry, wasn't impressed and decided to mete out her own brand of justice, burning Lynn's hand in the steam press. It was a shocking scene of violence – even more horrifying when it transpired that Lynn *was* innocent, and the real kidnapper was the baby's own mother who nobody suspected. From that moment, I was hooked – I *had* to know if that baby was going to be OK and if Lynn would ever be exonerated.

With a largely female cast, the soap was full of Women's Film storylines, with complicated, damaged or disagreeable characters who grew on you as you watched them suffer, grow and fail week after week. Characterisation was *Prisoner*'s strength – and the central characters – Bea, Lizzie, Doreen, Judy, Rita, Erica, Meg, Vera, Joan and Ann – were legendary. There was always a sense of excitement when a new prisoner was inducted, especially if their introduction involved a backstory – how would they react to their new surroundings, and would the other prisoners befriend or harm them? The prison felt a bit like a strict girls' school at times, with the wily prisoners always trying to get one over on the warders. Even though the stories could be quite harrowing, and not all of the characters got the endings they deserved, there was a sense of communal fun in many of the scenes that was endearing. One of the campest storylines involved a 'fish-out-of-water' character, 'nice' Dr Kate Peterson, who was sentenced for killing her husband. Well spoken and polite, Kate started standing up for prisoner's rights and got caught up in prison politics. However, the writers threw in a twist and retooled her as evil. Becoming increasingly strange and imperious, in one scene she was summoned before the Governor for insubordination. During the interview, Dr Kate reprimanded Mrs Powell, one of the prison officers, for interrupting her, telling the Governor, 'I do realise that these menials are necessary for running a place of this type.' When Mrs Powell cried out, 'Menials?' in disbelief, Dr Kate boomed, '*Silence!*' at her, and then offered to help the Governor run the prison: 'I find the idea of a joint venture rather challenging.' A few episodes later, Dr Kate appeared to have gone insane, and, with comically bulging eyes and bared teeth, she tried to strangle Judy, one of the show's best-loved characters.

In the UK, the programme went out in an unfashionable weekday late-night slot, with regional stations showing it at different times. The programme was cancelled at the slightest provocation (for example, if a moderately important sports game was on). With the cards stacked against it from the start, it is impressive that it quickly acquired an intensely loyal set of British fans who revelled in its unintentional camp. It was also a case of perfect timing – the UK's favourite 'bad' soap, *Crossroads*, had been cancelled in 1988. Liverpudlians, who are known for their sharp wit and love of taking the mick, adopted the soap as their own – a local radio station regularly telephoned Sheila Florance, who played Lizzie, and in 1997 homegrown drag star Lily Savage appeared in a musical, almost adult pantomime, version of the soap. I attended a performance at the Liverpool Empire Theatre and when Maggie Kirkpatrick, who played infamous prison warder Joan 'the Freak' Ferguson came onstage, the audience screamed for about thirty-six hours (perhaps I am exaggerating slightly). Many of the original cast members embraced their new fans and I love the fact that the show had an even more fabulous second life in the 1990s – with its stars achieving the international fame that they deserved.

Caged women! Lily Savage and Maggie Kirkpatrick (playing 'the Freak') in *Prisoner Cell Block H the Musical.*

LOUNGE ACTS

Another aspect of the ironic appreciation of the past involved musical tastes. In the mid-1990s a form of music called 'lounge' became popular, having its own section in music stores for a few years. Lounge was a rebranding of the 'easy-listening' music that had been ubiquitous in the 1950s to 1970s. It was often used as incidental music, playing in the background in films and television programmes, and it evoked a glamorous world of fast cars, cocktails, exotic holidays and hip detectives dressed in Carnaby Street fashions. There was also a futuristic version used in television series like *Space 1999* (1975–7) and *Star Maidens* (1976), making use of electronic instruments. Composers like Alan Hawkshaw, Roy Budd, Quincy Jones, Keith Mansfield, Syd Dale, Bruno Nicolai and Lalo Schifrin were the gods of lounge and their compositions, which had been long-abandoned in basement music libraries, were suddenly in demand, re-released on CD compilations with exciting names like *Ultra Lounge*, *The Sound Gallery*, *Blow Up* and *The Easy Project*. *The Sound Spectrum*, one of my favourites, contains music from the gangster film *Get Carter* (1971), the blaxploitation film *Gordon's War* (1973) and the children's television programme *Catweazle* (1970–71). Some of the hipper British nightclubs started hosting 'easy' nights and, in 1997, I recall hauling my friends off to one, called Tiger Lounge, in Manchester, proudly wearing an expensive retro-style shirt.

As well as rehabilitating old music, lounge parodied the present day. In 1995, a rather glum song called 'Wonderwall' reached number two in the UK pop charts. The song's writer, Noel Gallagher, was in a rock band called Oasis, along with his brother Liam. They resided at the cooler, edgier end of 1990s Britpop culture. 'Wonderwall' played homage to the past – the title is the name of a 1968 film, as well as the instrumental soundtrack of the film released by George Harrison. The video accompanying the Oasis song is in black and white, the performers look serious or bored, nobody has bothered to put on smart clothes and the lyrics appear to be about obsessive love, and feel as if they are the result of bitter experience. Liam looks genuinely crest-fallen when he sings that he doesn't believe that anyone feels the way he does. People interpreted the song as being about Noel's girlfriend, but he later said it was about an imaginary friend who is going to save you from yourself.

However, just a few weeks after 'Wonderwall' charted, a pop star called Mike Flowers released an easy-listening cover version that eclipsed the original, revealing a lot about the tastes of Generation X and their love of camp. Flowers drew on the clean-cut styles of 1960s light entertainers, wearing a thick blond wig with a side parting and a double-breasted jacket over a colourful shirt. In his version of the song, all of its melancholy and mystery is drained away. Instead, on the song's video, Flowers smiles and croons, turning 'Wonderwall' into a whimsical ballad. He is accompanied by three female backing singers in colourful gowns and a nine-piece orchestra in dinner jackets. The song is endowed with a sense of camp fun – Flowers sways his hips and, when he sings the line about nobody feeling the way he does, he makes a pearl-clutching gesture.

By Christmas 1995, the cover version of 'Wonderwall' had reached number two in the charts and it got to number one in Scotland. Its rise to popularity was helped by the fact that Radio 1 DJ Chris Evans made the Mike Flowers Pops version his song of the week, jokingly telling his listeners that it was the original, implying that the Oasis song was the cover. To be fair, the Mike Flowers version did sound as if it was from an older time, but even when people realised the joke they still liked the camp version. The serious music press didn't appreciate the joke, though. *NME* apparently called the Flowers version 'a pile of unrelenting donkey toss' and *Melody Maker* said it was 'stupid, sniggery and entirely craven'.[190] Once again, camp showed its capacity to annoy, although, in this context, that stance appears a little off-message.

I think there came a point where the fans of irony realised that they actually liked the thing they were making fun of. There is then a kind of double-think period where something is both bad and good, until, like me, you find yourself asking your husband to bring back 'any lounge CDs you can find' when he's on a business trip to Germany because you have exhausted all the ones in the British music stores (he came up trumps with a track called 'The Blues, the Beat and All That' by Horst Jankowski). We might start off by appreciating unintentional camp with a knowing sense of superiority, but beware: it is a bit like a magic cauldron – if you stare into it for too long, it will possess you.

Another key piece of lounge music was used at the start of the 2001 film *Ghost World*, which makes a number of compelling points about art and racism while tackling the late-'90s equation: irony + nostalgia = camp. *Ghost World* is based on a comic book of the same name, published between 1993 and 1997, so the main characters represent the last of the Generation Xers, although they would be early Millennials in the film. It follows the misadventures of Enid (Thora Birch) and Rebecca (Scarlett Johansson), two teenage social outcasts who have just left high school. The pair hate everything about the world they live in, especially mainstream culture with all its inauthenticity and consumerism. The girls visit a fake 1950s diner called Wowsville, which has rap music on its jukebox. They dub it 'the Taj Mahal of fake '50s diners' and joke that it feels like they've stepped into a time-warp. In another scene, Enid attends a blues night at a bar and is repulsed by the main act, an aggressively loud all-white band who claim to be 'authentic way down in the Delta blues' and then sing about having been 'picking cotton all day long'. The (white) audience love it, and Enid and her musical mentor, Seymour (Steve Buscemi), are the only people who find the band problematic.

Enid has to retake a remedial art class and she decides to exhibit a racist advertising poster from the 1920s which features a crude caricature of a Black man, as a piece of 'found art', aiming to highlight how the present day white-washes past incidences of racism rather than acknowledging its existence. Her art teacher loves the idea and wants to give Enid a scholarship, but, when the poster is displayed, school officials find it so offensive that the scholarship is revoked and she fails the class.

Despite the film's anti-racist message, there are aspects that raise questions relating to where appropriation starts and appreciation ends. During the opening credits of the film, Enid is shown dancing in her graduation gown while watching a sequence from the 1965 Bollywood film *Gumnaam* (meaning 'Unknown', inspired by Agatha Christie's *And Then There Were None*) that she has obtained on videotape. Bollywood films often begin with spectacular dance numbers, which sometimes have absolutely nothing to do with the plot. This is the case with *Gumnaam*, where masked dancers perform to the song 'Jaan Pehechaan Ho' ('Let's Know Each Other'). It is an amazing film sequence – the song is from a genre called Indian Rock and Roll, the main dancer is wearing a gold lamé dress with frills and matching shoes, the dancing involves lots of head shaking, the choreography is wild and everyone wears a fixed smile as if they are having the *best* time. At one point, the singer is so overcome that he collapses onto the floor. *Ghost World* is spot on with the way that old Bollywood films have been interpreted as camp. Another film, *Shalimar* (1978), has another weakly integrated pre-title scene set in the garishly decorated 'Ferguson's Dance School', where the teacher tries to show her students how to do the cha-cha-cha while singing her own version in a song called 'One Two Cha Cha Cha' – which has lyrics in Hindi and English and combines disco with sitar music. It is a very busy sequence, with the teacher continuously correcting the behaviour of her pupils while an assassination is carried out in the background. Interestingly, the sequence was cut from Western releases of the film, perhaps because it would be interpreted as setting the tone as too camp. Only the assassination survives. In 1997, 'One Two Cha Cha Cha' and another song from the same film, 'Baby, Let's Dance Together', made their way onto a lounge compilation album called *Further Inflight Entertainment*. These kinds of songs are camp, for me, and there are others from that genre that would come under the same category – 'My Name is Anthony Gonsalves' from the film *Amar Akbar Anthony* (1977) or 'Disco 82' from *Khud-Daar* (1982).

Anupa Mistry, a writer born in the north of England, now based in Toronto, has described how her parents, from Gujarati labouring diasporas of colonial East Africa, would use Indian cinema as a way to maintain a link to their memories of home. As a child, Mistry hated Bollywood films *because* they were camp.

> Bollywood's mise-en-scène is permanently fixed on camp's excess. It's in the aesthetic: sudsy dialogue, elaborate plot lines, tight shots on half-parted lips glossed in frosty pink, or bushy eyebrows trembling with anger, laborious deaths, wailing mothers, and song-and-dance routines that spuriously transport a flirting couple from the bustling streets of Mumbai to a picturesque Swiss village or British countryside.

However, she gradually came to embrace the camp of Bollywood, as a flash point of connection to a mythic homeland, and as an aspect of Bollywood that was rapidly changing.[191]

If Mistry's relationship to Bollywood has been complicated, the same is doubly true for non-Indian audiences. How should *they* appraise the films? Twenty years ago, my relationship to this kind of music was more straightforward – it was camp and I loved it. Today, though, I wonder if it is appropriate to enjoy as camp the past music of a culture to which I do not belong, particularly when I see unintentional camp and someone from that culture and time period may not have. The ironic enjoyment of something as camp can come across as dismissive, even offensive. This is especially the case given the pick-and-mix, magpie approach of the late-twentieth century, which takes its pleasure where it can find it but can be too eager for the next thrill to properly engage with anything. You can imagine the conversation: 'Oh, I love "Jaan Pehechaan Ho", it's so camp. Oh, no, I mean it as a compliment. I'm not making fun of anyone's culture. But it's hilarious. Well, no, I don't know what the lyrics mean. Wait, what are you tweeting about?'

I think Susan Sontag has a point when she says that 'Camp taste is, above all, a mode of enjoyment, of appreciation – not judgement. Camp is generous. It only seems like cynicism.' But Sontag's essay is rather lacking on issues of race and culture. I would like to think that my camp appreciation of "Jaan Pehechaan Ho" was the gateway to me engaging more seriously with Bollywood films, while making me consider the ways that my experience of them is different from their original intended audience.

POSTMODERNISM WIGS OUT

Developments in entertainment technologies meant that by the 1990s it was easier to access the culture of the past and other cultures than ever before. In the 1960s and 1970s, you were much more firmly rooted in your era and culture. If you wanted to watch a television show, you looked up when it was on in a listings magazine and then you made an appointment to watch the show at that time. If you missed it, well, too bad. On 30 October 1976, my husband watched the first episode of a *Dr Who* story called 'The Deadly Assassin'. It was so thrilling that afterwards he ran upstairs and wrote it all down because he didn't want to forget any of it. But, in later decades, you could record the programme and watch it over and over. Or you could rent an old film rather than hope that one of the few television channels might decide to put it on. If you wanted to watch a Bollywood movie, some video stores could help you out. This led to a Big Idea in the 1990s – rather than come up with anything distinctly new, elements of the past could be sampled, combined and reinterpreted and that in itself would be original. Around this time academics asserted that we were no longer in a modern era but a postmodern one. Postmodernism was somewhat cynical and ironic, even to the point of nihilism; it was sceptical of the idea of 'grand narratives' and saw reality as a mental construct. Whereas 'modern' storytelling presented a coherent, clear narrative (usually with some sort of moral message), clearly defined good and bad characters and just deserts being meted out at the end, postmodern stories were non-linear and ambiguous, inviting audiences to see their own meanings and presenting complex characters who barely understood their own motivations. Postmodernism celebrates pastiche, blending genres together, borrowing from the past and referencing what has gone before. An example would be *Pulp Fiction* (1994) which is set in the present-day (for the time) 1990s and, like *Ghost World*, has characters visiting a 1950s-themed restaurant. During this sequence, gangster's wife Mia Wallace (Uma Thurman) persuades Vincent Vega (John Travolta) to compete in a 'Twist contest' with her. To the tune of Chuck Berry's 'You Never Can Tell' – a hit in 1964 – the pair perform increasingly stylised and silly retro dance moves (the twist, the Batman, the monkey, the swim) all the while looking deadly serious. There is no single storyline but a set of inter-connected stories that play out in non-linear time. Characters have long conversations that do little to advance the plot, and it is difficult to identify who is meant to be a hero or villain. Parts of the film are funny while other parts are horrific. The director, Quentin Tarantino said, 'If a million people see my movie, I hope they see a million different movies.' It sounds like hard work, and it is.

Pulp Fiction could be seen as perhaps an extreme instance of 1990s postmodern culture and, apart from that one dance sequence, there's little in it that I find camp. But there were other cases of borrowing from the past, which more straightforwardly embraced the fashion excesses of earlier decades with the intention of making audiences laugh. *The Brady Bunch Movie* (1995) was based on a popular sitcom which ran from 1969 to 1974. The show's premise was based on a blended family with six children, and its up-beat theme was sung by the cast members, whose faces appeared in a grid of squares. The family lived in a kitsch-looking two-storey house, designed by Mr Brady, with an open staircase, internal brick features and a lawn made of artificial grass. There was only one bathroom and no toilet. The show covered topics like puberty and sibling rivalry in a light-hearted manner with a liberal sprinkling of teachable moments. While I was old enough to remember watching it (an episode involving a family holiday to Hawaii and a cursed idol had scared me), I had not seen it since the 1970s. Watching the movie and hearing the theme tune again unlocked a host of early childhood memories, resulting in a strong nostalgia ache that was strangely mixed with the camp pleasure of seeing the Brady family parading around in long-dead fashions.

Squares in squares – *The Brady Bunch Movie* captures the 1990s laughing at the 1970s.

The conceit of the 1995 film is that, somehow, the Brady family, living in the 1990s, act as though they are *still* living in the early 1970s (it is not explained how or why), so a lot of the humour is based on these 'innocents abroad' who persistently misunderstand 1990s social norms and references. Eldest sister Marcia is unaware that her best friend, Noreen, is in love with her or that Guess is a clothing brand. The family, who were pretty square even by 1970s standards, are now pure out-of-place camp, with their polyester shirts, giant wing collars, flares and dated language ('out of sight!').

The film was shot on the same stage at Paramount where the original series had been made and it reworked some of the storylines from the TV series, including one where middle child Jan is jealous of popular older sister Marcia. The film was so successful that it inspired merchandising – and in 1995 I proudly wore a T-shirt that had Jan's frustrated quote 'Marcia, Marcia, Marcia' on it. Of course, viewed from the 2020s, there's a further, unintentional level of humour in the film, in that the supposedly cool 1990s with their over-sized cell phones look almost as dated as the 1970s.

Other 1960s and 1970s series that were remade as films in the 1990s and 2000s included *Charlie's Angels*, *Starsky & Hutch*, *Bewitched*, *CHiPs*, *Dukes of Hazzard*, *Get Smart*, *Mission Impossible*, *The Mod Squad* and *Scooby Doo*. Additionally, the *Austin Powers* movie series (1997–2002) featured comedian Mike Myers as a British secret agent who had been cryogenically frozen in 1967, only to be thawed out thirty years later. The movie parodied the *James Bond* film series, particularly those starring Sean Connery in the 1960s, as well as spy television series like *Department S* and its spin-off *Jason King*. Dressed in Italian boots, a silver medallion in the form of a male symbol, a high-fastening velvet suit with frilly sleeves and a jabot (a seventeenth-century piece of neckwear with ruffles), Powers is a heavily distilled set of late-1960s tropes, with catchphrases like 'Groovy, baby', 'Oh, behave!' and 'You're very shagadelic'. His promiscuity is characterised as a funny flaw, made the more comedic due to his horrible teeth. The fish-out-of-water storyline sees Powers having to resume his spying while adjusting to life in the 1990s, which is depicted as a much less flamboyant time.

Despite the nostalgic bent of these films, it's unlikely that a substantial swathe of their target audience would have been old enough to have remembered the originals the first time around. It didn't matter, though – the films played on Generation X's love of irony and the 'so-bad-it's-good' aesthetic that had been used by directors like John Waters. Of course, there were commercial gains to be made. And so this knowing, intentional type of camp was perfected for a new generation, becoming the dominant form by the end of the millennium.

It didn't even have to be overtly nostalgic, although those references to the past were often there in the camp output of the era, just disguised slightly. A fitting example of the flavour of 1990s camp is US soap opera *Melrose Place* (1992–9), which had a modern aesthetic (an electric guitar soundtrack informed audiences how they should be feeling at any given point), but was firmly rooted in the dramatic conventions of the recent past. Centred on the lives of a set of hip young adults living in an LA apartment block, each episode was initially a self-contained story with a lesson-of-the-week, but when that proved unpopular, newer, more antagonistic characters were introduced and the narrative switched to traditional soap format. A hard-nut called Amanda (Heather Locklear, fresh from playing a bitch in *Dynasty*) moved into the building, then bought it, as well as becoming boss of the advertising agency where some of the other characters worked. As Queen Bee, Amanda worked her way through almost every male character in the show, torturing underling Allison by stealing her boyfriend and getting her fired. When visiting Allison (who had been blinded in a bomb blast) in hospital, Amanda says, 'Oh my God, Allison, you're gonna want to keep this flower arrangement. You should see it. It's bigger than a Buick.' In another scene, Amanda tells one of the show's hunks, Michael, 'Count your friends, Michael. Oops, done already?' The dialogue in *Melrose Place* was like an updated version of the 1950 film *All About Eve*, with characters regularly sassing one another with their incisive character analyses or simply observing the lunacy of the plot developments.

Towards the end of its second season, *Melrose Place* got into its stride, embracing full-on over-the-top campy storylines while drawing on the films of Bette Davis for inspiration. An episode called 'All About Brooke' had new character Brooke (played by *Sex and the City*'s Kristin Davis) assume the role of manipulative Eve Harrington in *All About Eve*. A high point occurred in the series three finale, which was driven by the problems of a character called Dr Kimberly Shaw (Marcia Cross) who was presumed dead after a car accident. It turned out she'd been alive all along, and she returned during a thunderstorm, pulling off a wig to reveal a gigantic scar down the side of her head, the result of brain surgery – the electric guitar hauntingly warning of trouble ahead.

Discarded by philandering Michael, Kimberly became increasingly hostile and unstable, and the writers pushed the character into darker places. She had Matt – the nice non-effeminate gay character – beaten up; she kidnapped a baby and tried to breastfeed it. Viewers loved it – what would she do next? In later decades, exploiting mental health issues for camp humour would attract much more criticism, but back then it was fair game. Kimberly started hallucinating a man called Henry whenever she looked in a mirror – 'I'm not insane, I'm not insane, no, no, no, no, no!' she cried, collapsing to the ground (later it is revealed that

She's not a well woman. Michael (Thomas Calabro) with troubled Kimberly (Marcia Cross) in *Melrose Place*.

Henry raped her mother and Kimberly killed him – a nod to the 1964 Alfred Hitchcock film *Marnie*). While driving, she sees Henry in the rearview mirror and threatens to kill herself, telling him, 'If you die, I'm free; if I die, it doesn't matter; if we both die, good riddance.' Viewers of a certain age might have recalled similar dialogue from the film *Dangerous* (1935), where Bette Davis plays Joyce Heath, an actress who wants to divorce her husband. He refuses while they are on a car journey. Joyce threatens to crash into a tree, saying, 'If you're killed, I'll be free. If I'm killed, it really doesn't matter. If we both die, good riddance.'

Kimberly went on to provide *Melrose Place*'s most gripping cliff-hanger finale – rigging the apartment with 'four fire bombs strategically placed' and then setting them off when everyone's storylines converged upon the building. 'I just hope my insurance covers mad bombers,' Amanda quipped, making light of the fact that one of the bombs did actually kill someone. Keith Marder, in the *Times Union* wrote that 'even for Camp Campy ("Melrose"), this season has been more like a trip to Camp Craziness' and Heather Locklear was reported as saying, 'It's fun to be over the top, but we've been way over the top. I think we'll definitely try to get back a little to the original show, but not the real, real original show, next year.'[192]

This did not prove to be the case – the show had become so removed from reality that, by the end of the following season, Kimberly had become a sex addict, was running her own psychiatric institute, and was then given multiple personality disorder, assuming personalities like Betsy – a 1950s housewife – and Rita – a biker. It feels a bit like the writers of *Melrose Place* had discovered a copy of the *Diagnostic and Statistical Manual of Mental Disorders* and were working their way through it. Mental health was awkwardly used as the basis for numerous zingers. One of Kimberly's love rivals, Sydney, calls her 'kookie-bird' and 'a vicious monster with so many screws loose she could start a hardware store'. And after Kimberly was released from psychiatric hospital Sydney asked, 'How's the electroshock going? It's putting an attractive curl in your hair.'

As a result of the bomb blast, Sydney's sister Jane was paralysed for a short time and used a wheelchair. Sydney had to reluctantly look after her and in one scene she wheels her out to the beach and leaves her there – parallels to *Whatever Happened to Baby Jane?* Later in that season, Jane and Sydney think they have killed Jane's violent boyfriend, Richard, and, rather than going to the police, they bury him in a shallow grave, echoing a scene from another Bette Davis film, *Hush. . . Hush, Sweet Charlotte* (1964). At the end of the episode, Richard's hand reaches up out of the ground, paying tribute to another camp classic, the horror film *Carrie* (1976). I think it's doubtful that most of the *Melrose Place*'s eighteen- to thirty-five-year-old target audience would have been aware of these postmodern inter-textual references, or how what was essentially a form of humour that had been appreciated by gay men from a generation or two earlier was given a wide-reaching platform and proved to be a hit with younger fans.

And *Melrose Place* was immensely popular, capturing the zeitgeist, despite being viewed as something of a guilty pleasure. During OJ Simpson's trial for murder, Judge Ito requested videotapes of the show for jurors. Other shows made fun of it but also acknowledged its hypnotic power. In the sitcom *Seinfeld*, the lead character, Jerry, dated a police officer who got him to take a lie detector test regarding whether or not he watched *Melrose Place*. Hooked up to a polygraph machine, the gruff operator interrogates Jerry with a series of questions: 'Did Kimberly steal Jo's baby? Did Billy sleep with Allisons' best friend? Did Jane sleep with Michael again?' Stone-faced, Jerry initially says, 'I don't know' but at the last question he breaks, screaming, 'Yes! The stupid idiot, he left her for Kimberly, he slept with her sister, he tricked her into giving her half the business, and then she goes ahead and sleeps with him again!' Knowing that he has blown his relationship with the police officer, he grabs his coat and walks out.

The romantic-comedy film *Reality Bites* (1994) also referenced the complicated relationship that audiences had with *Melrose Place*. *Reality*

Bites could be viewed as the ultimate Generation X film, focusing on five friends who have left school and are trying to make their way in the world. In one scene Vickie (Janeane Garofalo) confides in Lelaina (Winona Ryder) about her anxiety that she might become HIV+.

> Every time I sneeze, it's like I'm four sneezes away from the hospice, and it's like it's not even happening to me. It's like I'm watching it on some crappy show like *Melrose Place* or some shit, right? And I'm the new character, I'm the HIV/AIDS character, and I live in the building and I teach everybody that it's OK to be near me, it's OK to talk to me, and then I die. And there's everybody at my funeral wearing halter tops or chokers or some shit like that.

Lelaina consoles her: 'I know . . . it's gonna be OK.' After a pause she mock-earnestly says, '*Melrose Place* is a really good show.' They both laugh. *Melrose Place* represents a breakthrough of over-the-top, self-aware camp into the mainstream, and the conversations about it in *Seinfeld* and *Reality Bites* showed how people found it addictive, but were ashamed to admit it, and how that dilemma in itself was so trivial that worrying about it was funny.

YOU DON'T KNOW HER

While the camp plot devices on *Melrose Place* were aimed at a mainstream eighteen- to thirty-five audience, and their hag movie provenance generally went unacknowledged, for cultural output aimed at gay audiences, there was a more open recognition of the antecedents of camp. The 2003 film *Die, Mommie, Die!* – based on the 1999 play of the same name – starred female impersonator Charles Busch as performing artiste Angela Arden. Busch's plays and films have both celebrated and made fun of classic film genres, particular the Woman's Film. Busch has said:

> I'm not sure what [campy] means, but I guess if my plays have elements of old movies and old-fashioned plays, and I'm this bigger-than-life star lady, that's certainly campy. I guess what I rebelled against was the notion that campy means something is so tacky or bad that it's good, and that I just didn't relate to.[193]

In *Die, Mommie, Die!* Angela Arden is reminiscent of Hollywood film stars like Joan Crawford, Bette Davis and Lana Turner, while the storyline draws heavily on psychological thrillers like *Sunset Boulevard*, *Female on the Beach* (1955), *Whatever Happened to Baby Jane?* and *Dead Ringer* (1964), making use of identical twins, murder, LSD and a gigolo. The film was aimed at a gay-friendly audience and was a hit on the LGBTQ+ film circuit, winning awards at the Miami Gay & Lesbian Film Festival and Sundance in 2003, and the Glitter Award in 2004. The film was in on the joke from the start, as was its target audience. However, there was a very different response to another film, *Showgirls* (1995), which also took inspiration from a Bette Davis vehicle but was initially a critical and commercial failure, winning a clutch of 'Worst Film' awards. Its story is a strange and puzzling one, showing the limits of the relatively sophisticated 1990s audience to 'get' camp.

Showgirls is a rags-to-riches tale of unlikeable ingénue Nomi Malone (Elizabeth Berkley) who arrives in Las Vegas with nothing but anger issues and the ability to memorise complex dance moves, and ends up as the lead in *Goddess*, the top Vegas show. Nomi's rise mirrors that of Eve in *All About Eve*, which had Margo Channing (Bette Davis) as the older jealous star who gets replaced by Eve. In *Showgirls*, Nomi replaces Cristal Connors (Gina Gershon) as top performer, after pushing her down a staircase. So, this is essentially a recycling of a 1950s film, in a much more vulgar and superficially glitzy package, replete with gratuitous violence, nudity and swearing. *All About Eve* is camp but it is also a great film, relying on sparkling dialogue and characterisation, reflecting the relatively sophisticated world of respectable Broadway theatres. Alternatively, *Showgirls* depicts Las Vegas, with its soft-core sexuality, feather headdresses and excessive hedonism – it was the first big-budget film to receive an NC-17 rating in the US.

Melrose Place and *Die, Mommie, Die!* were campy – the writers knew what they were doing and their shows were homages to the camp plots and stars of the 1950s and 1960s. The camp in *Showgirls* on the other hand was, to an extent, unintentional. It seems incredible, but it was meant to be a serious film with an important message.

Mirror, mirror... Gina Gershon and Elizabeth Berkley in the misunderstood genius of *Showgirls*.

Joe Eszterhas, who wrote the script, called *Showgirls* a morality tale, claiming, 'The movie shows that dancers in Vegas are often victimized, humiliated, used, verbally and physically raped by the men who are at the power centers of that world.'[194] Just before the film was released, its director, Paul Verhoeven wrote a companion book called *Showgirls: Portrait of a Film*, which appeared to cast the film as a social commentary: 'In my films, I hold the mirror up to life. What you see is the sex and the violence that already exists in modern societies.' The essay in the book also suggested a postmodern reading of the film: 'We cannot pin these hidden drives down . . . It is as if there is no "real" reality. There are many realities.' Perhaps, with a different script and a different director, the film could have successfully conveyed those messages. Instead, it became the thing that it tried to critique and any sense of seriousness was quashed by its over-the-top acting, bizarre dialogue and unintentional humour.

In one scene, for example, Nomi is visited by two of her old co-workers from the strip club, the Stardust. By this point she has become established in the chorus line of *Goddess*, which has semi-nude performers but is relatively tame compared to the lap-dancing at the Stardust. The scene is sentimental, with tough-nut club owner Al Torres, having watched Nomi's performance, telling her she was 'real good' and tenderly holding her face. But as he walks away, he says wistfully, 'Must be weird not having anybody cum on you.' That kind of emotional non sequitur happens all the way through the film – scenes start as touching or shocking or funny but end in completely unexpected ways. The viewer is constantly wrong-footed. This could be seen as postmodernism, along the same lines of *Pulp Fiction*, with different genres mixed together and a storyline that allows for multiple interpretations. But, at the time, audiences and critics didn't see it that way.

And oh, but the critics were savage. James Berardinelli said *Showgirls* was 'predictable and poorly-written'[195] while Todd McCarthy described it as 'harsh, graceless and quickly tiresome'.[196] Elizabeth Berkley was particularly singled out for criticism, unfairly in my opinion. In *Entertainment Weekly*, Owen Gleiberman wrote, 'As an actress, Berkley is, to put it mildly, limited . . . She has exactly two emotions: hot and bothered.'[197] Janet Maslin in the *New York Times* said that Berkley had 'the open-mouthed, vacant-eyed look of an inflatable party doll'.[198] Poor Elizabeth's career suffered – her agent dropped her and she went from big-budget features to playing supporting roles in independent films like *Roger Dodger* (2002), *Moving Malcolm* (2003) and *Tail Lights Fade* (1999), none of which I have seen.

What's sad about the reaction to *Showgirls* is that it was not immediately celebrated as unintentional camp. Perhaps it was because it was aimed at too mainstream an audience and the reviewers in the national press were too entrenched in serious film criticism to appreciate its camp appeal. Instead, there was a pile-on, which now comes across as both cruel and inane. However, as with *Mommie Dearest* before it, gradually, there was a reappraisal. One of the first signs occurred in the satirical slasher film *Scream 2* (1997), when horror film nerd and retro fan Randy Meeks is stalked by a mask-wearing serial killer who telephones him, posing the same question he asks all his victims before he kills them: 'What's your favourite scary movie?' Randy wisecracks '*Showgirls*, absolutely frightening, what's yours?' Perhaps this helps to explain why, in her 1999 book *No Logo*, Naomi Klein noted that 'trendy twenty-somethings were throwing *Showgirls* irony parties, laughing sardonically at the implausibly poor screenplay and shrieking with horror at the aerobic sexual encounters'. The film became a staple on the midnight movie circuit and generated $100 million from video rentals. By 2015, it had a well-established camp following. Berkley introduced an open-air screening of *Showgirls* at Cinespia at Hollywood Forever Cemetery to an audience of 4,000 people. Receiving a standing ovation, she spoke to the crowd: 'This is such a special night . . . This is twenty years in the making . . . Tonight is like this magical, full-circle moment where I actually didn't get to experience the sweetness of a screening with a crowd that embraced it.' She then performed one of the iconic dance moves from the film, to shrieks of undisguised joy from the audience. Poet Jeffrey Conway said that the film completes the 'Trilogy of Camp', coming after *Valley of the Dolls* and *Mommie Dearest*.[199]

It has been argued that there are hidden depths to the film, if you know where to look. In the documentary *You Don't Nomi* (2019), aspects of the film's camerawork and production design were praised – the repeated use of mirrors and repetitive structuring devices, the doubling of different characters, the expressionist background imagery, which gave clues to plot developments. Perhaps, then, the problem with *Showgirls* was that it was *too* postmodern, even for the 1990s. There were too many ways to 'read' it, and despite the clever-clever reactions of audiences, *Showgirls* pushed up against their limits. It's interesting to see how those who were involved in *Showgirls* have responded to its rehabilitation as a camp classic. Paul Verhoeven seems to be resigned to its new status: 'Maybe this kind of ritualistic cult popularity isn't what I intended, but it's like a resurrection after the crucifixion.'[200] However, Eszterhas has claimed that the film was always meant to be funny, saying, 'We went through the script line by line, and we were really laughing at some of it. I defy people to tell me that a line like, "How does it feel not to have anybody coming on you anymore" isn't meant to be funny.'[201] He's right, but that doesn't really chime with the earlier claims about *Showgirls* being a morality tale or social commentary.

George Piggford has written of how those who cannot read the camp in a performance become disoriented and frustrated, whereas those who can see the camp will also be disoriented but they will revel in and celebrate the sensation.[202] Similarly, Peaches Christ, a drag performer and filmmaker who has performed in *Showgirls* parodies says, 'You either get it or you don't. But for those of us who get it, it can become our religion.'[203] The failure of *Showgirls* in the 1990s shows that the majority of people who made up mainstream audiences and critics still did not get it. Despite postmodernism and the success of soaps like *Melrose Place*, which smuggled in camp storylines through recycling hag movie plots, the 'so-good-it's-bad' appreciation of camp was still breaking through. It had certainly expanded from its core audience of gay men to now include younger, educated members of Generation X who appreciated irony, but the camp sensibility was still out of reach to many. It reminds me of the optical illusion picture where you can simultaneously see an old woman with a huge nose or a young woman with her head turned away. Many people in the 1990s were still mostly seeing the young woman. But in our final chapter, we will see how, in the twenty-first century, increasing numbers of people finally started seeing the old woman – and laughing at her.

CHAPTER 8

She's Gone Viral

Despite having more free time than most of my contemporaries, I've always felt a pang of regret because I never had children. Fortunately, I have a sister and three sisters-in-law who have nine children between them, so there have been plenty of opportunities to assume the camp role of 'fun uncle', namely Paul Lynde playing Uncle Arthur in *Bewitched* or Rosalind Russell in *Auntie Mame*. I like to think that I've been able to inject a little glamour and humour into the impressionable minds of these young people – none of them have complained about being encouraged to watch *Whatever Happened to Baby Jane?*, *Rosemary's Baby* or *Evil Under the Sun* during extended visits. In 2001, my husband and I took our thirteen-year-old niece Rachel and her mother, Alison, on holiday to the gay resort Provincetown (we hadn't realised it was Bear Week so that was a bit of additional education). Alison is one of those fabulous women who has more than a dash of Samantha from *Sex and the City* about her. On the first night she wore a devastating low-cut red dress, causing a clutch of American queens in an open-top car to skid to a halt and scream 'Honey, I *love* what you're wearing!' Afterwards we flew from Boston to New York and spent a few days in Manhattan. We walked to the Twin Towers of the World Trade

Center and boarded a ferry to Liberty Island. A street performer was at the side of the boat entertaining the waiting passengers before the boat disembarked. For some reason, he singled out my husband and Alison. 'What a lovely couple,' he exclaimed. 'Daddy, why don't you give your wife a kiss!' It was one of those moments when it was easier to comply rather than explain that they were brother and sister. The crowd went 'Ahhh!' as they awkwardly pecked at one another and we all laughed about it afterwards. It was a gloriously bright day in late August and the world felt perfect. The whole holiday was spent making camp jokes about everyone and everything we encountered, and Rachel was an apt pupil. Twenty years later, she is an author[204] and professional makeup artist who gives tutorials in how to look like the Bride of Frankenstein, Marlene Dietrich, Marie Antoinette, Cruella de Vil and Dorothy from *The Wizard of Oz*. I like to think that I had a small part to play in the wonderful adult she has become.

Another nephew, who is a terrible tease, assumed a drag persona when he was thirteen. Jasmine was a disdainful queen who enjoyed 'reading' her older relatives. She denied her entire family entrance to her 'fabulous revue show' because none of us were cool enough. I was told that my moustache made me look like ancient Corporal Jones (Clive Dunn) in the sitcom *Dad's Army* and that my shoes were 'knock-off'. My husband was called out for wearing an 'old fisherman's hat' and having a red spot on the end of his nose, and Jasmine then nicknamed her grandmother 'Pot of Gold' due to the apparent colour of her teeth. During Rachel's wedding, Jasmine sashayed around in lipstick, a feather boa and a woman's hat, generating quiet consternation from a couple of the older male members of the family. I suspect Jasmine, who has faded from view as time has gone on, was a way for my nephew to troll the entire family in different ways. But to me it indicates how camp has a much wider reach than it did during my own childhood. It no longer feels like it is on the margins.

—

We are almost at the end of our journey, and this chapter considers camp in the first decades of the twentieth century, a period where much of the world's population is now online and connected to one another through social media. It could be argued that we are living in kinder times. There have been efforts to address long-standing inequalities, with movements like Black Lives Matter and #MeToo focused around racism and sexual harassment, respectively. At the time of writing, thirty-four countries have legalised same-sex marriage and young people in particular hold more tolerant views on a range of social issues (although those who do not live up to similar standards might find themselves publicly targeted). Some forms of humour are increasingly viewed as problematic, particularly humour that mocks identity characteristics. At the same time, the world feels more fractured than ever. The early twenty-first century has been characterised by lack of trust in authority, strongly oppositional political stances, unwillingness to compromise and a combative mode of interaction, often played out on social media with unwavering zeal and sincerity.

These factors suggest that the early twenty-first century is a complicated environment for camp. Indeed, in 1996, Daniel Harris proclaimed the death of camp, writing that as forces of social stigma dissipate, camp begins to lose shape. He viewed camp as inextricably linked to oppression and argued that, once homosexuality began to become more widely accepted, the death of one would necessitate the death of the other. As earlier chapters have indicated, LGBTQ+ people had taken pleasure in camp, which was a form of both escapism and political protest. With increased acceptance and liberation, is camp now surplus to requirements? Or has it now become so mainstream that its impact is diluted and increasingly tedious? Can we even be camp, in a world where a bitchy comment, intended to be funny, might be seen as a micro-aggression and earn opprobrium from masses of people who have never met you. This is going to be a very tricky final chapter.

SHE IS DARK-SIDED TOO!

At the start of the 2000s, a new form of entertainment became dominant – reality television. It was a cost-efficient and often callous way of producing content – simply point a camera at a bunch of people and see what happens. One of the first of this genre, *Big Brother* was premised on a gameshow format – put people in a house, cut them off from the outside world and have one of them voted out each week (either by viewers or fellow contestants) until only one is left and wins a cash prize. Although the premise echoes Agatha Christie's *And Then There Were None*, the show's title was named after the malevolent leader in George Orwell's fictional dystopian novel, *1984*. In the book, Big Brother was an invented figurehead, designed to keep citizens in check in a society that was brutally controlled by a tiny elite. In *1984*, many words meant their opposite – the Ministry of Truth peddled propaganda whereas the Ministry of Love was where dissidents were tortured. It is fitting, then, that the term 'reality TV' is also disingenuous – this was reality in a sense that situations were manipulated by television producers, while events were heavily edited so that any contestant could be cast as a villain, victim or hero depending on the narrative that the producers thought would garner the most controversy and highest viewing figures. In later versions of reality television, the gameshow format was dropped and, in programmes like *The Real Housewives* series and *The Only Way Is Essex*, the cameras simply followed around a troupe of camp people, who, to an extent, role-played situations that had been suggested to them by the programme makers. Even some of the dialogue on reality TV felt inspired by traditional soaps. In 2010, during season twelve of the American version of *Big Brother*, a gay contestant called Regan riffed on Amanda's bitchy line from *Melrose Place* I quoted in the previous chapter, asking one of his rivals, 'How many people high-fived you, Rachel? Done counting already?'

The format had enormous potential to capture unintentional camp, as ordinary, non-media-savvy people from relatively sheltered environments were lured onto these shows, believing the promises of fame and fortune. There was usually over-subscription in terms of volunteers, so producers were able to hand-select people who were most likely to do something outrageous. Many of these programmes usually featured one gay man, a casting choice that was framed as inclusive and therefore progressive, although the kinds of gay men that were selected were often entertainingly camp and unlikely to present any sort of sexual threat to other contestants. And just having one gay contestant rendered them asexual – they couldn't pair off, unlike the heterosexual contestants. Camp reality show stars were popular among audiences – the winner of the second series of *Big Brother* (UK) was Brian Dowling, a self-described 'trolly dolly' (flight attendant), while in series seven, a contestant called Nikki Grahame gained something of a cult following due to her dramatic outbursts, complaining to the producers about a fellow contestant: 'Who *is* she? Who *is* she? Who *is* she? Where did you find her?'

In the US, a reality show called *Trading Spouses* used a formula that involved married couples swapping partners (not sexually) for a short period. Often, sets of couples with different lifestyles or belief systems were matched up. In 2005, a devout Christian, Marguerite Perrin from Louisiana, switched places with a New Age humanist, Jeanne D'Amico Flisher. Marguerite did not have a good experience with her new family, having difficulty with their beliefs and becoming increasingly erratic. Meanwhile, Jeanne had attempted hypnotherapy on Marguerite's eldest daughter, Ashley, who wanted to lose weight.

During the final scenes of the programme, the women were united with their own families. The Perrin family were shown excitedly waiting for Marguerite, eager to present her with gifts on her return. But the reunion took an unexpected and highly camp turn as Marguerite tearfully went into a five-minute meltdown, believing that her family had been exposed to pagan beliefs in her absence. The reality television format was geared to produce these moments – the more people are placed under stress and try to keep it together, the bigger the explosion will be when they can finally bear no more. As a horror-film soundtrack played, Marguerite performed a rant that was both shocking and hilarious, describing her experience with the D'Amico Flisher family as the 'worst time of my life'. She then called it 'dark-sided' and screamed, 'It's not of God! It's not Christians! . . . She's tampered in dark-sided stuff! Yes! Yes! She did! The entire house is dark-sided. She is dark-sided *too!*' Marguerite appeared to be working herself up into a frenzy, ripping up Jeanne's letter, which allocated the reward of $50,000 to the family, screaming 'I want *nothing*, I want God and my family. This is tainted, I don't want it . . . I give it up to God. I'm a God Warrior. And I don't want anyone with tainted *anything* and beliefs doing anything with my family!' She recited a litany of the beliefs of her host family: 'Gargoyles, psychics, everything's ungodly! . . . they only believe in the moon and the gods and the this and the that! . . . Astrology! Tarot card readings!' Marguerite then turned on the camera crew, ordering them to leave: 'Every dark-sided person get outta my house, if you believe in Jesus you can stay here.' During this extraordinary tirade, Marguerite's family looked on in horrified silence. Gradually, she appeared to calm down, although she continued to relay her opinions and experiences as the camera crept out of the house and then pointed upwards to focus on the moon – one of Marguerite's most hated symbols. An angelic chorus then played, and subtitles noted how Jeanne had allocated the money to the family (including $20,000 for Marguerite to have gastric bypass surgery), with the final sentence revealing, 'Upon further review, Marguerite has decided to accept the money.' The music ended with a terrifying, cynical, low chord.

The sequence is endlessly watchable. Overnight, Marguerite became notorious, with people posting videos of themselves online, miming to her monologue, or mixing her speech to music.

Marguerite described how, when the Perrin family watched their 'Psycho Mom' on television, they cried. 'It was very sad for the world not to see Marguerite Perrin happy because my friends and family know me like that.'[205] Marguerite's unusual phrasings took on a life of their own, with people phoning her house to scream 'God Warrior' and 'gargoyles' at her. She appeared on T-shirts, bracelet charms, bumper stickers, magnets and pins. Marguerite was the subject of global ridicule, but then she experienced something rare and fascinating – that moment when someone sees themself through the eyes of others, realises that they are camp, and finds it funny. Marguerite told *Esquire*, 'I can see how people felt the way they felt. I get it. I totally get it.'[206] She also defended her host family, claiming that she liked them and everyone on the show had been edited badly. When someone created a bobblehead doll of her and it was auctioned on eBay, she unsuccessfully put in a $70 bid for it. She then appeared on *The Tonight Show with Jay Leno*, who presented her with the bobblehead doll as a surprise gift. She even returned to *Trading Spouses* for a second go.

However, life took a tragic turn and, in 2007, Marguerite's daughter, Ashley, died in a car accident. Marguerite was devastated, unable to leave her bed, and none of her friends were able to get through to her.

And then something amazing happened. Members of the gay community, who had been the most appreciative of Marguerite's camp meltdown, reached out to her, sending notes of condolence and flowers in a genuine expression of love and concern. Considering Marguerite's strongly religious views, it might be assumed that she would not want any association with gay people, let alone be seen as a gay icon. But this was not so. Marguerite said that her gay fans:

> . . . weren't scared to talk about me losing Ashley and saying I'm sorry to hear about that . . . I was pretending like I was happy and I was OK. They would not leave me alone.

> You couldn't help but talk to them and be OK with them. The people that write those little memes and do those little things, I love that. That's what got me out of bed after Ashley's death.

In 2019, after visiting a church in New York, Marguerite was spotted by a group of gay men who introduced themselves. They hugged her and offered their condolences. Marguerite was later photographed waving a rainbow flag, posing with other people who were celebrating Pride, telling a fan, 'Never stop being true to yourself, and never stop screaming.'[207]

Of all of the individual stories in our story of camp, the God Warrior most emphatically illustrates its potential to surprise, to subvert the narrative, and to bring out the good in people – when camp is part of a journey of self-discovery it is truly a beautiful thing.

LEAVE BRITNEY ALONE!

In 1997, Daniel Harris had warned that reverence of celebrities would give way to ridicule, and this prediction was to become more prescient than ever in the 2000s, as magazines like *Heat* and bloggers like Perez Hilton made mincemeat of their stars, particularly young women, whose bodies were subjected to scrutiny like never before. There was a toxic atmosphere around celebrity 'gossip', and, as the bad-girl protagonist Lace in the 1975 exploitation film *Switchblade Sisters* warns, 'It's gonna turn out baaaaaad!'

So now I would like to introduce you to a twenty-six-year-old pop star called Britney Spears, who, in November 2007, was not having a good time. Spears had been dancing since the age of three and was known for her energetic, sexualised moves that had propelled her to stardom. However, recently, life had been tough for Britney – she had been photographed driving with her son on her lap rather than in a car seat, she had started divorce proceedings and her aunt Sandra had died of ovarian cancer. There were signs that she was going through a mental health crisis – she had rather publicly shaved her head and had spent time in a drug rehabilitation facility. It felt as if Britney was following a well-established camp narrative, of the beautiful, talented young star who gets messed up by the entertainment industry, following in the uncertain footsteps of Judy Garland before her. Was Britney going to be the latest in a long line of troubled female stars to get lost forever in the Valley of the Dolls?

It was not, perhaps, a well-thought-out plan for Britney to perform live, in front of millions, at the 2007 MTV Video Music Awards. It was supposed to be a comeback (I hate that word, it's *return!*) but just before the performance she was in a state of panic, crying backstage, aware that she had not rehearsed enough, and unhappy with the way her hair and body looked. The performance was not one of her best. It is not a complete disaster, but she looks uneasy, even distracted, her moves are sluggish at times, her lip-syncing is off and the energy and precision she was known for are missing. It's a bit on the amateurish side, but, considering the circumstances, it's amazing she got through it at all.

Predictably, the press crucified her. The *New York Post* called her performance 'totally lame, pathetically lip-synched', while the *New York Times* said, 'she was awful. Visibly nervous, she tottered around the stage'. Most cruelly, Spears's body was mocked, with ABC News claiming, 'those abs of yore are now just a memory', the *New York Post* writing that 'she jiggled like jello' and *E-Online* questioning 'her decision to flaunt her semi-gelatinous middle in a black sequined bra-and-panty number'. Body shaming of women was de rigueur in the 2000s, so this was nothing we hadn't seen before. But then, suddenly, one young person's camp sensibility gave this narrative a surprising turn.

Cara Cunningham (who recently transitioned) lived with her grandparents in Tennessee. She had been home-schooled after years of bullying and online she posted videos about a range of topics, under the name Chris Crocker. Sometimes she performed as Earl Annie Edna, a parody of an obnoxious talk-show host. Cara *loved* Britney and viewed the media pile-on with increasing horror. There were even online suicide countdowns. Suddenly, something snapped inside.

In close-up, with a blanket as a backdrop, wearing black eye-liner and with her hair dyed blonde, Cara gave a heartfelt monologue addressing those who had attacked Britney. She described Britney's recent woes, noting that she was making journalists money so it was unprofessional to publicly bash someone when they are going through a hard time. As Cara continued to speak, she became increasingly agitated and emotional. The monologue ended with the following anguished words: 'Leave Britney *alone*. Please! Leave Britney Spears alone! Right *now!* I mean it! Anyone that has a problem with her, you deal with me, because she is not well right now.' It was not a restrained plea. Cara screams with rage and there are several points when she is so overcome that she breaks down in tears. It was a raw, ugly speech and Cara looks into the camera so it appears that she is directly berating the viewer. If you turned the sound down you might guess that Cara was reacting to a news report of impending nuclear war. The effect was both disturbing and unintentionally hilarious. Cara posted it to her YouTube account.

'Leave Britney Alone' went viral almost immediately, being interpreted as camp due to Cara's sincere but over-the-top delivery. There were also the grandiose aspects of the rant, which made Cara appear delusional – when she said, 'anyone that has a problem with her, you deal with me' – it seemed unlikely that Cara would be able to defend Britney against her many detractors, including major media outlets. Even the statement 'she is not well right now' could be read as an observation about Cara, as opposed to Britney.

The reaction to 'Leave Britney Alone' was as immense and cruel as the reaction to Britney's MTV Awards performance, overshadowing the attention that Britney had been receiving. Cara became famous overnight, was made fun of on late-night talk shows and parodied on the animation show *South Park*. Fox News compared the fabric backdrop in the video to one used in terrorist Osama bin Laden's videos, upping the camp stakes considerably. On numerous occasions, Cara was attacked, both online by anonymous sources and also physically, with one man waiting for two hours outside a bar to beat Cara up, calling her 'an embarrassment to the community'.[208] The mark Cara left on the queer community was so significant that, ten years later, on an episode of the sitcom *Will & Grace*, Will performs a lip-sync to 'Leave Britney Alone' in a contest in a gay bar.

'Leave Britney Alone' is an example of what author Michael Strangelove calls 'Camp 2.0'.

> The old camp performers of the mid-Twentieth century saw themselves as performers, and they weren't in the business of revealing themselves and engaging in the audience. The medium of the Internet is changing identity politics. Chris Crocker gets wrapped up in all of this and is significant in this new early wave of performing and emoting.[209]

From this point on, *anyone* could potentially achieve fame through camp. You no longer needed to be a movie star or recording artist. All you needed was a camera and an internet connection. In a world where everyone can project their voice online, the messages that get heard are going to be the ones that stand out. Perhaps they are more insightful than others, or the speaker might be distressingly beautiful, or the message itself might be an extreme example of unintentional camp. Many of us perform versions of ourselves online, we turn up the volume in numerous ways, we exaggerate our emotions and over-state our opinions. We communicate in soundbites and a lot of the time we appear to be utterly sincere and committed to our beliefs. All of these things are the base ingredients for camp and the internet's plethora of voices means that hyperbole is rewarded with attention. Those tweets where people put a 👏 handclap 👏 emoji 👏 between 👏 each 👏 word 👏 are camp. When people write 'I am shook' or 'screaming, crying, shitting, rolling on the floor' or 'this gives me life' they are being camp. If camp is exaggerated sincerity that fails, then you will find it in abundance online as people compete to have their voices heard.

Although Cara was widely ridiculed for her video, it could be argued that she was ahead of her time. She told *NPR*, 'If people just read the transcript and didn't pay attention to how I looked or that I was screaming and just read what I said, there's nothing comical about it.'[210] And in the years that followed there began to be a much-needed shift in attitudes, with more people questioning the ways that young women are treated, both in the entertainment industry and in news reporting. Looking back, Cara was right – the treatment of Spears was a disgrace, shining a harsh spotlight back on a cruel society. Additionally, since then, it is less likely that people who sound or look trans, non-binary or androgynous would be laughed at as camp. Unless such people are trying to be funny, there are now a clearer set of limits around how we respond to unintentional camp. We are not laughing *at* so much. But are we laughing *with?*

IT'S ACTUALLY CERULEAN

The mid-2000s saw some aspects of camp on safer ground, thanks to the inspirational over-achievements of one Anna Wintour, a fashion journalist who took over editorship of London *Vogue* in 1985, and then moved to US *Vogue* a few years later. Her somewhat uncompromising and authoritarian management style had earned her the nickname 'Nuclear Wintour', and in 2003 a former personal assistant, Lauren Weisberger, wrote a roman à clef novel called *The Devil Wears Prada*, which focused on Andrea (Andy) Sachs, an idealistic journalist who becomes junior assistant to Miranda Priestly, the editor-in-chief of the fictional magazine *Runway*. A film version of the book came out in 2006, with Meryl Streep starring as Miranda.

Streep's performance is divine – she plays Miranda as Versailles royalty – impatient, bored, imperious, reeling off lists of intricate demands that are largely impossible to fulfil, let alone memorise, without pausing for breath and capped off with, 'That's all.' Miranda's sarcastic ripostes cross the line from workplace banter to Human Resources intervention: 'Details of your incompetence do not interest me'; 'Please, bore someone else with your questions'; 'By all means, move at a glacial pace. You know how that *thrills* me.'

As the fish out of water, we are given the outsider perspective through the eyes of Andy (Anne Hathaway), feeling her panic and frustration as she is forced to compromise her values in order to

Deal with it. Miranda Priestly (Meryl Streep) and assistant Andy Sachs (Anne Hathaway) in *The Devil Wears Prada*.

keep working for Miranda – a job that holds the promise of leading to better things. In the film's most iconic scene, the High Priestesses of *Runway* agonise over which of two near-identical belts they should use in a photoshoot and Andy commits the sackable offence of laughing at them. This causes Miranda to give Andy a dressing-down of mammoth proportions, along with a lesson in how fashion works. She picks on Andy's 'lumpy blue sweater' and tells her that it's actually *cerulean*, a colour which was used in 2002 by Oscar de la Renta, and was then picked up by eight different designers, after which it trickled down to department stores and then the clearance bin that Andy fished it out of.

> That blue represents millions of dollars of countless jobs, and it's sort of comical how you think that you've made a choice that exempts you from the fashion industry, when, in fact, you're wearing a sweater that was selected for you by the people in this room . . . from a pile of 'stuff'.

Runway's art director, Nigel Kipling (Stanley Tucci), is one of the most brainwashed employees of *Runway*, swanning about as if he's curing cancer while reminding Andy that she's working for a multi-million-dollar industry. Andy is suitably chastened and gradually gives in to the cult of fashion, becoming the best-dressed employee ever. However, by the end she realises that she is unable to follow Miranda's instinct for cut-throat decision-making and gives it all up. It is a happy ending of sorts, although Andy loses her boyfriend, Nate (Adrian Grenier), who didn't like the way that the job took over her life.

While it could be mistaken as a romantic comedy, the film's heart is much darker, and there is an ambivalence about the undertaking. The world of *Runway* is represented as tantalising, glamorous and an important cog in a system that encourages people to keep buying stuff, even if they don't strictly need to. In one scene, Nigel tells Andy how the magazine was a 'shining beacon of hope' for him as 'a young boy growing up in Rhode Island with six brothers, pretending to go to soccer practice when he was actually at sewing class and reading *Runway* at night under the covers with a flashlight'. However, at other times, the workplace culture of *Runway* is shown to be problematic – the backstabbing and lack of basic civility, the vicious fat-shaming – despite being a healthy weight, Andy is called fat by her colleagues, including Miranda, and she is pressurised by Nigel, the most sympathetic *Runway* minion, into changing her lunch choices. The film's ambiguity has even resulted in a kind of rehabilitation of Miranda. In 2018, Harling Ross wrote that Andy's boyfriend, Nate Cooper, was the worst part of *The Devil Wears Prada*,[211] while in 2019 Asmita claimed that Nate was the 'real villain', citing his lack of support towards Andy.[212] Diandra Malivindi of *Elle* Australia went one further and actually viewed Andy as the villain of *The Devil Wears Prada*, pointing out her 'high-horse mentality' and 'sense of entitlement'.[213] Jonathan Norcross notes that Miranda could never have obtained her position without making difficult choices, such as betraying someone you care about.[214] Having worked for a range of bosses over the years, the 'it's a high-pressure job' excuse doesn't cut it with me – Miranda is definitely the devil. She's hilarious. But she's evil. Of course, there's something camp in reappraising *Devil Wears Prada* so that the heroes are seen as villains, even if it comes off as a little on the nihilistic side.

A softer-centred take on high fashion was found with *Ugly Betty*, a US television series which ran from 2006 to 2010. It was a remake of a Colombian series *Yo soy Betty, la fea* (I am Betty, the ugly one), which had aired from 1999 to 2001. *Betty, la fea* was a telenovela – a serial drama similar to soap operas. However, telenovelas tend to run over the course of six to twelve months and usually tell a single self-contained story, rather than having numerous open-ended intertwining plots. Because they have a planned beginning, middle and end, telenovelas tend to be faster-paced than soap operas, resulting in an arguably even more dramatic style, with storylines

In the eye of the beholder. America Ferrera as Ugly Betty.

borrowed from fairy tales (mistaken parentage, the Cinderella character). In other words, telenovelas are prime material for camp. *Betty, la fea* was a Cinderella comedy, with the titular Betty becoming secretary to Armando Mendoza, a wealthy, handsome playboy who is president of a clothing company, Eco Moda. The American version was one of more than a dozen remakes that had been shown in other countries, and it aimed to stay true to its telenovela roots, casting a young American woman, America Ferrera, as Betty. Ferrera's parents were from Honduras in Central America, and Betty was a Mexican-American woman from Queens, New York, whose father had settled in the US without legal paperwork. The series was developed by a first-generation Cuban-American, Silvio Horta, and one of its executive producers was the Mexican-American actress Salma Hayek, who also played roles in the series, and had become famous after appearing in a Mexican telenovela called *Teresa*.

The American version has a lot in common with the original Colombian series. Betty is still the sweet naïve new girl, now working at a fashion magazine called *Mode*, where a new boss, hunky Daniel Meade, has been installed as editor-in-chief. Betty wears braces, spectacles and frumpy clothes that are the antithesis of *Mode*. However, unlike the telenovela, Betty's ethnicity is played as camp. In the first series, Betty's family often have a super-campy telenovela playing on their television in the background, a recursive nod to the show's origins. And on her first day at *Mode* Betty shows up wearing a bright-red poncho, emblazoned with the word 'Guadalajara' (the name of a Mexican city) on it, thinking she will fit in as she had observed one of *Mode*'s models wearing a poncho earlier. Amanda, a conventionally pretty, bitchy receptionist, who is Betty's opposite in every sense of the word, greets her with, 'Oh. My. God. Hi, are you the before? The before and after? The photoshoot?' Betty is non-plussed, so Amanda asks, 'Are you de-liv-er-ing some-thing?' enunciating each syllable separately, as if talking to someone who can't speak English, then asks, 'Where do *you* come from?' Later, Amanda gives Betty fashion advice, 'You may want to take the Betty-wear down just a notch. The human piñata look may be all the rage in Queens, but in SoHo they'll arrest you for crimes against humanity.' These sequences demonstrate this era's complex relationship with camp and inclusivity. Betty's culture is mined for its camp – the audience is led to laugh at her poncho, but when Amanda openly mocks her, we are reminded how racist such attitudes are.

Gradually, as the soap progresses, Betty loses her braces and embraces a geek chic style. Compared to *Devil Wears Prada*, *Ugly Betty* is kinder, although this is perhaps because its longer running time enables its characters to lose their sharp edges. The camp is on the surface – in the quips of the *Mode* employees, the outrageous clothes, the discrepancy in the set design between Betty's kitsch family home and the austere, futuristically styled *Mode* offices, and the mocking of the telenovela genre. But look deeper and the show has a lot to say about gender, ethnicity, sexuality and social class. The characters do a lot of growing and learning over the course of the four seasons. Betty's sister, Hilda, offers a different 'flavour' of Latina camp – representing a sexy 'spitfire', wearing tight clothes, with big hair and lots of makeup. But Hilda is an updated version of the camp Latina, typified by women like Lupe Vélez and Carmen Miranda. She is not a stereotype – her defining characteristic being her commitment to her family and love of her teenage son; when he comes out as gay, Hilda has nothing but love for him.

In the years that followed *Ugly Betty*, mainstream US television drama increasingly embraced camp. Ryan Murphy's musical comedy-drama series *Glee* (2009–15) was based around a show choir at a high school, while his anthology series *American Horror Story* (starting in 2011) made use of a repertory cast who played different characters in each season. Other Murphy series with high camp content included *Scream Queens* (2015–16), *Pose* (2018–21), *The Politician* (2019–20), *Feud* (from 2017), *American Crime Story* (from 2016) and *Ratched* (from 2020). Murphy's shows demonstrate a strong respect for camp history with many of them paying homage to cultural touchstones, including some rare gems. For example, the eighth series of *American Horror Story – Apocalypse* (2018) – stars Joan Collins playing a rich actress called Bubbles McGee. In a flashback, Bubbles is shown acting in a terrible horror film called *A Christmas to Dismember* where she plays a character who kills her husband and is then herself terrorised by a serial killer dressed as Santa Claus. However, this is based on a real film called *Tales from the Crypt* (1972) where Joan Collins played exactly the same character in the same storyline. And in another scene in *American Horror Story*, Joan's character berates her maid for burning the champagne by leaving it in the freezer – a nod to Joan's stint on *Dynasty* where burnt champagne was the ultimate faux pas.

Other series by Murphy are based on real-life characters – *Feud* focuses on the relationship between Bette Davis and Joan Crawford, while *Pose* is set in the 1980s/'90s Harlem ball scene. These series have a camp sensibility, larger-than-life characters, plenty of queer visibility, snappy dialogue and over-the-top situations. As with *Ugly Betty*, the camp is seamlessly integrated into dramatic storytelling that often has a social conscience. For example, the second series of *American Horror Story – Asylum* (2012) – is set in a mental institution in 1964. One of the main arcs of the story involves a journalist, Lana Winters, who wants to expose the mistreatment of inmates at the asylum. However, Sister Jude, the nun who runs the asylum, finds out that Lana is a lesbian and has her committed, where she undergoes aversion therapy. The show was praised for highlighting the violence that LGBTQ+ people experienced, and continue to experience, under the guise of medical treatment. However, other aspects of *AHS: Asylum* involved alien abduction, Nazi experiments and a serial killer who dresses as Santa Claus (what is it with all the killer Santa Clauses?) In one memorable episode, Sister Jude, who has become a patient in her own asylum, and is heavily sedated, hallucinates a performance of the jolly 1964 song 'The Name Game', a hit for Shirley Ellis. Amid a series that is bloody and grim, it is an oddly light-hearted, if surreal, moment. One understanding of camp is that it is all style over substance – a colourful package, adorned with ribbons and bows but with nothing inside. However, as we have seen throughout this book, camp has always had the potential to be more than this, to make political statements, to provoke thought, to encourage social change. One of the defining aspects of early twenty-first-century camp is the way that the package increasingly contains matters of importance.

When researching this part of the book, I expected that Murphy would be able to provide a wealth of celebratory quotes about the value of camp, both to his own work and to society more generally. However, in an interview Murphy gave for the *New Yorker* in 2018, I was slightly staggered to read that he *hates* the word camp, viewing it as a lazy catch-all that is used to marginalise gay artists and their ambitions, so they are framed as niche. His understanding of camp seems to be based on its meaning as the accident you can't look away from and he argues that it is not a term used to describe a melodrama made by a straight man. Even when camp is used as a compliment, he sees it as containing an insult, suggesting smallness. Instead, he prefers the term *baroque* which means big.[215] To me, Murphy's work *is* a celebration of camp and he has played an enormous role in making it a mainstream mode of entertainment. My take is that we should acknowledge camp's importance in the history of queer identity and protest rather than let detractors define what it stands for. Still, Murphy's dislike of the word camp is a twist worthy of one of his shows, and an indication of the complicated relationship that some gay men continue to have with it.

START YOUR ENGINES

Another chief reason for camp's high profile in the twenty-first century is a statuesque (six-foot-three) drag queen called RuPaul Andre Charles. One of her catchphrases is, 'You better work!' – a sentiment that she has embodied for decades with a CV that stretches back into the mists of time. However, her breakthrough came in 2009 when she produced and hosted the television series *RuPaul's Drag Race*, which has since won a bouquet of Emmys, numerous plaudits and extremely healthy viewing figures. Appearing first on the niche channel Logo, which targeted LGBTQ+ audiences, in 2017 the show moved to VH1, making it available to ninety million homes in the US. The show has been franchised, with spin-off versions in Canada, New Zealand, Australia, UK, the Netherlands, Israel, Italy, the Philippines, Sweden, Thailand, France and Spain.

Drag Race employs a format that has been used successfully in numerous reality shows like *America's Next Top Model*, *The Apprentice* and *The Great British Bake Off*. In each episode contestants are given a different challenge, such as performing in a musical, talent show, gameshow, film or advert. Other challenges involve the contestants displaying their makeup, design or sewing skills, or telling jokes as part of a comedy roast or stand-up routine. Contestants also take part in a runway challenge, wearing an outfit they have designed themselves. This part of the show is an homage to the Harlem ball scene, with RuPaul choosing a different category for each episode (JetSet Eleganza, Ugliest Dress Ever, Baby Drag Realness, etc.). At the end of the episode, a panel of judges pick a winner and a pair of losers, who then have to battle it out to remain in the game. Usually, the losing contestants have to 'lip-sync for their lives', performing a dance routine while mouthing lyrics to a song, usually by a female vocalist.

Drag Race is suffused in a warm pink glow of camp and RuPaul acknowledges the influences of the ball scene in Harlem. In one mini-challenge, contestants are informed that 'the library is now open' and are required to put on a ridiculous pair of glasses to 'read' each other, with RuPaul reminding them that 'in the great tradition of *Paris Is Burning*, reading is *fundamental*'. Reading involves the contestants insulting one another, although this must be done in a way that evokes humour rather than simply being savage.

Like *Melrose Place* in the previous chapter, there is humour to be found in people's secret enjoyment of *Drag Race*. On the long-running US comedy show *Saturday Night Live* in 2017, a sketch had macho mechanics admitting they loved *Drag Race* and engaging in a dance-off. While *Melrose Place* was secretly enjoyed by the Gen X girls in *Reality Bites* or urbanites like Jerry Seinfeld, for *Drag Race* the secret fans are butch, working-class straight men. The appeal of *RuPaul's Drag Race* is phenomenal, stretching well beyond the expected target audience of gay men, and is an indication that camp humour has become mainstream. No wonder then that RuPaul's DragCon, the trade fair of drag culture, is particularly popular with young women and girls. In 2017, there were 40,000 attendees at the LA convention, which had a children's area. My old school friend Kathryn told me, 'After all these years, *finally*, I have something to talk about with the women who cut my hair!' If anyone has made camp mainstream, it is RuPaul.

RuPaul has viewed drag as making fun of everything, as a way of mocking gender, to remind people and culture to not take itself seriously[216] – a view that echoes one of the key aspects of a camp sensibility, certainly for much of the twentieth century. However, RuPaul's vision for *Drag Race* has sometimes clashed with twenty-first-century social justice movements that foreground notions of equality and inclusion and are sometimes expressed in ways that are straightforwardly serious and, particularly on social media, can appear decidedly earnest or even confrontational.

One area where this has happened relates to the ways that trans people are talked about. In recent years, the media had often taken a mocking stance with journalists regularly making jokes about their appearance or sexual organs. Terms like *tranny*, *she-male* and *gender-bender* had been used pejoratively, and trans people had tended to be represented as militant, as receiving special treatment lest they be offended, as victims or villains, or involved in transient relationships or sex scandals.[217] In 2014, *RuPaul's Drag Race* featured a mini-challenge called 'Female or She-male', which involved contestants having to identify whether someone was a 'biological' or 'psychological' woman. The term *she-male* had also been used as a pun on the word email in a regular catchphrase on the show, 'You've got she-mail.' The term was criticised and RuPaul was quoted as saying, 'Don't you dare tell me what I can do or what I can't – say or can't do. It's just words, like, "Yeah, you hurt me!" Bitch, you need to get stronger.'[218] However, Logo removed the episode from its platform and committed not to have the term appear in the programme again. Similarly, *tranny* was excised from the show, reflecting similar criticisms.

The controversy indicates one of the difficulties that camp humour has faced in the twenty-first century. Drag queens are meant to be offensive, their sharp wit has been honed over years of parrying taunts, using humour as a way of staying on top of or defusing a situation that could easily escalate into violence. Drag queens are tough cookies – their attitude is to demonstrate that no insult can hurt them because they are invincible and, if you try, they will come back with something much more devastating. Ultimately, camp is meant to be funny but if the audience isn't laughing, is it still camp? RuPaul acknowledges, 'When someone doesn't get the joke or feels offended by it, it's a lose-lose situation, because you can't explain a joke. It isn't funny if you explain it.'[219]

Another aspect of *RuPaul's Drag Race* involves its references to women. RuPaul often says that the winning contestant will have 'Charisma, uniqueness, nerve and talent' – words that form an acronym that has a misogynistic interpretation. Contestants are flippantly referred to as bitches, hoes and sluts, while the word *fishy*, which is meant to refer to the legitimacy of the queens' performance as a woman, is arguably derived from the supposed odour of female genitalia. In a season eleven mini-challenge, contestants had to show their 'boobography' by taking part in a potato sack race. This involved them bouncing up and down while wearing enormous fake breasts for comic effect. Hence, from some feminist perspectives, *Drag Race* could be cast as a bunch of men making fun of women, along with adolescent joking about their body parts. Does it matter that they are mostly gay men, many of whom have been bullied or rejected for being 'effeminate' as children? Along with the camp there is a rather earnest thread to *Drag Race*, similar to *Ugly Betty* and Ryan Murphy's shows, which advocates acceptance, self-love and liberation. Often, in the series finale, the contestants are asked to speak to a childhood picture of themselves. It is a segment that usually involves tearful recollections and heartfelt emotions.

Drag Race has also been criticised for only allowing gay men to be drag queens rather than including trans, heterosexual or female contestants, something that later seasons have strived to rectify. In 2018, RuPaul commented on a contestant from the previous year called Peppermint who was trans but had not had breast implants. RuPaul attracted criticism by saying that he probably wouldn't have accepted a contestant who had transitioned – 'You can identify as a woman and say you're transitioning, but it changes once you start changing your body.'[220] Again, this is an area that later seasons of the programme have tried to address. So, season three of *Drag Race* UK featured a female contestant called Victoria Scone, while season fourteen of the American version had two Black trans women, Kerri Colby and Kornbread Jeté, as well as a heterosexual man called Maddy Morphosis. But such attempts at inclusiveness have resulted in further criticisms from some quarters. Perhaps it could be argued that when gay men in drag call themselves bitches, they are recasting the word to give it a positive meaning, but if heterosexual men can perform in drag then is this more clearly an insult to women?

In February 2022, there was a camp controversy over an episode of *Ant & Dec's Saturday Night Takeaway*. A staple of the UK's weekend light entertainment for twenty years, the two presenters, Anthony McPartlin and Declan Donnelly, had been friends since the late 1980s when they acted in a BBC children's drama called *Byker Grove*. On *Saturday Night Takeaway*, for the start of a new series, a song called 'We Werk Together' was introduced by RuPaul and performed by the winning contestants from the first three seasons of the UK version of *RuPaul's Drag Race* – The Vivienne, Lawrence Chaney and Krystal Versace. Then, to the delighted screams of the studio audience, Ant and Dec appeared in drag, as Lady Antoinette and Miss Donna Lee. Although accomplished presenters, the boys were somewhat out of their comfort zones, but they were certainly able to hold their own among drag royalty. 'We Werk Together' was a catchy song, with a litany of positive messaging – lyrics included 'don't be bitter, just be better', 'we are family', 'proud forever' and 'live in the light'. Proceeds of the song went to the charity the Trussell Trust, which supports 1,300 food bank centres and campaigns for long-term change to prevent poverty.

While the vast majority of people who reacted to the performance were positive, there were fifty-nine complaints to the TV watchdog Ofcom, with some viewers claiming that the performance was misogynistic, degrading and disgusting, that it involved a parade of sexist stereotypes, a pornified mockery of women, and appropriated and parodied female identities. On Twitter, some complaints were tagged with #womanface, with posters arguing that drag was no different to blackface, the practice of non-Black people putting on makeup to appear black. Defenders of drag, like Nishant Upadhyay, have argued that:

> . . . it is completely wrong to compare drag with blackface . . . Drag is an exploration of gender, while blackface is rooted in violent histories of anti-blackness . . . It is an assertion of racial power over black folks, whereas drag is a challenge to patriarchy. The comparison is ahistorical.[221]

I can see Nishant's point, although some aspects of *Drag Race*, like the potato sack contest, don't seem as much of a challenge to patriarchy as just having a laugh about women's breasts.

The existence of female drag queens rather complicates the 'woman-face' criticism. Female drag queen Holestar believes that, while feminism did wonderful things for women, it suppressed opportunities for women to be camp, with a few exceptions. Holestar characterises women like Shirley Bassey and Dolly Parton as drag queens, who have kept female camp alive. Holestar explains: 'I like camp, I like over-the-top. I wanted to reclaim all that to the female body. I wanted to bring that back and say, "Why can't women do this? Why can't women be ridiculous and camp?"'[222] Another female drag queen, Victoria Sin, says 'What's important to make clear is that, for me, drag is not performing a woman, drag is performing femininity.'

As the most visible face of camp, drag queens have become a flashpoint for a complicated set of concerns around identity, sex, sexuality, gender and humour. Drag queens who read stories to children have been targeted by right-wing protest groups who have accused them of proselytising, while one interpretation of feminism is that drag is demeaning to women. In fifty years will drag queens be viewed as corrupting children, or similar to blackface, or will they be seen as good, clean, harmless fun? Only time will tell. For this key manifestation of camp, the stakes have never been higher.

SNAKES AND SISSIES

I've been arguing in this chapter that camp has become mainstream, although the examples I've given have tended to originate from countries that have English as a first language. Should camp be viewed as primarily an English-speaking phenomenon and, if so, where does that leave other cultures? *Snakes on a Plane* (2006) is an example of a film that went viral before it had been released, due to its title, which was also its premise, and the casting of Samuel L Jackson (who had appeared in *Pulp Fiction* and three other Quentin Tarantino films) in the lead role as a 'bad-ass' Blaxploitation-style hero. Irony was so entrenched in popular culture by 2006 that nobody needed to have it explained to them that the film was going to be a self-aware, camp, postmodern parody of disaster movies like *Zero Hour!* (1957) and *Airport* (1970). Even before anyone had seen the film, people were making T-shirts, their own trailers and websites based upon what they wanted to see. As fan expectations grew, additional shooting was carried out, including giving Jackson's character a line that had become popularised on the internet: 'Enough is enough! I have had it with these motherfucking snakes on this motherfucking plane!' Ultimately, the film was unable to live up to the enormous buzz it had generated, with the founder of New Line, Robert K Shaye, admitting it had been a dud despite high expectations. The failure of *Snakes on a Plane* is a prudent reminder that the best camp doesn't have to try, it just is. However, there's another aspect of the film that reveals an interesting point about recognition of camp across different cultures.

Samuel L Jackson in *Snakes on a Plane*. What could possibly go wrong?

The film critic Jim Emerson wrote a column about *Snakes on a Plane*, which considered how it was marketed in countries where the concept of 'it's so bad it's good' was not as widespread as in the UK or US.[223] In Venezuela, he wrote, the newspaper adverts for the film framed it like any old run-of-the-mill straight-to-DVD movie, trying to appeal to the horror concept of snakes on a plane, rather than acknowledging the irony or camp premise. Emerson argues that in some countries, the majority of the viewers would see *Snakes on a Plane* simply as a bad plane movie. Are we to believe Susan Sontag that 'Camp taste is by its nature possible only in affluent societies, in societies or circles capable of experiencing the psychopathology of affluence'? Emerson's observation suggests a divide between cultures based on the extent that the populace recognises or celebrates camp.

This brings us to China and its controversy over 'sissy boys'. In the twenty-first century, feminine-presenting young men have been an increasingly popular part of Chinese culture, particularly adored by young women and girls. Take the multitalented Cai Xukun, a songwriter, singer and dancer who won the reality show *Idol Producer* and led the boyband Nine Percent. Every track on his EP *1* topped the Chinese music charts. With pouting lips, flawless skin and a penchant for high fashion, KUN, as he is known to fans, is certainly camp to my eyes. In the video for his song 'Pull-Up', he sprawls louchely on a rococo sofa, plays with a cocktail olive, fondles his chest and makes innumerable costume changes. He has been photographed wearing makeup with his dark hair dyed a rather bracing shade of blond. He is not alone – many of the male contestants of *Idol Producer* and other shows like *Youth With You* and *The Coming One* have a gender-fluid appearance, sometimes wearing flamboyant eye-shadow, lipstick and foundation. The trend came from a form of South Korean music called K-pop, which often features male singers who are not traditionally masculine, and it is something that has been popular in Anglo-American culture since the 1970s, with pop stars like David Bowie, Boy George, Prince and Robert Smith being famed for their androgynous style. In China, these boys

Sissy boys! Cai Xukun on *Idol Producer*, April 2018.

have also crossed over into acting, appearing in film or television adaptions of 'boys' love' fiction novels, a genre from Japan which features homoerotic relationships between young men. The actor Zhang Zhehan went largely unnoticed when he played traditionally masculine roles, but he found instant stardom when he appeared in the television series *Word of Honor* in 2021, playing alongside Gong Jun, who was implied to be his romantic partner. Commenting on his rise to fame, Zhang's female fans created a meme – 'manning up for a decade failed, but [he] succeeded as a wife overnight'.[224]

Homosexuality is not illegal in China, but its rulers do not strictly approve of it. In 2016, images of men kissing and holding hands were banned from the media, resulting in depictions which were more subtly coded – longing looks and romantic gestures, as well as male characters who were feminine in manner and appearance. To counter this, since 2019, young men's tattoos, earrings and ponytails were blurred out online. And on 2 September 2021, the campaign was stepped up further when the government banned the appearance of what they called sissy men or *niang pao* (girlie guns) in the media. Broadcasters must 'resolutely put an end to sissy men and other abnormal esthetics' decreed China's National Radio and TV Administration. Some people have argued that the real target is the big tech companies whose revenue has been boosted by hosting these kinds of stars,[225] while others have pointed to a desire for China to be seen as a powerful country, with the implication that femininity is weakness.[226]

This was a request rather than a law, but it seems to have had some effect. Within weeks, KUN had butched up, abandoning his natty black turtlenecks and blond quiff, to instead sport facial hair and baggy jeans. Will it work? Paradoxically, it could be argued that the ban weakens China's standing among other countries, making it look reactionary and frightened, and, in any case, censorship can often make a banned product more alluring. If there's one thing this book has shown, it's that oppression of queerness tends to result in more camp, rather than less. Camp always has a way of kicking right back.

WHEN CAMP GOES WRONG, NOTHING GOES RIGHT

If camp is everywhere, this can only be a good thing? Perhaps not. Bruce LaBruce paints a picture of camp in the twenty-first century that suggests it has become so ubiquitous that it has become detached from having gay significance. Instead, he says that camp can be co-opted, commercialised and, most ironically of all, trivialised.[227] Camp can also become little more than a marketing strategy, designed to get us to buy stuff. Adverts have always had the potential to be camp – in the UK, an advert that was first aired in 1980 for a product called Shake n' Vac is still fondly remembered by those of a certain age. The advert featured a woman shaking scented powder over her carpet a little *too* enthusiastically, then vacuuming it up while tonelessly singing, 'Do the Shake and Vac and put the freshness back' in a somewhat flat voice. Although the camp in the advert is likely of the unintentional sort, more recent ads have purposefully upped the camp quotient to cash in on our knowing delight, in order to sell products that are, in some ways, the antithesis of camp. In 1999, I remember being dismayed when clothes chain Gap had a dance troupe perform a series of Bob Fosse-inspired 1960s moves to the splendid track 'Wild Elephants', just to get people to buy their bland clothes. The advert called itself khaki a-gogo, for me it was khaki a-no-no; khaki is *many things* but it is not camp. Then, in 2005, the Sammy Davis Jr camp classic 'Rhythm of Life' from the film *Sweet Charity* (1969) was used to sell the manly alcoholic beverage Guinness, while worst of all, in 2011, Heineken co-opted 'Jaan Pehechaan Ho' from *Gumnaam* – three of my favourite pieces of 'lounge' music now tainted, dark-sided, not Christian, not of God!

In earlier chapters we saw how camp was employed as a form of radical action against right-wing forces, indicating that if camp is to be political it is more likely to be used by progressives. However, there are aspects of camp that indicate that it could be gainfully, or even painfully, used by conservatives. To my eyes, such politicians have more potential for unintentional camp, compared to liberals or progressives. Exhibit A is the 2008 Republican vice-presidential nominee, Sarah Palin. When *CBS Evening News* host Katie Couric asked Palin which newspapers she read, Palin replied, 'Um, all of them, any that have been put in front of me over these years.' With her folksy 'mama bear' persona, beauty pageant history and gleeful lack of preparation during interviews, she was ripe for parody, with Tina Fey's impersonation of her on *Saturday Night Live* being uncannily accurate. When asked about foreign policy in Russia, Palin said, 'They're our neighbours and you can actually see Russia from land here in Alaska, from an island in Alaska.' Fey spun gold with this, claiming, 'I can see Russia from my house.' Of course, as we've seen earlier in this chapter, the best way of reacting to being outed as camp is to go along with it, so Palin said that Fey's impersonation was hilarious, she dressed as Fey for Halloween and even appeared on *SNL* herself.

Voters may not have bought Palin's ticket, but, in 2017, enough of them ticked Donald Trump's box, resulting in a surprise Republican win, despite him gaining fewer votes than his competitor, Hillary Clinton. It could be argued that Trump was the campest person alive in 2017. He looks and behaves like a resident of the dystopian and decadent Capitol in Suzanne Collins's *The Hunger Games*. With his vulgar manner, love of gold, over-application of orange makeup and oddly teased hairstyle, he certainly had a uniquely camp look. One of his favourite films is *Sunset Boulevard*, which he finds 'just incredible'.[228] At his rallies, Trump would lead performances of Village People songs like 'YMCA' and 'Macho Man', as well as the plaintive Dolly Parton hit 'Jolene' and, more recently, 'Do you hear the people sing?' from the musical *Les Misérables*.[229] Then there were his tweets. Here's a classic from 28 March 2014: 'Healthy young child goes to doctor, gets pumped with massive shots of many vaccines, doesn't feel good and changes – AUTISM. Many such cases!' We can laugh at the camp exclamatory writing style, but then wonder how many children will miss out on vaccines due to claims that have been refuted by the medical science community. Trump was banned from Twitter in January 2021 'due to the risk of further incitement of violence', after his followers invaded the US Capitol when he lost the 2020 election. The invasion resulted in several deaths. Heed the warning – in the wrong hands, camp can be deadly, especially when parts of your audience don't have the ability to recognise it.

Bruce LaBruce has talked about how conservatives like Sarah Palin and Donald Trump have engaged in reactionary burlesque, with views that are exaggerated and put across in a way that is stylised but has no substance. They function as a crude spectacle by pretending to be on the side of the masses, yet offer them policies that are directly antithetical to their needs.[230] And Constance Grady has noted how Trump made camp more about politics than aesthetics, turning camp's sense of playfulness and transgression into cruelty. The camp perspective that everything is ridiculous, nothing matters and nihilism is fun is fine for art – but when that sense of camp comes into politics, it becomes dangerous.[231] LaBruce admits that his essay ends on a depressing and unhopeful note, arguing, like Daniel Harris, that camp has 'lost its essential qualities of esoteric sophistication and secret signification, partly owing to the contemporary tendency of the gay sensibility to allow itself to be thoroughly co-opted, its mystery, and therefore its power, hopelessly diffused'. I certainly wouldn't deny that in the last two decades it feels that camp's popularity has attracted what I'd call 'the wrong set'. But I recall Andy Medhurst's comment about camp being a tenacious tigress and I want to believe that it will pull through and slash with a bejewelled claw at its would-be captors, as it has always done before.

It was Trump's presidency that partly inspired the Metropolitan Museum of Art to make camp the theme of its annual Gala in 2019. The curator of the exhibition, Andrew Bolton, described Trump as 'a very camp figure'. He went on to say that 'since I have been working on the show, I have started to think it is everywhere, and that all fashion is on some level camp'. Concerned that camp's popularity had all but rendered it invisible, his goal was to make it visible again.[232] The resulting exhibition, *Camp: Notes on Fashion*, opened on 9 May, containing over 250 objects, including an original copy of Molière's *Les Fourberies de Scapin* (which contains the first known printed usage of camp as a verb), along with exhibits on Oscar Wilde and Christopher Isherwood, oodles of naked male statues, a whole room devoted to Susan Sontag, and outrageous outfits designed by the likes of Jeremy Scott, Vivienne Westwood, Walter Van Beirendonck and Jean Paul Gaultier.

The exhibition was a triumph and, on 11 August, the MET tweeted that it had welcomed half a million visitors. However, the opening Gala suggests that not everyone had got the memo, although perhaps this related to the perennial problem that people have in defining exactly what camp is. Dylan Hafer noted that the camp theme meant that the only rule this year was 'don't be boring', but, despite this sounding simple, some of the stars in attendance had more trouble than you'd think, with poor Kim Kardashian disgracing herself by dressing in the same outfit she'd worn for a *Vogue* cover shot. Ashely Graham also got it wrong by looking gorgeous but having an outfit that contained no drama, and Halsey failed by thinking that putting on a large red dress would be enough to be camp (it wasn't).[233] However, Hafer's list of who got it right is telling: Lady Gaga, Billy Porter, Janelle Monáe and Katy Perry. They all understood the assignment – Katy Perry essentially dressed up as a chandelier, while Billy Porter was carried in on a velvet-draped litter by a crew of topless hunky men in gold. His outfit involved a gold costume and headdress, making him look like a pharaoh. When he descended from the litter, he spread out his arms to reveal enormous golden wings. As Julian Clary would say – what an entrance! And, of course, Joan Collins arrived at the Gala as the character she played in *Dynasty*. Wearing an all-white feathered gown, topped with a tiara and diamonds, she teased her appearance via Maison Valentino's Twitter feed with a short video where she announced, 'I'm Alexis Morell Carrington Colby Dexter Rowan and I'm wearing Valentino Haute Couture for the Met Ball.' Anyone who criticised what *she* was wearing did so at their own risk.

And that's how it's done. Billy Porter is 💯 at the MET Gala 2019.

Not everyone approved of the Gala night. Li Edelkoort called the event a violent act of haughtiness and criticised those present for their lack of historic insight into camp. Edelkoort also hated the 'vomiting waste of wealth' on display, becoming rather cross at it all. She compared the Gala to the poverty she witnessed around her in her day-to-day life. Thinking of Marie Antoinette, she even viewed the event as the tipping point, the beheading of culture – a point that was confirmed when Jared Leto arrived with his own severed head.[234] Perhaps that's a little fanciful and, in the months that followed, impoverished New Yorkers did not set up guillotines in Times Square. However, Edelkoort makes an important point about camp's relationship to inequality and sustainability – the Gala occurred on the same day that the UN reported that human abuse of the environment will result in the loss of one million species. There is something obscene about the super-rich shelling out to have designers dress them in ridiculous outfits that they'll only wear for a couple of hours. Camp can often involve excess – but in the context of a climate crisis, some people would say that extreme materialism isn't funny. And if no one's laughing, it's not camp.

The Gala at least got people talking about camp, even if the old definitional conversations were rehashed. And, as a result of this focus, what followed was a reappraisal of camp, with new perspectives and a more diverse set of voices talking about it. Take, for example, Hafizah Geter's article about Black camp.[235] Geter viewed Black people as being erased from camp, with the MET Gala being one further example in a long line of this practice. She describes the camp cakewalk dances and goes on to list Black culture's ongoing contribution to camp through the ages:

> Our Camp includes Josephine Baker's banana skirt performances, Blaxploitation films, voguing, and Carnival. We've got Camp luminaries like Grace Jones, Erykah Badu, Bootsy Collins, Lil' Kim, Missy Elliot, Busta Rhymes, André 3000, and Lorraine O'Grady's 'Art Is . . .' movement. Our Campiest Camp of all is the excess of a Black congregation's Sunday best – the zoot suits, the bright colors, the big hats.

Rona Cran also frames Black experience in a discussion of the history of camp, starting by mentioning Little Richard's performance of 'Tutti Frutti' in 1956, and ending on two music videos by the rapper Lil Nas X, 'Old Town Road' (2019) and 'MONTERO (Call Me By Your Name)' (2021).[236] The former (which was the longest-charting number one song on the Billboard Hot 100) is a blend of country music and hip-hop, featuring people in full-on country drag – sequins, tassels and chaps – whereas the latter is a hip-hop and electropop song that has the biblical Adam kissing a serpent, judged by versions of himself in blue Marie Antoinette wigs. He is killed when someone throws a butt plug at him, then rides down a stripper pole to hell and performs a lap-dance for Satan while dressed in Calvin Klein underwear and thigh-high boots with stiletto heels. Cran writes that Lil Nas X claims camp transgression for Black queerness, confirming that camp is much more than a quirky outfit. If there is one defining aspect of camp in the early years of the twenty-first century, it is its inclusivity – that includes recognition of camp as *always* having had a strong connection to Black culture, but it also includes acknowledging the utilisation of unintentional camp by conservatives for political leverage. We are living in strange times, and so our story reaches a somewhat ambiguous conclusion, with camp now a part of our daily experience but also being pulled in many different directions at once. Its continuation is by no means a foregone conclusion and my hope is that, in writing this book, I can help people to recognise and challenge the less benevolent uses of camp, and to inspire its use in movements for good. And, in these serious times, I would also hope to stress the importance of *not* always being earnest. To riff on a famous RuPaul quote, if you can't laugh at yourself, how in the hell are you gonna laugh at someone else?

AND FINALLY

Here we are, right at the end. I hope you've learnt a few things on the journey, raised an amused eyebrow on the way, and that you've been moved to seek out some of the music, art, television, films and other cultural objects that I've written about in this book. I also hope I've inspired you to embrace camp, to recognise the camp in yourself and the camp all around you.

So, what's next for camp? Channelling fortune-teller Criswell from Chapter 5, I see a set of possible futures, based on where society might be heading. Imagine, if you will, a world where science and technology have solved most of our problems, and democracy is much less likely to be gamed than it currently is, leaving us in a glorious utopia where everyone has more than enough. We can all be healthy and beautiful, and nobody has to work unless they want to. All of that leisure time and luxury would make princesses out of everyone and I think the ensuing world would be excessively camp, a high-tech version of Versailles, with endless diversions, sexual fluidity, outrageous fashions and shrieks of laughter ringing out everywhere as our robot servants sassed us with their AI algorithms. International conflicts would be resolved through dance-offs and although now largely devoid of political meaning, in this world, camp humour would be viewed as central to our wellbeing. It would even be seen as having therapeutic value and parents would anxiously monitor their children, expressing concern if they did not show an early appreciation of camp: 'Little Lulu's so serious – where did we go wrong?'

Or consider a world where power and wealth are concentrated in the hands of a tiny super-elite, who, fearful of losing their grip, are compelled to devise increasingly oppressive ways to retain their position. The usual distraction tactics – nationalism, wedge issues and scapegoating of minorities must be employed, along with mass surveillance and violent punishment to stymie rebellion. Homosexuality, along with any form of gender 'deviance' would, of course, be outlawed. As it has always done, camp would go underground, being used to mock and subvert. And like all authoritarian regimes, unintentional camp would be in the DNA of this kind of society – snazzy uniforms and military parades, mass public displays of emotion, kitsch propaganda – although people wouldn't be allowed to comment on its existence – camp itself also being against the law and punishable by death.

Of course, there may be some sort of terrible disaster – a zombie virus, a comet collision, robots becoming our self-aware overlords, or, more realistically, climate catastrophe brought about by our over-consumption – so we'd all be struggling for survival. Camp humour would be used by some as a coping strategy, to get us through the worst of it, but I think most of the time we would be far too busy for camp, unintentional or otherwise, in this grim world.

Finally, there's a business-as-usual scenario, whereby the world continues to be a shaky battleground of ideologies and new camp sites are continually being pitched. In this world some people will be delightfully oblivious to their camp and others will be fervent camp followers. Film and music critics will remain extraordinarily bad at spotting or appreciating camp, always being last to get the joke. And, of course, nobody will ever be able to agree on what camp actually is so it will keep on surprising us, meeting each new era and trend with a knowing laugh. It will continue to entertain, perplex and infuriate, just as it always has done. As Criswell predicted in *Plan 9 from Outer Space*, 'remember, my friend, future events such as these will affect you in the future'.

Before I set pen to paper, I thought I knew camp. It had formed the basis of my friendships while my family had provided plenty of examples of it. But I hadn't realised how maddeningly complicated it was, how many different faces it had and how much it has changed. The more I looked, the more fascinating it became. And, despite all the complexities and backlashes, what I've also realised is that a world without camp would be a very boring one indeed. We're only here a short time and some of it is going to be rather dreary while other parts will be quite ghastly. At times, we're going to get picked last. Sometimes we won't even get picked at all. A camp attitude will help us to redefine what it means to win. It will bring splashes of colour to the most boring day and let you endow others with the priceless gift of laughter. So camp it up while you can, darlings, it'll make your stay here much more fun.

Now, be gone, before someone drops a house on *you!*

Notes on the Text

CHAPTER 1: HELLO, PUSSYCAT

1 LaBruce, Bruce. 'Notes on Camp – and Anti-Camp'. *The Gay & Lesbian Review*, 2014

2 Friedman, Vanessa. 'Met Costume Institute Embraces "Camp" for 2019 Blockbuster Show'. *New York Times*, 9 October 2018

3 Fred. 'Hurst and DeVars "Bits of Millinery"' (review). *Variety*, 58.5, p.24, 26 March 1920. Quoted in Richard Dickon Edwards' *Ronald Firbank and the legacy of camp modernism*. Unpublished PhD Thesis, Birkbeck, University of London, 2022

4 Parker, Stanley. 'After the Theatre'. *Illustrated Sporting and Dramatic News*, 2 August 1940

5 'The Oz Bowl Game'. *TIME*, 15 January 1965

6 'A reluctant adieu to Expo 67'. *Christian Science Monitor*, 1967

7 Sontag, Susan. 'Notes on "Camp"'. *Partisan Review*, 31(4): 515–530, 1964

8 Booth, Mark, *Camp*. Quartet Books, London, 1983, pp.15–16

9 Core, Philip, *Camp, The Lie that Tells the Truth*. Plexus, London, 1984, p.7

10 LaBruce, Bruce. 'Notes on Camp – and Anti-Camp'. *The Gay & Lesbian Review*, 2014

11 Newton, Esther, *Mother Camp: Female Impersonators in America*. Prentice-Hall, Englewood Cliffs, New Jersey, 1972, p.23

12 Babuscio, Jack, 'Camp and the Gay Sensibility' in Richard Dyer ed. *Gays and Film*. British Film Institute, London, 1977, pp.40–57

13 Halperin, David, *Saint Foucault: Towards a Gay Hagiography*. Oxford University Press, Oxford, 1995, p.29

14 McMahon, Gary, *Camp in Literature*. McFarland, Jefferson, NC, 2006, p.14

CHAPTER 2: YOUR ACTUAL FRENCH

15 Foufelle, Dominique, *The Little Book of Versailles*. Editions du Chêne, Vanves, 2017, p.36

16 Ibid., p.52

17 Ibid., p.84

18 Booth Mark, *Camp*. Quartet Books, London, 1983, p.40

19 Foufelle, Dominique, *The Little Book of Versailles*. Editions du Chêne, Vanves, 2017, p.100

20 Ibid., p.120

21 Jacobsen, Helen, *Inspiring Walt Disney: The Animation of French Decorative Arts at the Wallace Collection*. Philip Wilson, London, 2022

22 Harvey, Keith. 'Describing camp talk'. *Language and Literature* 9(3): 240–60, 2000

23 Ward, Edward, *The Secret History of London Clubs*. J Dutton, London, 1709

24 Norton, Rictor, *Mother Clap's Molly House: The Gay Subculture in England 1700–1830*. Gay Men's Press, London, 1992

25 Knowles, James, *The Nineteenth Century and After*. Leonard Scott, New York, 1901, p.276

26 Boswell, James, *Journal of a Tour to the Hebrides with Samuel Johnson, LL.D.* Henry Baldwin, Oxford, 1785

27 Kelly, Ian, *Beau Brummell: The Ultimate Dandy*. Hodder and Stoughton, London, 2005, p.157

28 LaBruce, Bruce. 'Notes on Camp – and Anti-Camp'. *The Gay & Lesbian Review*, 2014

29 McKenna, Neil, *Fanny & Stella: The Young Men Who Shocked Victorian England*. Faber and Faber, London, 2013, p.165

30 Ibid., p.110

31 Brophy, Brigid, *Black and White: A Portrait of Aubrey Beardsley*. J. Cape, London, 1968

32 Freeman, Chris. 'Oscar Wilde and the Limit of Camp'. *The Gay & Lesbian Review* 26(6): 20–21, 2019

33 Holland, Merlin, and Hart-Davis, Rupert, eds., *The Complete Letters of Oscar Wilde*. Henry Holt, New York, 2000

34 Alberge, Dalya. 'Sworn enemies: the real story of Old Bailey clash that ruined Oscar Wilde'. *Guardian*, 24 January 2021

35 Baldwin, Brooke. 'The Cakewalk: A Study in Stereotype and Reality'. *Journal of Social History*. Oxford University Press, 15 (2): 205–18, 1981

36 Ibid.

37 Geter, Hafizah. 'Black Phenomena: On Afropessimism & Camp'. *Bomb Magazine*, 23 September 2021

38 Jones, LeRoi, *Blues People: Negro Music in White America*. William Morrow, New York, 1963, pp.85–6

39 Morgan, Marjorie. 'From slavery to voguing: the House of Swann'. National Museums Liverpool, online, February 2021

40 'Negro Dive Raided Thirteen Black Men Dressed as Women Surprised at Supper and Arrested'. *Washington Post*, 13 April 1888

41 Joseph, Channing Gerard. 'The First Drag Queen Was a Former Slave: Who fought for queer freedom a century before Stonewall.' *The Nation*, 31 January 2020

42 Currie, Netisha. 'William Dorsey Swann, the Queen of Drag'. *National Archives*, 29 June 2020

43 Geter, Hafizah. 'Black Phenomena: On Afropessimism & Camp'. *Bomb Magazine*, 23 September 2021

44 Sontag, Susan. 'Notes on "Camp"'. *Partisan Review*, 31(4): 515–30, 1964

CHAPTER 3: COCKTAILS AND LAUGHTER

45 Bolton, Paul. 'Education: Historical Statistics'. House of Commons Library, online, 27 November 2012

46 Undergraduate Degree Results. Gov.uk, online, 29 July 2022

47 Hoare, Philip, *Noël Coward, A Biography*. Sinclair-Stevenson, London, 1995, p.59

48 Petridis, Alexis. 'Leaders of the banned'. *Guardian*, 12 April 2002

49 Nallon, Steve. 'Fun and Games with Noël Coward'. www.nallon.com/?p=700

50 Baker, P. 'A year to remember? Introducing the BE21 corpus and exploring recent part of tag change in British English'. *International Journal of Corpus Linguistics*, 2023

51 Elder, Robert K, *The Best Film You've Never Seen: 35 Directors Champion the Forgotten or Critically Savaged Movies They Love*. Chicago Review Press, Chicago, 2013

52 Bilow, Rochelle. 'The Exciting History and Origin of the Cocktail Umbrella'. *Bon Appétit*. 21 March 2014

53 A rather rich concoction, consisting of brandy, crème de cacao, double cream and ice, garnished with caster sugar, nutmeg and cinnamon.

54 Battersby, Eileen. 'Brideshead besmirched'. *Irish Times*, 8 January 2009

55 Mitford, Nancy, *The Pursuit of Love*. Hamish Hamilton, London, 1945

56 Thompson, Laura, *Life in a Cold Climate*. Head of Zeus, London, 2004

57 Mitford, Diana, speaking in *Nancy Mitford: A Portrait by her Sisters*. BBC, London, 1980

58 Member of the Most Excellent Order of the British Empire. An award for outstanding achievement or service to the community.

59 Kumar, Naveen. '7 Black Artists Who Turned Camp into a Cultural Revolution'. *Them*, 19 April 2019

60 Sowinska, Alicja. 'Dialectics of the Banana Skirt: The Ambiguities of Josephine Baker's Self-Representation'. *Michigan Feminist Studies*, vol. 19, 2005–6

61 Ibid.

62 Rose, Phyllis, *Jazz Cleopatra: Josephine Baker in Her Time*. Doubleday, New York, 1989, p.24

63 Klein, Christopher. 'Josephine Baker's Daring Double Life as a World War II Spy'. History.com, 15 March 2021

64 Strong, Lester Q. 'Josephine Baker's Hungry Heart'. *The Gay & Lesbian Review*, September–October, 2006

65 Day, Elizabeth. 'Mr nice guy'. *Guardian*, 13 April 2008

66 '*The Mouse Trap* by Agatha Christie'. *The Times*, 3 May 1955

67 Thompson, Laura, *Life in a Cold Climate*. Head of Zeus, London, 2004, pp.86–88

CHAPTER 4: DOLLY, DIVA, SISTER, HAG

68 Harris, Daniel. 'The Death of Camp: Gay Men and Hollywood Diva Worship, from Reverence to Ridicule'. *Salmagundi* 112, pp.166–7, 1996

69 Dyer, Richard, *Heavenly Bodies: Film Stars and Society*. St Martin's Press, New York, 1986, p.176

70 Frank, Steven. 'What does it take to be a gay icon today?' AfterElton.com, 25 September 2007

71 Walters, Barry. 'An icon for the ages'. *The Advocate*, 13 October 1998

72 'Seance at the Palace'. *TIME*, 18 August 1967

73 Goldman, William. 'Judy Floats'. *Esquire*, January 1969

74 Kaiser, Charles, *The Gay Metropolis 1940–1996*. Houghton Mifflin, New York, 1997, p.198

75 Duberman, Martin, *Stonewall: The Definitive Story of the LGBTQ Rights Uprising That Changed America*. Dutton, New York, 1993

76 Goodman, Amy. 'Stonewall Riots 40th Anniversary: A Look Back at the Uprising that Launched the Modern Gay Rights Movement'. *Democracy Now!*, 26 June 2009

77 Loughery, John, *The Other Side of Silence: Men's Lives and Gay Identities: A Twentieth-Century History*. Henry Holt and Company, New York, 1998, p.316

78 *Peyton Place* was an American soap opera, which ran from 1964 to 1969, adapted from a 1956 book of the same name. Barbara Perkins and Lee Grant, who both starred in *Valley of the Dolls*, had long-standing roles in it.

79 Crowther, Bosley. 'The Screen: "Valley of the Dolls" Opens: Susann's Little Women Led Astray Again'. *New York Times*, 16 December 1967

80 Ebert, Roger. 'Valley of the Dolls'. *Chicago Sun-Times*, 27 December 1967

81 Liebenson, Donald. 'Why Valley of the Dolls Still Sparkles at 50'. *Vanity Fair*, 13 December 2017

82 Berger, John, *Ways of Seeing*. Penguin, London, 1972, p.47

83 Schneider, Dan. 'Whatever Happened to Baby Jane?' www.hackwriters.com/BabyJane.htm

84 Considine, Shaun, *Bette and Joan: The Divine Feud*. Warner, London, 1989, p.324

85 Ibid., p.314

86 Ebert, Roger. 'Clash of the screen divas'. *Chicago Sun-Times*, 16 February 2008

87 Considine, Shaun, *Bette and Joan: The Divine Feud*. Warner, London, 1989, pp.331–2

88 '*Sextette* Review'. *Variety*, 31 December 1977

89 Canby, Vincent. 'Screen: Mae West, 87, Does an Encore: Trying for 6th Marriage'. *New York Times*, 8 June 1979

90 Harris, Daniel. 'The Death of Camp: Gay Men and Hollywood Diva Worship, from Reverence to Ridicule'. *Salmagundi* 112, p.188

91 McNeil, Liz, and Warner, Kara, 'Faye Dunaway Opens up about Movies, Men, and the problem with "Mommie Dearest"'. *People*, 4 October 2016

92 Medved, Harry and Michael, *Son of Golden Turkey Awards*. Angus and Robertson, Sydney, 1986, p.118

93 Harris, Daniel. 'The Death of Camp: Gay Men and Hollywood Diva Worship, from Reverence to Ridicule'. *Salmagundi* 112, p.188

94 *Room 101*, series 4, episode 7, 3 September 1999

95 Dowell, Ben. 'Secret drugs menu of TV chef Fanny'. *Guardian*, 10 September 2006

96 Kinser, Jeremy. 'Exclusive: Donna Summer Denied Making Antigay Remarks That Hurt Her Career'. *The Advocate*, 17 May 2012

97 'Donna in the Pulpit'. *Gay Times*, October 1984, p.20

98 'Bronski Beat'. *Gay Times*, November 1984, pp.41–3

99 Block, Adam. 'Summer and Smoke'. *The Advocate*, 23 July 1985

100 Kinser, Jeremy. 'Donna Summer Disputed Antigay Remarks in 1989 Letter to ACT UP'. *The Advocate*, 12 June 2012

101 'Donna Summer Files Libel Suit Against Magazine'. *AP News*, 2 October 1991

102 Midler, Bette, at the Continental Baths. www.youtube.com/watch?v=UOrzpQeJyKI

CHAPTER 5: CLENCHED FISTS ON LIMP WRISTS

103 Cassandra (Connor, William). 'Yearn-Strength Five'. *Daily Mirror*, 26 September 1956

104 Betty White Interview, on *The Joy Behar Show*. HLN, 3 May 2011, www.youtube.com/watch?v=i-wTJ2hQCK8

105 Russo, Vito, *The Celluloid Closet: Homosexuality in the Movies*. Harper and Row, New York, 1981

106 'Larry Grayson: Door that inspired catchphrase uncovered'. *BBC News*, 12 March 2019

107 Hall, Sarah. 'Letters show Monty as "repressed gay"'. *Guardian*, 26 February 2001

108 Brown, Mark. 'Library books defaced by prankster playwright Joe Orton go on show'. *Guardian*, 11 October 2011

109 Hughes, Kathryn. 'Portable Magic by Emma Smith review – a love letter to reading'. *Guardian*, 28 April 2022

110 Fox, James. 'The Life and Death of Joe Orton'. *Sunday Times*, 22 November 1970

111 Pettitt, Josh. 'Joe Orton's prank play on homosexuality turned down by Hampstead church'. *Ham&High*, 9 November 2012

112 Davies, Russell, ed., *The Kenneth Williams Diaries*. Harper Collins, London, 1993, p.307

113 Chesters, Laura. 'Islington Museum buys collage by Joe Orton's lover at auction'. *Antiques Trade Gazette*, 23 September 2016

114 Yardley, William. 'Storme DeLarverie, Early Leader in the Gay Rights Movement, Dies at 93'. *New York Times*, 29 May 2014

115 Carter, David, *Stonewall: The Riots that Sparked the Gay Revolution*. St Martins Press, New York, 2004, p.160

116 Deitcher, David, ed., *The Question of Equality: Lesbian and Gay Politics in America since Stonewall*. Scribner, New York, 1995, p.67

117 Carter, David, *Stonewall: The Riots that Sparked the Gay Revolution*. St Martins Press, New York, 2004, p.178

118 Ibid., p.188

119 France, David, dir., *The Death and Life of Marsha P. Johnson*. Netflix, 2017

120 Shephard, Benjamin. 'Sylvia and Sylvia's Children: A Battle for Public Space', in Mattilda Bernstein Sycamore ed. *That's Revolting! Queer Strategies for Resisting Assimilation*. Soft Skull Press, New York, 2004, pp.123–40

121 Laczko, Rob. 'Remembering Sylvia – The Mother of the Riot'. *Out in Jersey*, June–July 2010, p.4

122 Thompson, Howard. 'Stage: Watergate humour'. *New York Times*, 21 July 1973

123 Dyer, Richard. 'It's Being So Camp As Keeps Us Going'. *Playguy*, 1976

124 Maltin, Leonard, *Leonard Maltin's Movie and Video Guide*. Signet Books, New York, 2003

125 From publicity material for the film *Vampira: The Movie*.

126 Waters, John. 'A Bad Influence Picks his "Role Models"'. *NPR*, 3 June 2021

127 Waters, John, *Crackpot: The Obsessions of John Waters*. Fourth Estate, London, 1988, pp.116–23

128 Slater-Williams, Josh. 'John Waters on camp, Trump and being Mr Know-It-All'. *The Face*, 27 August 2019

129 Fitzgerald, Lucy. 'Does Hairspray (2007) still "hold" up?' *Glasgow Guardian*, 23 September 2021

130 Waters, John, *Shock Value*, Fourth Estate, London, 1991, p.2

131 Corbett, Ken. 'More life: Centrality and Marginality in Human Development', in Aron, Lewis and Harris, Adrienne, eds. *Relational Psychoanalysis: Volume 2: Innovation and Expansion*. Routledge, New York/London, 2016, p.448

132 Slide, Anthony, *Some Joe You Don't Know. An American Biographical Guide to 100 British Television Personalities*. Greenwood, Westport, 1996, p.122

133 'Too knowing'. *Gay News' Gay Guide*, 13 December 1979, p.xii

134 Britton, Andrew. 'FOR interpretation – Notes Against Camp'. *Gay Left* 7, Winter 1978/9 pp.11–14

135 'Are You Being Stereotyped?' *End of Part One*, 1980 www.youtube.com/watch?v=A1THgABWUxw

136 Rigelsford, Adrian, Brown, Anthony, and Tibballs, Geoff, *Are You Being Served? The Inside Story*. KQED books, San Francisco, 1995, p.29

137 'Are you being unfair?' *Daily Express*, 12 October 1977

138 'Gay pickets chase Inman show'. *Gay News*, 15 December 1977, p. 2

139 'New Zealand'. *Gay News*, 1 June 1978, p.1

140 'The Distorting Mirrors'. *Gay News*, 5 May 1977, pp.19–21

141 'CHE pays a call on John Inman'. *Gay News*, 17 November 1977, p.10

142 'Limp wrists a boon'. *Gay News*, 15 June 1978, p.12

143 '"Have you heard the one about the queer who . . .?" The homosexual as a figure of fun'. *Gay News*, 25 March 1976, p.13

144 Medhurst, Andy. 'Camp' in Medhurst, A, & Munt, S R, eds. *Lesbian and Gay Studies: A Critical Introduction*. Cassell, London, 1997, p.281

CHAPTER 6: CAMP IN A COLD CLIMATE

145 Dave Marsh. 'The Flip Sides of 1979'. *Rolling Stone*. 27 December 1979

146 Lawrence, Tim. 'Disco and the queering of the dance floor'. *Cultural Studies* 25(2): 230–43, 2011

147 Sclafani, Tony. 'When "Disco Sucks!" echoed around the world'. *TODAY NBC*, 10 July 2009

148 Behrens, Andy. 'Disco Demolition: Bell-bottoms be gone!' *ESPN* Chicago, 12 July 2009

149 Lupsha, Jonny. 'Solid gold toilet stolen from palace reminiscent of Hussein's opulence'. *Wondrium Daily*, 3 October 2019

150 Newby, Debbie. 'Denver business capitalizes on popular tv series Dynasty'. *Toronto Star*, 25 October 1986

151 Clover, Carol J, *Men, Women and Chainsaws: Gender in the Modern Horror Film*. Princeton University Press, Princeton, 1992

152 Peitzman, Louis. 'The Nightmare Behind the Gayest Horror Film Ever Made'. *Buzzfeed*, 21 February 2016

153 Maurice, Emma. 'Paul O'Grady relives horrifying homophobic police raid on Lily Savage show at London's legendary Royal Vauxhall Tavern'. *Pink News*, 26 January 2021

154 Derdeyn, Stuart. 'Scott Thompson's Buddy Cole Monologues addresses psychic fallout of AIDS era'. *Vancouver Sun*, 9 September 2019

155 Riseman, Abraham. 'The Kids in the Hall's Scott Thompson Used Gay Provocateur Buddy Cole As an Essential Megaphone'. *New York Magazine*, 9 February 2017

156 Derdeyn, Stuart. 'Scott Thompson's Buddy Cole Monologues addresses psychic fallout of AIDS era'. *Vancouver Sun*, 9 September 2019

157 Riseman, Abraham. 'The Kids in the Hall's Scott Thompson Used Gay Provocateur Buddy Cole As an Essential Megaphone'. *New York Magazine*, 9 February 2017

158 Bray, Abbie. 'Julian Clary discusses frosty encounter with Joan Collins. "We had a tricky time."' *Express*, 5 June 2022

159 Belfield, Alex. *Julian Clary 'Fisting Norman Lamont' Comedy Awards Gag – BBC Interview & Life Stories*. www.youtube.com/watch?v=2is1nmRPgHI

160 Potter, Lynda-Lee. *Daily Mail*, 15 December 1993

161 'Comedian Clary is ditched by awards'. *Edinburgh Evening News*, 11 December 1998

162 '3AM: Number 65: Julian Clary'. *Daily Mirror*, 24 August 2002

163 Baker, Stuart, *Voguing and the House Ballroom Scene of New York 1989–92*. Soul Jazz Books, London, 2011

164 Parkerson, Michelle. 'Paris Is Burning'. *Black Film Review*, 6(3), 1992, p.26

165 bell hooks, *Black Looks: Race and Representation*. South End Press, Boston, 1992, p.150

166 Ibid., p,148

167 Ibid., pp.154–5

168 Tucker, Ricky, *And the Category Is . . .: Inside New York's Vogue, House and Ballroom Community*. Beacon Press, Boston, 2021 p.16

169 Fratti, Karen. 'Billy Porter says "Pose" Season 2 isn't about "Madonna Bashing" – But It's Complicated'. *Bustle*, 10 June 2019

CHAPTER 7: JUST LITTLE BITS OF HISTORY

170 Gale, George. 'When being gay should be a crime'. *Sunday Mirror*, 14 December 1986, p.6

171 Junor, John. *Sunday Express*, 30 November 1986

172 Alison Park, Caroline Bryson, Elizabeth Clery, John Curtice and Miranda Phillips. (2013) *British Social Attitudes 30*, London: NatCen Social Research, p. 16

173 Worsthorne, Peregrine. 'The oppressive face of modern liberalism'. *Sunday Telegraph*, 3 January 1988, p.22

174 Jarman, Derek. 'An offer Sir Ian was honour bound to refuse?' *Guardian*, 4 January 1991, p.34

175 Lucas, Ian. 'The Color of His Eyes: Polari and the Sisters of Perpetual Indulgence' in Livia, Anna and Hall, Kira eds. *Queerly Phrased*. Oxford University Press, Oxford, 1997, p.1

176 Peake, Tony, *Derek Jarman: A Biography*. Little Brown, London, 1999, p.484

177 Ross, Andrew. 'Uses of Camp' in Bergman, D, ed., *Camp Grounds*. Massachusetts Press, Massachusetts, 1993, pp.54–77

178 Long, Scott. 'The Loneliness of Camp' in Bergman, D ed., *Camp Grounds*. Massachusetts Press, Massachusetts, 1993, pp.78–91

179 Meyer, Moe, ed., *The Politics and Poetics of Camp*. Routledge, London, 1994, p.5

180 Medhurst, Andy. 'Camp' in Medhurst, A, & Munt, S R, eds., *Lesbian and Gay Studies: A Critical Introduction*. Cassell, London, 1997, pp.274–293

181 Butler, Judith, *Gender Trouble, Second Edition*. Routledge, London, 1999, p.172

182 Nussbaum, Martha C. 'The Professor of Parody'. *The New Republic*, 22 February 1999

183 Nicholson, Rebecca. 'Workin' it! How female drag queens are causing a scene'. *Guardian*, 10 July 2017

184 Laver, James, *Taste and Fashion*, Chapter 18. George G Harrap, London, 1937

185 LaBruce, Bruce. 'Notes on Camp – and Anti-Camp'. *The Gay & Lesbian Review*, 2014

186 'Victoria Wood "favourite" video wins new fans on Twitter'. *BBC News*, 30 December 2017

187 'Blair gets soap in his eyes over Deirdre plea'. *Independent*, 1 April 1998

188 'Prisoner Girls' Night of Glory'. *TV Week*, 29 March 1982, p.16

189 Spikeyroberto, 'Prisoner Cell Block H . . . Did the walls wobble?' www.youtube.com/watch?v=OBQuf6QpXeQ

190 Sawle, Chris. 'Not forgotten: Mike Flowers and the easy revival'. *Backseat Mafia*, 19 December 2020

191 Mistry, Anupa. 'The shared faith of Bollywood's diasporic camp aesthetic.' *cléo* 3(2) Summer 2015

192 Marder, Keith. 'Next season, "Melrose Place" needs a serious reality check'. *Times Union*, 26 April 1996

193 Dodds, Richard. '"Psycho Beach Party" goes from a Joke to a Play'. *Times-Picayune*, 16 November 1990

194 Keesey, Douglas, *Paul Verhoeven*. Taschen, Cologne, 2005, p.36

195 Berardinelli, James. 'Showgirls'. www.reelviews.net/reelviews/showgirls

196 McCarthy, Todd. 'Showgirls'. *Variety*, 22 September 1995

197 Gleiberman, Owen. 'Showgirls'. *Entertainment Weekly*, 6 October 1995

198 Maslin, Janet. 'Film Review'. *New York Times*, 22 September 1995

199 Conway, Jeffrey. *You Don't Nomi*, dir. Jeffrey McHale. RLJE Films, 2019

200 Shaw, Jessica. 'Party girls: "Showgirls," "Pride and Prejudice"'. *Entertainment Weekly*, 22 March 1996

201 'The Nerve Interview: Joe Eszterhas'. Nerve.com, 15 September 2006

202 Piggford, George. '"Who's that Girl?" Annie Lennox, Woolf's Orlando and Female Camp Androgyny', in Fabio Cleto ed. *Camp: Queer Aesthetics and the Performing Subject – A Reader*. Edinburgh University Press, Edinburgh, p.297

203 Christ, Peaches. *You Don't Nomi*, dir. Jeffrey McHale. RLJE Films, 2019

CHAPTER 8: SHE'S GONE VIRAL

204 Duffy, Rachel, *Creative Makeup: A step-by-step guide to expressive makeup from fantasy to full illusion*. David & Charles, Newton Abbot, 2022

205 Fernandez, Maria. 'Swapped spouse gains notoriety'. *Los Angeles Times*, 18 November 2005

206 Kirkland, Justin. 'God Warrior Remains a Beloved Meme, But Marguerite Perrin Isn't Afraid of Dark-Sided Stuff Anymore'. *Esquire*, 8 November 2019

207 Megarry, Daniel. 'The heartwarming story of how "God Warrior" Marguerite Perrin became an LGBTQ ally'. *Gay Times*, 2019

208 Pruitt-Young, Sharon. 'Chris Crocker, "Leave Britney Alone" video creator, reflects on what's changed'. *NPR*, 27 June 2021

209 Volpe, Allie. '"Leave Britney Alone": Chris Crocker 10 years later'. *Rolling Stone* Australia, 14 September 2017

210 Pruitt-Young, Sharon. 'Chris Crocker, "Leave Britney Alone" video creator, reflects on what's changed'. *NPR*, 27 June 2021

211 Ross, Harling. 'I Have a Lot of Pent-Up Feelings About Nate in "The Devil Wears Prada"'. *Repeller*, 5 November 2018

212 Asmita. 'Just A Reminder That The Real Villain of "The Devil Wears Prada" Was Andy's Boyfriend, Nate. That's All'. *ScoopWhoop*, 9 July 2019

213 Malivindi, Diandra. 'Let's Be Honest, Andy Sachs Was The *Real* Villain In "The Devil Wears Prada"'. *Elle* Australia, 11 August 2021

214 Norcross, Jonathan. 'Why Identifying the True Villain in "The Devil Wears Prada" Depends on Where You Are in Life'. *Collider*, 3 May 2022

215 Nussbaum, Emily. 'How Ryan Murphy became the most powerful man in TV'. *New Yorker*, 7 May 2018

216 Framke, Caroline. 'How RuPaul's comments on trans women led to a Drag Race revolt – and a rare apology'. *Vox*, 2 March 2018

217 Baker, Paul. '"Bad wigs and screaming mimis": Using corpus-assisted techniques to carry out critical discourse analysis of the representation of trans people in the British press', in Hart, C, and Cap, P, eds. *Contemporary Critical Discourse Studies*. Bloomsbury, London, 2014, pp.211–236

218 '"Bitch, you need to get stronger" – RuPaul Responds To Activists Who Call Drag Race "Transphobic"'. *Queerty*, 22 May 2014

219 Duffy, Nick. 'RuPaul: I wouldn't have dropped "she-mail" joke'. *Pink News*, 3 June 2015

220 Aitkenhead, Decca. 'RuPaul: "Drag is a big f-you to male-dominated culture"'. *Guardian*, 3 March 2018

221 Jonze, Tim. '"I'm just trying to make the world a little brighter": how the culture wars hijacked Drag Queen Story Hour'. *Guardian*, 11 August 2022

222 Nicholson, Rebecca. 'Workin' it! How female drag queens are causing a scene'. *Guardian*, 10 July 2017

223 Emerson, Jim. 'High camp: Does it translate?' rogerebert.com, 23 August 2006

224 Wang, Shuaishuai. 'How "sissy men" became the latest front in China's campaign against big tech'. *The Conversation*, 10 September 2021

225 Ibid.

226 Gao, Helen. 'China's Ban on Sissy Boys is Bound to Backfire'. *New York Times*, 31 December 2021

227 LaBruce, Bruce. 'Notes on Camp – and Anti-Camp'. *The Gay & Lesbian Review*, 2014, p.12

228 Nuzzi, Olivia. 'The Final Campaign'. *New York Magazine*, 23 December 2022

229 Glancy, Josh. 'Dancing Donald adds Les Mis to his high-camp playlist'. *Sunday Times*, 20 November 2022

230 LaBruce, Bruce. 'Notes on Camp – and Anti-Camp'. *The Gay & Lesbian Review*, 2014 pp.12–3

231 Grady, Constance. 'Camp, the theme of this year's MET Gala, is almost impossible to define. Here's our best effort'. *Vox*, 3 May 2019

232 Friedman, Vanessa. 'Met costume Institute embraces "Camp" for 2019 Blockbuster show'. *New York Times*, 9 October 2018

233 Hafer, Dylan. 'The Met Gala worst-dressed list: Does anyone understand camp?' *Betches*, 7 May 2019

234 Edelkoort, Li. 'The beheading of culture is irrevocable'. *de zeen*, 17 May 2019

235 Geter, Hafizah. 'Black Phenomena: On Afropessimism & Camp'. *Bomb Magazine*, 23 September 2021

236 Cran, Rona. 'LGBT+ history: the story of camp, from Little Richard to Lil Nas X'. *The Conversation*, 7 February 2022

Acknowledgements

Thanks to Vidisha Biswas, Rose Green, Grace Harrison, Vicki Heath Silk, Candida Lacey, Tony McEnery, Dhruti Modha and David Watkins for their encouragement and help in making this book happen. Also, thanks to Lancaster University library and ProQuest for providing hard-to-get resources.

Index

About the Author

Paul Baker is a Professor of English Language at Lancaster University and has written over twenty books, for both academic and popular audiences. These include *Fabulosa: The Story of Polari* and *Outrageous! The Story of Section 28 and the Battle for LGBT Education*. Paul is a Fellow of the Royal Society of Arts and a Fellow of the Academy of Social Sciences.